PEARL HARBOR

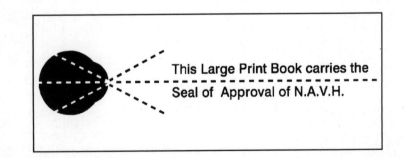

This Large Print Book carries the
Seal of Approval of N.A.V.H.

PEARL HARBOR

FDR LEADS THE NATION INTO WAR

STEVEN M. GILLON

THORNDIKE PRESS

A part of Gale, Cengage Learning

Detroit • New York • San Francisco • New Haven, Conn • Waterville, Maine • London

GALE
CENGAGE Learning

LIBRARY OF CONGRESS CATALOGING-IN-PUBLICATION DATA

Gillon, Steven M.
  Pearl Harbor : FDR leads the nation into war / by Steven M. Gillon.
    p. cm. — (Thorndike Press large print nonfiction)
  Originally published: New York : Basic Books, c2011.
  Includes bibliographical references.
  ISBN-13: 978-1-4104-4660-2 (hardcover)
  ISBN-10: 1-4104-4660-3 (hardcover)
  1. Pearl Harbor (Hawaii), Attack on, 1941. 2. Roosevelt, Franklin D.
(Franklin Delano), 1882–1945. 3. World War, 1939–1945—United States.
I. Title.
D767.92.G55 2012
940.54'26693—dc23   2011049773

Published in 2012 by arrangement with Basic Books, a member of
Perseus Books Group, LLC.

This book is dedicated to Abbe Raven

CONTENTS

PREFACE

President Franklin D. Roosevelt learned of the Japanese attack on Pearl Harbor at 1:47 p.m. on December 7, 1941. By that time the following day, FDR had finished delivering his war message to a joint session of Congress. It is hard to think of any other twenty-four-hour period that so radically transformed America and its role in the world. Japan's assault on a quiet Sunday morning transformed a precarious peace into a total war. In this incredibly short frame of time, one era ended and a new one began. Pearl Harbor was the defining event of the twentieth century — it changed the global balance of power, set the stage for the Cold War, and allowed the United States to emerge as a global superpower.

There is no shortage of books about Pearl Harbor or about Franklin Roosevelt, but there is surprisingly little written about how FDR responded in the hours immediately after the attack. The standard accounts of Pearl Harbor focus on the broad diplomatic, military, and political forces that conspired to produce the worst military failure in American history. They explain why the attack took place, trace the failure of American intelligence, and depict the nature of the carnage in Hawaii. But because they are painted on such a broad canvas, many of these panoramic accounts have little room to offer an intimate glimpse into the nature of Roosevelt's leadership in the hours that followed.

Even the finest Roosevelt biographers move quickly from the moment that FDR learned of the bombing to his war message the following day. In *FDR: The War President,* Kenneth Davis fills 804 pages with details of the Roosevelt presidency between the years 1940 and 1943, but he devotes only 5 pages to the twenty-four hours following the attack. Likewise, Doris Kearns Goodwin dedicates only a few paragraphs to the day's events in her Pulitzer Prize–winning *No Ordinary Time.*

Focusing on the first twenty-four hours of crisis allows me to tell familiar stories in an unfamiliar way and provide a new perspective on the inner workings of the presidency. It is based on the belief that the first twenty-four hours are critical to understanding the nature of leadership. It is during those first few hours that the die is cast. Those hours represent a test of presidential character. Dependable information is scarce. Situations are fluid, changing by the minute. A president has little time for reflection. Decisions need to be made. Process is abandoned. It all comes down to the judgment and instincts of one man, forced by circumstance to make momentous decisions that can alter the course of history.

Writing about "great men" has fallen out of favor among many professional historians, but events like Pearl Harbor remind us of the centrality of presidential leadership. While there are impersonal forces that shape the tide of history, there are also defining moments when individuals matter. Pearl Harbor was one of those defining moments.

History in macrocosm often appears more coherent than it actually is; in microcosm, contingency, uncertainty, and luck — both good and bad — play much larger roles than we might like to acknowledge. We think of the commander in chief as presiding over a vast and sophisticated communications system. But on the afternoon of December 7, 1941, intelligence was scarce and difficult to obtain. How big was the Japanese force?

How much damage did it inflict? Did the U.S. Navy, which FDR believed was on full alert, anticipate the attack and manage to repel the invaders? Initially, military officials in Hawaii were reluctant to give details of the damage assessment, even to the president, because they could not find a secure line and worried about Japanese eavesdropping. Much of the information they did provide — that some of the planes had swastikas painted on them, for example — would later be proved false.

It is against this backdrop of confusion and chaos that FDR's leadership must be judged. FDR was forced to make every major decision based on instinct and his own strategic sense of right and wrong. There were no instant surveys to guide his actions, no twenty-four-hour television coverage offering him a glimpse into the national mood. Making matters worse, the president's advisers were anxious and divided.

Although he lacked accurate information, Roosevelt exercised enormous power in the hours and days that followed the attack. While the entire nation looked to the White House for leadership, partisan differences disappeared, and former isolationists began clamoring for war. Roosevelt exercised nearly complete control over the flow of information. With the exception of a few radio reports that made it to the mainland, there was little or no independent information about events in Hawaii. All the major news outlets rushed to the White House to find out what had happened. As *Newsweek* reported that week, "The White House was the only funnel for information."[1]

One of the extraordinary aspects of the hours after Pearl Harbor was Roosevelt's ability to manage the news in the wake of the attack. Unlike the Kennedy assassination, or the terrorist attacks on September 11, 2001, when television spread the word around the country and the globe within minutes, news about Pearl Harbor spread slowly, trickling out over the radio in the afternoon. The attack took place during the traditional Sunday dinner hour on the East Coast and in the Midwest, which meant that most people did not have their radios on. The unseasonably warm weather across the nation drove many people outside, and away from their radios, for picnics and other activities. It was not until later in the afternoon, when the "extra" editions of daily newspapers hit the streets with their screaming headlines, that the entire nation learned of the assault.

Nonetheless, FDR was still able to deceive the public and Congress about the extent of the carnage. Although the president had detailed damage and casualty reports by the end of the day, he refused to release them — not only to the press but also to lawmakers in Washington. He deliberately downplayed the effectiveness of the Japanese attack when he met with a bipartisan group of congressional leaders on the evening of December 7.

There were good reasons for FDR to be deceptive: He worried that if the Japanese realized what a devastating blow they had delivered, they would launch a land assault against Hawaii. He also needed to maintain public morale and feared details of the devastation could panic the American people. Based on comments he made that evening, it seems that FDR also worried that the public would blame him for the disaster, undermining his authority when he needed it most to rally the nation behind him. It is revealing that Roosevelt's successful leadership depended on a level of deception that would be unacceptable by today's standards.

There is, however, no evidence that FDR deceived lawmakers or the American public about a critical and much-contested point surrounding the Pearl Harbor attack: the fact that it came as a surprise. The public's fascination with conspiracy theories has distorted much of the writing about Pearl Harbor. The conspiracy theories popped up even before the war was over, with the appearance of John Flynn's self-published *The Truth About Pearl Harbor,* and they have continued up to the present, with the 1999 release of Robert B. Stinnett's *Day of Deceit.* Most of these books focus on a single question: Did FDR use the attack on Pearl Harbor as a "back door" to war? In other words, was FDR the mastermind behind a massive government conspiracy to push a reluctant nation into battle? Over the years, conservative critics of Roosevelt and a few historians have promoted the so-called backdoor theory, but it has failed to gain much credibility. All the evidence shows that FDR and the men around him were genuinely shocked when they learned of the attack. They may have been naive and gravely misjudged Japanese intentions and capability, but they were not guilty of deliberate deception.[2]

Having secured an unprecedented third term in 1940, FDR had served as president for 3,200 days (8 years, 9 months, and 3 days, or 76,800 hours) when the Japanese bombed Pearl Harbor. His entire presidency had been engulfed in crisis. His presidency began amid a worldwide economic depression, with millions of Americans out of work and underemployed, the financial system in crisis, and the political establishment in paralysis. By 1939, the conflagration in Europe, and the growing threat of Hitler's armies, threatened the global balance of power and seemed destined to pull a reluctant nation into another European war.

Despite the length of his presidency, and the great crises that he confronted, FDR remains an elusive figure. "I am a juggler," Roosevelt once said about his approach to governing. "I never let my right hand know what my left hand does." His administrative style was often chaotic. He refused to establish clear lines of authority, allowed aides to fight each other for his attention, and frequently turned to outside advisers for advice. After nearly three years of working with Roosevelt, Secretary of War Henry Stimson wrote, "The President is the poorest administrator I have ever worked under. . . . He is not a good chooser of men and does not know how to use them in coordination." Vice President Henry A. Wallace, even before he was dumped in

1944, noted that Roosevelt "looks in one direction and rows the other with utmost skill."[3]

Critics complained that Roosevelt's style was deceptive and manipulative, while supporters defended his deviousness, claiming it was necessary to navigate the conflicting currents of American public opinion. Either way, his style makes it hard to pin him down. Because he had the habit of telling people what they wanted to hear, it is not always easy to divine what he was really thinking. Henry Morgenthau, a Dutchess County neighbor who served as secretary of the Treasury, described Roosevelt as "weary as well as buoyant, frivolous as well as grave, evasive as well as frank . . . a man of bewildering complexity of moods and motives."[4]

Roosevelt, for all his outward charm and warmth, remained distant and elusive even to those who knew him best. He formed few real friendships. He used people, and when they no longer served a purpose, he discarded them. Marguerite "Missy" Le-Hand, who loved FDR and served him loyally for many years, once observed that he "was really incapable of a personal friendship with anyone."[5]

A relatively thin paper trail complicates

the task of understanding FDR's inner motives. Because he died in office in 1945, he left no memoirs. The office of the presidency was far less bureaucratic in Roosevelt's day than it is now. Most business was conducted informally. In fact, FDR was the first chief executive to conduct much of the nation's business by phone. He also discouraged note taking at meetings, fearing that it would prevent people from being open and candid. As a result, the Roosevelt administration produced fewer documents than the "modern" presidencies that followed. For example, the Clinton presidential library houses 80 million pages of documents. John F. Kennedy served less than three years, but his library houses more than 48 million pages. The FDR Library, by comparison, contains only 17 million pages of documents, despite his much longer presidency.

December 7, however, may be the most well-documented day of the Roosevelt presidency. Perhaps understanding the momentous events that were taking place, Roosevelt defied his own policy and allowed a stenographer to take detailed notes of his conference with congressional leaders that evening. As a result, we have a full transcript of the meeting. A few of the president's advisers also left detailed notes of their actions that day. For example, Treasury head Morgenthau continued his practice of having a secretary listen to his phone calls, writing a transcript of all conversations. Secretary of War Stimson kept a detailed diary of all his White House activities.[6]

Most valuable are the volumes of testimony produced by a series of government investigations into the Pearl Harbor disaster. Less than two weeks after the attack, FDR signed an executive order establishing a commission, headed by Supreme Court Justice Owen Roberts, to determine why the United States was so unprepared. The commission interviewed 127 witnesses before laying blame at the feet of Admiral Husband Kimmel and General Walter Short, the local commanders in Hawaii.

The commission, however, failed to silence critics who claimed that important evidence had been omitted. To settle the matter, numerous federal agencies conducted their own separate investigations — six in all — during the war, each one reaching different conclusions about who was responsible. After the war, Congress tried to settle the questions by establishing a joint committee to investigate the disaster. In 1946, the committee released forty volumes of testimony. By the end of the series of investigations, every major player close to the president testified, often more than once. Taken together, testimony by FDR's advisers runs thousands of pages. While most of the questioning focused on the events that led up to the attack, the testimony also sheds a great deal of light on Roosevelt's thinking and actions on December 7.[7]

By the evening of December 7, fear and uncertainty had gripped the capital. No one knew what would happen next. Would the Japanese invade Hawaii? During dinner on the evening of December 7, a White House butler overheard FDR speculating about the possibility of a Japanese invasion on the West Coast that could advance as far east as Chicago. That fear would later lead to one of the greatest mistakes of his presidency: the internment of Japanese Americans living in the West.

FDR can also be blamed for failing to pay close attention to the growing crisis in the Pacific in the months leading up to the Pearl Harbor attack. Roosevelt liked to act as his own secretary of state, but he was unusually passive in dealing with the Japanese threat. Distracted by events in Europe, he delegated responsibility to Secretary of State Cordell Hull and other lower-level officials. The result was a policy of drift and indecision.

But in the hours and days after the attack, he reassured a shaken government and inspired a nervous nation. Despite the enormity of the defeat at Pearl Harbor, and its potential consequences, Roosevelt remained steady and sure-minded. "Through it all the President was calm and deliberate," a cabinet member observed. "I don't know anybody in the United States who can come close to measuring up to his foresight and acumen in this critical hour." Eleanor Roosevelt, who peeked in on the president a few hours after the attack, observed her husband's "deadly calm" composure.

It is impossible to fully appreciate Roosevelt's deft handling of the crisis without exploring his character — the often intangible aspects of his personality that allowed him to remain optimistic in the midst of tragedy and calm in the wake of defeat. The last time Eleanor witnessed a similar expression on her husband's face was in August 1921, as he lay paralyzed from the waist down while a doctor informed him for the first time that he suffered from polio. That private crisis inspired the same iron will, dogged determination, and unquestioned optimism that the nation would witness in the face of its greatest military defeat.

1

"YOUR BOYS ARE NOT GOING TO BE SENT INTO ANY FOREIGN WARS"

Franklin Roosevelt likely started his day on December 7, 1941, in typical fashion. At 8:15 a.m. his valet, Arthur Prettyman, would have come into the bedroom, announced the time, and then helped FDR to the bathroom. Roosevelt would then have returned to his bed, where, propped up by pillows, he would take his breakfast on a tray sent up by the White House kitchen. Most mornings, Roosevelt ate a boiled egg along with two pieces of bacon and toast. While FDR ate, Prettyman would set up a table next to the president's bed with a small coffee percolator. "One of the President's real joys," reported Missy LeHand, "is to make his own coffee."[1]

While eating his breakfast, Roosevelt could look out his bedroom windows, which offered an unobstructed view of the Washington Monument to the south. From this spot, the president would read each morning the latest dispatches from abroad and scan a handful of papers: the *New York Times, New York Herald Tribune, Baltimore Sun, Washington Post,* and *Washington Herald.*[2]

Roosevelt's limited mobility required him to gather within arm's reach many of the objects that he needed throughout the day. This left his living and work space in a state of perpetual clutter. Atop the white painted table next to the bed were aspirin, nose drops, a glass of water, pencils, reminder notes, an old prayer book, a pack of cigarettes, an ashtray, and a couple of telephones. No one was allowed to tidy this table. On a shelf above the table rested a six-by-three-inch alligator-covered case that contained a clock and a barometer. On the floor below sat a small basket where Eleanor would often leave him notes, memorandums, and articles she wanted him to read. "I have a photographic impression of that room," recalled Secretary of Labor Frances Perkins. "A little too large to be cozy, it was not large enough to be impressive."[3]

At some point during the morning FDR's valet helped him get dressed. He slipped on a pair of flannel slacks and an old gray pullover sweater that had once belonged to his son James. Prettyman then wheeled him into the adjacent Oval Study. With the exception of a visit to the White House physician's office, the president would conduct all of the nation's business from this small room on December 7.

While the Oval Office represented the seat of power, Roosevelt preferred the comfort of his private study on the second floor. Speechwriter Robert Sherwood described the Oval Study as "the focal point of the nation and, in a sense, of the whole world" during FDR's presidency. Lined with mahogany bookcases, the room was stuffed with ship models, maritime pictures, books, and stacks of paper. White woodwork-framed walls were painted in a color that a White House architect described as "a sort of schoolhouse tan." On them hung portraits of his mother, Sara, who had died three months earlier, and his wife. An oval dark-green chenille rug covered most of the floor, while an odd assortment of tables, floor lamps, and chromium ashtray stands contributed to the clutter. The leather sofas and chairs had once been used by Theodore Roosevelt on the presidential yacht the *Mayflower*. A pipe organ occupied one corner of the room. FDR had received it as a gift, and although he never learned to play it, he also refused to get rid of it.[4]

The study was FDR's favorite room in the White House. It was where he found solace in the massive stamp collection he had inherited from his mother, which contained a million stamps preserved in 150 matching albums. It was also where he unwound in the evening, inviting his many houseguests to join him for cocktails. A tradition dating back to when FDR was governor of New York, the cocktail hour was the time at the end of the day when he gathered with a few close aides, and the numerous houseguests, to reflect on the day, share stories, and exchange jokes. No official business was permitted. The president insisted on mixing the drinks himself, experimenting with new concoctions of gin and rum, vermouth and fruit juice. He had a special cocktail for each day and always ordered the appropriate ingredients ahead of time. "He mixed the ingredients," reflected Sherwood, "with the deliberation of an alchemist but with what appeared to be a certain lack of precision since he carried on a steady conversation while doing it."[5]

In addition to the informality of the room, Roosevelt no doubt appreciated its convenience. The Oval Study was ideally set up for a man who could not walk. His bedroom and bathroom were just off to one side. It was an easy room for him to navigate, and he could do so without assistance. Roosevelt needed help in the morning getting out of his bed and into the wheelchair, but he was capable of transferring himself from his wheelchair to his more comfortable working chair.

Roosevelt used a wheelchair only for transportation, and he designed it specifically for that task. A simple device crafted from the frame of a regular kitchen chair, it was mounted on a sturdy base with two large wheels in the front and two smaller ones in the back. The large wheels were nineteen inches in diameter, which made it easier for him to slide from the wheelchair to a stationary chair. They also allowed him to turn in a very small circumference. There was a small platform for him to rest his feet and a retractable wood and glass ashtray attached beneath the seat. Since it did not have arms, the chair was narrow enough to fit through most doorways.[6]

FDR's dynamic leadership over the next twenty-four hours obscures the fact that every aspect of his life was made more difficult by his polio. He required assistance to perform the simplest of tasks that most people take for granted — getting dressed, climbing in and out of bed, moving around his home. But he needed little help in making momentous decisions that would impact the lives of millions of Americans.

On the morning of December 7, Roosevelt was tired, sick, and in desperate need of a vacation. He had twice delayed his traditional Thanksgiving trip to Warm Springs, Georgia, where he wanted to enjoy the warmer weather and therapeutic baths. He finally managed to slip out of town by train on November 28, hoping for a ten-day respite. Shortly after he arrived at the "little White House," however, his secretary of state, Cordell Hull, had called, asking him to return to Washington. A large Japanese armada was on the move in the Pacific, and no one was sure where it would strike. Roosevelt returned to Washington on December 1. Not only had he failed during his short trip to procure much-needed rest, but his chronic sinus infection had flared up, leaving him congested while his head throbbed in pain.

Reading the headlines on the morning of December 7 may have only aggravated his discomfort. Clearly, Japan was going to strike somewhere in the Pacific. The *Washington Post* reported that Tokyo's patience was coming to an end, while the *New York*

Times predicted that an attack on Thailand was "imminent." There seemed little reason for Americans to worry. The *Times* reassured readers that the United States Navy, in the midst of a three-year expansion, was first-rate. It quoted Secretary of the Navy Frank Knox who, in his annual report released on December 6, announced the U.S. Navy "has at this time no superior in the world."[7]

It was ironic that Roosevelt's attention was focused on the Pacific this morning because for the previous two years he had used all of his juggling skills to nudge the nation closer to war in Europe. Since coming to office in 1933, Adolf Hitler had been consolidating power at home by asserting it abroad. Tapping into a deep well of resentment that Germans felt toward the West for imposing a punitive peace following World War I, he had repudiated the Versailles Treaty of 1919, withdrawn from the League of Nations in 1933, and unilaterally announced in 1935 that Germany would rearm. His Nazi Party had suspended constitutional rights and initiated systematic persecution of Jews living in Germany. One of Hitler's lieutenants, Alfred Rosenberg, announced that he wanted to see the head of a Jew impaled upon every telephone pole along a railroad line between Berlin and the North Sea.[8]

The events in Europe were clearly troubling to Roosevelt. An internationalist at heart, he recognized that the modern technology of warfare meant that America could no longer count on the vast geographic separation provided by two oceans to isolate the nation from events elsewhere in the world. His internationalist roots traced back to his earliest years. As a child, Roosevelt had traveled extensively throughout Europe, making his first trip at the age of three. He had also read the influential works of Alfred T. Mahan, who extolled the importance of sea power. During the Spanish-American War in 1898, FDR conspired with a few friends to run away to Boston and enlist in the navy. A bad case of scarlet fever foiled his plans, however. While a student at the prestigious Groton School and later at Harvard, he debated international issues and gloated in his cousin Theodore's exploits.

His fascination with world affairs and his love of the sea made him an ideal choice to serve as assistant secretary of the navy during the Wilson administration. His new job instilled in him a strong belief that a great power such as the United States should play an important role in world affairs. He lobbied for a dramatic expansion of the navy, argued for military intervention in nearly every crisis, and pushed the administration to enter World War I. After the war, he strongly supported Wilson's plan for a League of Nations, believing that collective security provided the best protection against future wars.

In 1920, Democrats chose Roosevelt as their vice presidential nominee. Although the country had turned against Wilson's idealism, and the Senate had rejected American participation in the League of Nations, Roosevelt refused to bend to public opinion. In his acceptance address, he warned that the United States must accept the fact that "modern civilization has become so complex and the lives of civilized men so interwoven with the lives of other men in other countries as to make it impossible to be in this world and not of it."[9]

Roosevelt watched with alarm as Hitler consolidated power in Europe and began threatening his neighbors. FDR harbored no illusions about Hitler, or his intentions. "The situation is alarming," Roosevelt told diplomats shortly after Hitler assumed power. "Hitler is a madman and his counsellors, some of whom I personally know, are even madder than he is." Roosevelt, fluent in German, had read the original version of Hitler's *Mein Kampf,* which contained virulent anti-Jewish comments that were purged from later editions. On the flyleaf of an American edition of the book, published in 1933, FDR wrote, "This translation is so expurgated as to give a wholly false view of what Hitler really is or says. The German original would make a different story."[10]

But while events in Europe alarmed the president, the Great Depression had monopolized his attention throughout much of the 1930s. When he took office in March 1933, one in four Americans was without a job. Each month, thousands of farmers and business owners went bankrupt. By March 3, the day before Roosevelt took office, thirty-eight states had shut down all of their banks, and the remaining ten states were moving to close theirs. Normal business and commerce ground to a halt. A Roosevelt adviser, Rexford Guy Tugwell, wrote in his diary, "Never in modern times, I should think, has there been so widespread unemployment and such moving distress from cold and hunger." By 1937, even after launching an aggressive program to combat unemployment and revive America's industrial engine, Roosevelt was still lamenting that a third of the nation was "ill-housed, ill-clad, ill-nourished." Confronting such overwhelming economic problems, Roosevelt had little time to dwell on the growing crisis in Europe.

Hitler, in the meantime, spent the '30s expanding his reach within Europe. In March 1936, the Nazi leader ordered German troops into the Rhineland, the strategic buffer that lay between France and Germany. And Hitler was not the only fascist leader threatening world stability during the 1930s. In 1935, Italian fascist leader Benito Mussolini launched an invasion of the independent African state of Ethiopia. In 1936, both leaders directly intervened in Spain's civil war, allowing General Francisco Franco to come to power.

Hitler accurately predicted that the distracted West would respond feebly to his aggression. In 1938, he pressed Europe to the brink of war. In March, he forced Austria into *Anschluss* (union) with Germany. Later that fall, the Nazi dictator threatened to invade Czechoslovakia when it refused to give him its Sudetenland, a mountainous region bordering Germany inhabited mostly by ethnic Germans. Hoping to avoid confrontation, the West sacrificed the Sudetenland on the altar of appeasement, agreeing to a gradual transfer to German control. Abandoned, the Czechs surrendered, demobilized their army, and allowed Germany to shear off the Sudetenland.

Six months later, German troops completed their rape of Czechoslovakia. Armed columns poured over the Czech border, smashing Western illusions that Hitler could be appeased. Within weeks, the British government reversed course, announcing that it was committed to the defense of Poland.

It became increasingly difficult for Roosevelt to ignore the growing crisis in Europe. He recognized that Hitler presented a long-term threat to America, and he believed the best way to restrain further aggression was for the United States to participate in collective security arrangements with the Western democracies. But in the United States, disillusion with World War I and concern about jobs at home intensified deeply entrenched isolationist sentiment. Popular writers, who claimed that selfish business interests had conspired to lead the United States into World War I, whipped popular disenchantment with World War I into a frenzy.

Congress reinforced the isolationist sentiment by passing restrictive neutrality legislation. In 1935, Congress imposed an automatic embargo on American arms and ammunition to all parties at war. The following year, Democrats and Republicans joined together to add a ban on loans to belligerents. Two years later, lawmakers banned American ships from war zones, prohibited Americans from traveling on belligerent ships, and extended the embargo to include not just armaments but also the oil, steel, and rubber needed for war machines. Foreign belligerents could buy such goods only if they paid for them in cash and carried them in their own ships.

For the next few years, Roosevelt struggled to find a way to work with the Western democracies to restrain Hitler without arousing isolationist sentiment. It was not an easy task. In October 1937, FDR had tested the depth of isolationist sentiment in a speech denouncing the "reign of terror and international lawlessness" that threatened the peace. "When an epidemic of physical disease starts to spread, the community approves and joins in a quarantine of the patients in order to protect the health of the community." But public reaction to the speech proved mixed, and Roosevelt quickly backed away from the internationalist implications of his "quarantine" message. "It's a terrible thing," he said, "to look over your shoulder when you are trying to lead — and find no one there."

Even if he wanted to influence events in Europe, FDR had little tangible support to offer. At the time of the Munich agreement, the U.S. Army consisted of 185,000 men and ranked eighteenth in the world. Not only was it no match for Hitler's Germany, but it was smaller than the armed forces of Sweden and Switzerland.

The limits of FDR's influence on events in Europe became obvious when the Germans and Russians concluded a nonaggression pact on August 23, 1939. The agreement provided for the partition of Poland and for Soviet absorption of the Baltic states, as well as territory in Finland and Bessarabia. With his eastern flank now secured, Hitler unleashed his fire and steel on the Polish people on September 1, 1939. In a potent display of military skill and power, the Germans conducted a *Blitzkrieg* (lightning war), as 1.5 million men streamed into Polish territory. "Close your hearts to pity," Hitler told his generals. "Act brutally." Two days later, honoring their commitments to Poland, Britain and France declared war on

Germany. World War II in Europe had begun.

Ambassador to France William Bullitt called Roosevelt at 2:50 a.m. Washington time to tell him the news. "Well, Bill, it has come at last," FDR said. "God help us all." Roosevelt propped himself on his pillow, lit a cigarette, and telephoned his secretaries of state, war, and the navy. They rushed to their offices. "I think a good many of us had a somewhat sleepless night," Roosevelt remarked to reporters the following morning.[11]

By late 1939, American sympathy was clearly with Great Britain and France, but most people continued to believe the Allies could defend Europe without U.S. assistance. The British, who claimed the largest navy in the world, would strangle the German economy. France's 800,000-man standing army was considered the most powerful in Europe. Many military strategists believed the French Maginot Line, an extremely well-developed chain of fortifications along the French-German border, could resist any invasion. The calm that settled over Europe during the winter of 1939–1940 only added to the detachment. For six months after the fall of Poland, Hitler's armies remained largely silent. Many

Americans believed that Hitler's thirst for conquest had been satisfied and a larger war averted. Isolationist senator William Borah snorted, "There's something phony about this war."

Roosevelt, however, was convinced that Hitler and his generals were determined to conquer the democracies in Europe before the United States could build its defenses. "My problem," he wrote editor William Allen White in December 1939, "is to get the American people to think of conceivable consequences without scaring [them] into thinking that they are going to be dragged into this war." In November 1939, Roosevelt achieved a partial victory when he convinced Congress to pass a revised Neutrality Act that lifted the arms embargo against belligerents. It retained a cash-and-carry provision and stipulated that shipments could move only in foreign vessels. The new law also forbade American merchant ships from entering a broad "danger zone" that included most of the major shipping lanes to Europe.[12]

A German offensive in April 1940 shattered the false confidence that Hitler's appetite for expansion had been appeased. On April 9, the Nazi *Blitzkrieg* overran Denmark, and German troops swarmed over

Norway. A month later, Hitler's armies swept over the Netherlands, Luxembourg, and Belgium. On May 13, German panzers bypassed the Maginot Line, crossed the Meuse River, and entered French territory.

The once-powerful French army crumbled after six weeks of fighting. On June 15, the French premier called Winston Churchill, who had been chosen British prime minister just ten days earlier. "We have been defeated," he said. "The Battle of France is over," Churchill told a somber Parliament. "I expect that the Battle of Britain is about to begin."

Churchill was right. Beginning in the summer of 1940, Hitler hurled his Luftwaffe (air force) at the British, hoping to destroy coastal installations in preparation for a cross-Channel invasion. The Royal Air Force fought back, managing to keep the Germans at bay. Frustrated, Hitler ordered the bombing of RAF bases and the terror bombing of London. From September to November, nearly 250 German bombers dropped their deadly cargo over London every night. The British people, though badly battered, refused to break.

Over the course of the summer, American isolationism was diminishing. The fall of France had changed the military calculus in

Washington. The images of Hitler's brutality, combined with Roosevelt's warnings about the dangers of isolationism, started to turn public opinion at home. In May, only 35 percent of Americans favored aiding the Allies. By August, the figure had risen to 60 percent.

Taking advantage of the shift in public mood, Roosevelt pushed through Congress an extension of the Selective Service Act and a dramatic increase in military spending. Total appropriations for the army and navy topped $17 billion, more than nine times the figure for 1939. By the fall of 1940, the navy had 210 ships committed for construction, including 12 aircraft carriers. Congress also supported the president's proposal for 50,000 airplanes.[13]

Roosevelt was convinced that America's survival was directly linked to the fate of Britain. "If Great Britain goes down," he said, "all of us in the Americas would be living at the point of a gun." Roosevelt understood that if Britain fell, Hitler would soon direct his fury against the United States. Over the next few months, Roosevelt publicly announced his support for a series of controversial measures that pushed the nation closer to war. He supported a plan to exchange U.S. Navy destroyers for access to British military bases in the Western Hemisphere. FDR understood the importance of sending America's limited resources to help Britain, especially since most people believed that it could not survive for long with or without American aid.[14]

Realizing that most members of his administration disagreed with his ardent internationalism, Roosevelt decided to shake up his cabinet in an effort to recruit like-minded men who shared his view of the European crisis and who, ideally, could also forge bipartisan support for his policies. He looked to the progressive wing of the Republican Party and found two aging disciples of his cousin Theodore Roosevelt's muscular view of American foreign policy. During the summer of 1940, Roosevelt named the seventy-two-year-old Henry L. Stimson as the new secretary of war. Stimson was joined by another aging pillar of the Republican establishment, publisher Frank Knox, sixty-seven, who became FDR's new secretary of the navy.

Stimson was perhaps the most influential member of the Republican foreign policy establishment. This would be his second tour of duty as secretary of war — he had served in the same capacity under William

Howard Taft. After the United States entered World War I, Stimson, nearing fifty, joined the military with the rank of colonel. He was so proud of his service that afterward he preferred that people refer to him as "the Colonel." Upon returning from the war, he served in the Coolidge administration before Herbert Hoover named him secretary of state in 1929.

An unabashed internationalist, Stimson believed the world would be a better place if the United States assumed the responsibilities of a global superpower. American business interests should expand around the world, government policy should be designed to further those interests, and the power to shape foreign policy should be vested in the presidency.[15]

Roosevelt also named to his cabinet another stalwart Republican leader, Frank Knox, who had fought alongside Theodore Roosevelt as a Rough Rider during the Spanish-American War. One of his most treasured possessions was a bullet-ridden sombrero, which he claimed to have worn as he charged up San Juan Hill. Like Stimson, he volunteered during World War I and, at the age of forty-three, enlisted in the army as a colonel. During the 1930s, he emerged as a tough critic of FDR's New

Deal programs, dismissing them as "alien and un-American." His strong opposition earned him a place on the Republican ticket as the vice presidential nominee in 1936. Although he had been critical of Roosevelt's domestic reforms, he shared TR's bullish views of America's role in the world and supported FDR's policy of aiding the Allies.[16]

Roosevelt could count on Knox and Stimson to support his efforts to aid Britain; moreover, as prominent Republicans, they provided him with political cover. As he nudged America toward providing aid to Britain, Roosevelt realized he needed to build support across the political aisle and garner as many congressional votes as possible.

Complicating the situation, 1940 was an election year, and Roosevelt faced the difficult decision of whether to seek an unprecedented third term in office. Had it been a typical year, Roosevelt likely would have retired from politics at the end of his second term. Instead, he decided to campaign for a third term. He believed that the global situation was too precarious, and the need to defeat Hitler too important, for him to simply step aside.

It became clear early on in the campaign

that issues of war and peace would decide the outcome. Growing concern about the deteriorating situation in Europe pushed the Republican Party to abandon its isolationist moorings and nominate little-known Wendell Willkie, a forty-eight-year-old Wall Street lawyer and utilities executive. Initially, Willkie expressed support for Roosevelt's defense policies and focused his attacks on the perceived failures of the New Deal. But in August, trailing badly in the polls, Willkie shifted gears. Three days after publicly supporting Roosevelt's destroyers-for-bases deal, Willkie condemned the move as "the most arbitrary and dictatorial action ever taken by a president in the history of the United States." Over the next few months, he sharpened his attacks. Early in October, charging the president was leading the country into war, Willkie warned that a Roosevelt reelection would mean "wooden crosses for sons and brothers and sweethearts." The Republican promised that he would not send "one American boy into the shambles of another war."

By mid-October, polls showed Willkie gaining ground in key states with large electoral votes, including Illinois, Indiana, and Michigan. The president decided to douse the flames with deception. In late

October, in what became the most quoted statement of the campaign, Roosevelt told a crowd in Boston, "I have said this before, but I shall say it again and again and again: Your boys are not going to be sent into any foreign wars." In the past he had always qualified the statement by saying, "except in cases of attack." He now said the disclaimer was not necessary. "It's implied, clearly. If we're attacked, it's no longer a foreign war."[17]

However disingenuous, Roosevelt's reassurances worked. He fended off Willkie's late surge and won reelection handily.

The president interpreted the election as an endorsement of his pro-British policies, and he responded by pushing for more aid. Churchill privately warned Roosevelt that the war was draining money from the British Treasury and that the "moment approaches when we shall no longer be able to pay cash for shipping and other supplies." A few days after Christmas, Roosevelt responded by unveiling a "Lend-Lease" proposal, which would allow the United States to provide Britain with valuable war matériel. After the war, Britain would repay the United States in kind. Roosevelt compared Lend-Lease to a garden hose one lends to a neighbor whose house is on fire. Urging the United States to "be the great arsenal of democracy," Roosevelt insisted that aiding the British was the best way to keep America out of the war.

Isolationists in Congress battled to defeat Lend-Lease. "Lending war equipment is a good deal like lending chewing gum," Senator Robert Taft grumbled. Isolationists formed the America First Committee to organize opposition to Roosevelt's actions. Led by a diverse group that included Taft, aviator hero Charles Lindbergh, and socialist Norman Thomas, committee members rejected the idea that Hitler posed a threat to American security.

However, the momentum of war was influencing American attitudes about the nation's role in the struggle for Europe. Polls showed more than 60 percent of the American public supporting Lend-Lease. Internationalists organized the Committee to Defend America by Aiding the Allies. Headed by Kansas newspaper editor William Allen White, the group called for unlimited aid to Britain. "Every time Hitler bombed London, we got a couple of votes," declared a congressional Lend-Lease supporter. The proposal quickly passed in both the House and the Senate. Both houses also passed legislation approving Roosevelt's request for $8 billion in additional funds to rearm the nation, while authorizing a one-year draft — the first peacetime conscription in American history.

Roosevelt was clearly maneuvering the nation into a war with Germany. He allowed the American navy to provide support for British ships, knowing that the policy would provoke lethal confrontations with the German U-boats that patrolled the Atlantic. The policy represented an escalation of what had already become an undeclared naval war in the North Atlantic. Three months earlier, in September 1941, a U-boat had attacked the USS *Greer,* an American destroyer that had been chasing the German submarine for hours. The president used the *Greer* incident to denounce the Germans as the "rattlesnakes of the Atlantic." The following month, a U-boat torpedoed the destroyer *Kearny,* killing eleven. "America has been attacked," Roosevelt blustered. "The *U.S.S. Kearny* is not just a Navy ship. She belongs to every man, woman and child in this nation." On October 30, an attack on the *Reuben James* resulted in the loss of ninety-six men. In response, Roosevelt ordered all ships engaged in escort duty to "shoot on sight" any

German submarines appearing in waters west of Iceland.

Public anger at the sinking of American ships provided Roosevelt with the support he needed to repeal the neutrality legislation. On November 13, 1941, Congress voted by a narrow margin to permit American merchant ships to sail through war zones to British and Russian ports. The last remaining restrictions on American actions had been removed. As a *New York Times* editorial declared, "The Battle of the Atlantic is on."

Sitting in the privacy of his study on Sunday morning, December 7, FDR could take satisfaction in having moved public opinion closer to his internationalist view of the war in Europe. Most Americans wanted to avoid getting involved in the conflict, but at least they now realized that America had a stake in the outcome. Meanwhile, as Roosevelt pushed the nation to the brink of war in Europe, the first bombs were about to fall in the Pacific.

2
"Do not let the talks deteriorate"

On Sunday morning, December 7, it was events in the Pacific, not Europe, that were weighing heavily on FDR. Tensions between Washington and Tokyo had mounted through the 1930s as Japan took advantage of the situation in Europe to expand its influence in Asia. Preoccupied with their own survival, European colonial powers could spare few resources to protect their Asian possessions.

By the 1930s, Japan had emerged as a major military power in Asia. Bragging the third-largest navy in the world, Japan's leaders were determined to establish a "Greater East Asia Co-Prosperity Sphere" by seizing control of large areas of Siberia, Manchuria, and eastern China. Acting on its ambitions, Tokyo captured Manchuria in 1931, established a puppet government, and dispatched colonists to settle the land. In 1937, Japan intensified and broadened its invasion,

49

bombing Chinese cities and killing thousands of civilians. In Nanking, Japanese troops slaughtered 100,000 Chinese. In December, in the midst of a full-scale military attack against China, Japanese war planes sank the American gunboat *Panay,* killing two American sailors and wounding thirty. Though Roosevelt privately considered responding with economic sanctions, he did nothing once Japan apologized.

During the 1930s, the United States criticized Japanese aggression in the Far East and refused to recognize their claim to territory in China. But Roosevelt always stopped short of taking any action. Henry Stimson had set the course of American policy in the region when he served as secretary of state in the Hoover administration. The so-called Stimson Doctrine stated that the United States would not recognize any arrangements imposed on China by force. Even before he took the oath of office in March 1933, Roosevelt had endorsed the main principles of the doctrine. Like many Americans, Roosevelt clung to a romantic image of the Chinese — an image reinforced by his ancestors' ties to the China trade. "I always had the deepest sympathy for the Chinese," adviser Raymond Moley recalled FDR saying. "How could you expect me not to go along with Stimson on Japan?"[1]

Regardless of his personal feelings, the reality was that the United States lacked the power to challenge Japanese predominance in East Asia. Economic power was the only effective weapon in the American arsenal. Japan depended on the United States for a long list of strategic materials, especially oil — 80 percent of Japanese oil came from the United States. But Roosevelt stopped short of using that leverage, consumed as he was with Europe, and dismissed the idea that Japan represented any real threat to American interests.

That changed in 1940 when, encouraged by Hitler's conquests, a new Japanese government headed by Premier Fumimaro Konoye decided it could solve its problem of dependence on imports by seizing oil fields in the Dutch East Indies, British rubber plants in Malaya, and tin mines in French-controlled Indochina. Tokyo's new military government pressured London to close supply routes through Hong Kong and Burma and to remove the British garrison from Shanghai. It also pressed France to shut the Indochina border. Suddenly, what had been a largely regional problem had the potential of exploding into a global conflict.

In response to the growing Japanese

threat, Roosevelt decided to relocate the American Pacific Fleet from California to Pearl Harbor on the Hawaiian island of Oahu. The British had been pressuring FDR to deter the Japanese, and his military advisers hoped that the fleet's presence would send a strong message to the Japanese to tame their aggression. In reality, the fleet was never strong enough to undertake offensive operations, and its presence was largely symbolic.[2]

The more pressing question was whether to impose economic sanctions on Japan, especially an embargo on oil shipments. Hard-liners, including Stimson, Treasury Secretary Morgenthau, and Interior Secretary Harold Ickes, lobbied for a total embargo on oil shipments. Roosevelt, however, was engaged in a delicate balancing act: He wanted to use economic leverage to temper Japanese aggression, but he did not want to trigger a confrontation that would draw attention and resources away from the European theater. "It is terribly important for the control of the Atlantic," Roosevelt told Harold Ickes in early July, "for us to keep peace in the Pacific. I simply have not got enough Navy to go around — and every little episode in the Pacific means fewer ships in the Atlantic." He never lost sight that Germany posed a greater threat to American interests than Japan. As he cautioned an adviser, war with Japan would mean "the wrong war in the wrong ocean at the wrong time."[3]

Roosevelt felt he had to take some action, so on July 26, 1940, he agreed to a limited embargo on the export of high-octane aviation gasoline and premium grades of iron and steel. Both Stimson and Ickes felt the limited embargo did not go far enough. They wanted a ban on all gasoline, but FDR preferred a go-slow approach, saying that he wanted "to slip the noose around Japan's neck, and give it a jerk now and then."[4]

The two nations were trapped in a cycle of escalation. Japan responded to the limited embargo by occupying the northern portion of Indochina. In September, Roosevelt upped the ante by signing an order banning the export of all iron and steel. He also announced a $100 million loan to China on September 27. Two days later, Japan countered by signing a treaty with Germany and Italy, the so-called Tripartite Pact, in which the three nations pledged to come to one another's help in the event of an attack "by a power not already engaged in war." Japan designed the treaty to prevent the United States from either aiding Britain in its battle against Germany or opposing its plans to dominate Asia. Japan hoped that the threat of a two-front war would deter the United States from taking further steps toward confrontation.[5]

Yet despite Japanese escalation throughout the winter and spring of 1940–1941, FDR largely left the problems in the Pacific on the back burner. Although he liked to think of himself as his own secretary of state, he allowed his foreign policy team to deal with the Japan problem. His civilian and military advisers, however, were deeply divided. Administration hawks continued to press for an embargo on all oil shipments, not just the high-octane oil needed for airplanes. Some military leaders urged caution, warning that cutting off oil would only force Japan to seek it somewhere else, possibly threatening the Dutch East Indies, Burma, and even the Philippines. More worrisome, the military realized that the United States was not prepared to fight a war in Asia and feared a confrontation would drain needed armaments from the European theater.[6]

Roosevelt wanted to buy time. In early 1941 Tokyo replaced its ambassador to the United States with Admiral Kichisaburo Nomura, an advocate of improved relations with America. Roosevelt welcomed the appointment, received Nomura cordially, and made a personal appeal for peace. "There is plenty of room in the Pacific area for everybody," he reasoned. "It would not do this country any good nor Japan any good, but both of them harm to get into war."[7]

Roosevelt suggested that Nomura sit down with Secretary of State Cordell Hull to see how relations could be improved. Hull, a courtly former distinguished senator from Tennessee, had served as FDR's secretary of state since 1933. Tall and thin, with a thatch of white hair, Hull was seventy-one years old, but looked even older. Weakened by the spread of tuberculosis, his health was already failing. The president often bypassed Hull on critical decisions, relying instead on trusted surrogates to conduct his foreign policy. Hull complained to colleagues about "that man across the street who never tells me anything." FDR hired Hull to sell his foreign policy to Congress, not to make it. While praising Hull publicly, FDR privately dismissed him as "gloomy, sanctimonious, and unimaginative." Hull's lisp — he had difficulty pronouncing the *cr* sound — was a source of amusement for the president. "If Cordell says, 'Oh Chwrist' again I'm going to scream," FDR whispered to Frances

Perkins. "I can't stand profanity with a lisp."[8]

Despite meeting fifty times over the next nine months, Hull and Nomura made no progress. Hull, who showed little patience or respect for Japan or its envoys, was convinced that negotiations would do little to slow the drive toward war. Japan, he later told the Joint Congressional Committee investigating the attack on Pearl Harbor, "had a long record of duplicity in international dealings." He once referred to Tokyo's envoys as "pissants." Japan had embarked on "a mission of conquest of the entire Pacific," he claimed. Since Japan was closely tied to Germany, Hull deemed its leaders dishonest and unreliable. Revealing a well-earned reputation for being stubborn and inflexible, he insisted that Japan remove all troops from China and Indochina, renounce its ties to the Axis powers of Germany and Italy, and abandon its strategy of using force to create a sphere of influence in the Pacific.[9]

While engaged in negotiations with the United States, Japan continued its aggression, sending 125,000 troops into southern Indochina. FDR hoped to avoid a confrontation with Tokyo, but he did not want their belligerence to go unpunished, so he chose to give the noose another "jerk." On July 26, 1941, Roosevelt signed an order requiring the Japanese to apply for an export license before each shipment of oil and gasoline. FDR, however, made it clear that he planned to continue the shipments; he just needed to send a strong signal to Japan that it was in danger of losing these vital resources if it continued its aggression. He tried to tighten the noose, but not so much that it left him with no further options. When asked specifically by the Treasury Department about how to handle Japanese requests for petroleum, FDR responded that he was "inclined to grant the licenses for shipment as the applications are presented."[10]

In this case, however, bureaucratic confusion resulted in a misdirected policy. After issuing the order, FDR left town for a secret meeting with British prime minister Winston Churchill off the coast of Newfoundland. While he was away, a subcommittee chaired by Assistant Secretary of State Dean Acheson had the final authority to make decisions about the export licenses. In Roosevelt's absence, Acheson unilaterally made the decision, in clear contradiction of the president's orders, to freeze all exports, including oil. With typical arrogance,

Acheson said his action would not provoke war in the Pacific, because "no rational Japanese could believe that an attack on us could result in anything but disaster for his country."[11]

FDR learned of the export freeze only when he returned to Washington on August 17. He chose to let it stand, even though it ran contrary to his original order. Roosevelt probably worried that reversing the policy would be perceived as appeasement. By the fall of 1941, American attitudes toward Japan had hardened. A survey in September showed that 67 percent of Americans were willing to risk war with Japan. Now that Japan and Germany were linked, would appeasement of Japan be perceived as weakness toward Germany? At the same time, the Chinese were pressuring FDR to maintain the tough line.[12]

The embargo shocked the Japanese and reminded them of their economic vulnerability. The action increased the power of hawks who called for dramatic action. One Japanese leader remarked that the nation was "like a fish in a pond from which the water was gradually being drained away." For now, Tokyo enjoyed naval superiority in the Pacific, but how long would that last, given the naval buildup that Congress had authorized the previous year? The emperor gave Prime Minister Konoye a month to negotiate an end to the embargo. Konoye, who desperately wanted to avoid war, pleaded for a private meeting with FDR. His request was turned down. Hull later claimed that Roosevelt refused the request, but most likely the president was simply consumed with events in Europe.[13]

FDR was also distracted during this critical period by a great personal loss. On September 7, his mother passed away after a short illness. Eleanor had called Franklin from Hyde Park on September 5 to tell him that Sara was very sick and that he needed to come immediately. Despite the pressing problems in Washington, he boarded an overnight train, arriving at Hyde Park the following morning. He spent all day by her side and she seemed to improve, but that evening she slipped into a coma. Franklin stayed with her through the night and into the next morning when, near noon, two weeks before her eighty-seventh birthday, Sara passed away.[14]

A grief-stricken FDR went into seclusion at Hyde Park for days. The *New York Times* reported that he "shut himself off from the world more completely than at any time since he assumed his present post." A few days later, while sorting through his mother's belongings with his secretary Grace Tully, he discovered a box that Sara had carefully tucked away containing a lock of his hair, toys, and other items from his childhood. As tears started pouring down his face, he asked Tully for a private moment. It was the only time that anyone had ever seen FDR cry.[15]

When he returned to Washington, the president hoped to send a signal to Japan that he was still open to negotiations. He wanted to avoid precipitating a war with Japan while the situation in Europe remained so precarious. What he really needed to know was: What was Japan's motive? Were they determined to continue their conquest, or was it possible to at least slow down their advance and achieve some temporary truce? At the very least, Roosevelt needed time to build up forces in the Philippines, which had been an American protectorate since the Spanish-American War. According to both European and Asian intelligence, Germany was pressuring Japan to fulfill its obligations under the Tripartite Pact and force both the Americans and the British to transfer valuable resources to the Pacific theater.[16]

Unable to reach an agreement to end the

embargo, Konoye resigned his post on October 16 and was replaced by the hard-line war minister General Hideki Tojo. "I am a bit worried over the Japanese situation," Roosevelt wrote King George VI on the day Konoye resigned. "The Emperor is for peace, I think, but the Jingoes are trying to force his hand." He had reason to be worried. Tojo told the Japanese privy council that "a policy of patience and perseverance was tantamount to self-annihilation." Japanese leaders agreed that negotiations with the United States would continue until November 25. If no settlement could be reached, Japan would likely resort to war.

In early November, the Japanese government announced that it was sending a special peace envoy, Saburo Kurusu, to Washington. At the weekly cabinet meeting, Hull warned that "relations had become extremely critical and that we should be on the outlook for an attack by Japan at any time." The cabinet was unanimous in its belief that the American people would support going to war if Japan attacked British or Dutch possessions in Asia. FDR seemed less convinced. He understood that war with Japan was likely, but he hoped that peace negotiations between the two nations could, at the very least, delay hostilities until a time when the United States was in a better military position to fight a two-front war. Although Hull held out little hope of finding a peaceful settlement, Roosevelt instructed him to keep the talks going as a means of preventing conflict. "Do not let the talks deteriorate," he told his secretary of state. "Let us make no more of ill will. Let us do nothing to precipitate a crisis."

Official peace talks commenced on November 10 and continued over the next eleven days. There was little hope of any breakthrough in the discussions. Hull was rigid and patronizing to Japan's envoys. He was less interested in the details of the discussion, instead using the occasions to lecture his counterparts on the importance of moral principles. It did not help that Hull had a mild speech impediment, while Nomura, who insisted on holding the discussions in English without a translator, was partially deaf.[17]

Once again, Roosevelt was distracted at a critical time in the process. On November 15, John L. Lewis, the fiery head of the United Mine Workers, ordered a strike that paralyzed the entire steel industry and threatened FDR's rearmament plans. Although generally sympathetic to organized labor, FDR eventually took a hard line, threatening to send in troops if the miners did not return to work. On November 22, Lewis backed down, agreed to compulsory arbitration, and ended the strike. The whole affair consumed the president's energy and attention at a time when he could least afford it.

Two days earlier, on November 20 — Thanksgiving Day — the Japanese representatives made their "final effort" at averting war. The proposal called for a six-month cooling-off period that would return relations to what they were before the embargo. In return for an end to the oil embargo, Japan would agree to no further expansion. But Japan refused to end its occupation of China, which had been a key stumbling block. In Hull's mind, to accept the Japanese proposal was "unthinkable." "It would have made the United States an ally of Japan and Japan's program of conquest and aggression and of collaboration with Hitler. It would have meant yielding to the Japanese demand that the United States abandon its principles and policies. It would have meant abject surrender of our position under intimidation," he told the Joint Congressional Committee.[18]

Roosevelt continued to search for a compromise. He seized on the idea of a modus vivendi in which the two nations would make mutual pledges that their policies were directed toward peace. The United States would also make a major concession. Instead of making Japanese withdrawal of China a precondition of any agreement, it would simply state that the conflict between Japan and China be "based upon the principles of peace, law, order, and justice." The agreement would remain in force for three months. At the very least, it would delay what almost everyone saw as the inevitable.[19]

Roosevelt scribbled out the main points of the compromise on a piece of paper and gave it to Hull. But his conciliatory response never made it back to the Japanese. It ran into strong opposition from the hawks in his cabinet and from America's allies.[20]

On November 26, Hull issued the formal response to the Japanese, sticking close to his hard line. He informed the envoys that the U.S. oil embargo would continue and demanded that Japan "withdraw all military, naval, air and police forces from China and from Indochina." The note omitted any reference to a truce or to the conciliatory language that FDR had initially suggested.

A tired, sick, and exhausted Hull lacked the energy and desire to engage in the delicate acts of diplomacy with envoys he considered dishonest and morally inferior. "I have washed my hands of it," he told Stimson, "and it is now in the hands of you and Knox, the Army and Navy." Perhaps convinced that Japan would never dare risk war with the United States, Hull intentionally drew a line in the sand that Japan would never accept. Probably he, like Acheson, simply assumed that Japan would back down.[21]

Concerned about Hull's hard line, FDR's military advisers weighed in and made sure that he was fully aware of the risks involved in a war with Japan. Chief of Naval Operations (CNO) Admiral Harold "Betty" Stark and Army Chief of Staff George Marshall, both recently handpicked to join the FDR team, wanted to delay war with Japan for as long as possible.

Both men had impressed FDR with their skill, poise, and independence. Roosevelt met his future CNO for the first time in 1914 when Stark, a navy lieutenant, was assigned to escort the future president and current assistant navy secretary to the family vacation home in Campobello. Stark skillfully maneuvered the ship through the treacherous waters near the compound. They stayed in touch over the next few decades, and when FDR needed someone to oversee the expansion of the navy, he passed over fifty more senior officers and appointed Stark, promoting him from vice admiral to admiral.

George Marshall, a descendant of John Marshall, the third and legendary chief justice of the Supreme Court, caught FDR's attention in 1938 when, as a low-ranking brigadier general, he accompanied a group of his superiors to the White House for a meeting with the president. FDR asked the group if they shared his enthusiasm for a new fleet of large planes. They all nodded in agreement — all except Marshall. His stone-faced expression must have caught Roosevelt's attention. "Don't you agree, George?" Roosevelt asked. "No, Mr. President, I do not agree with you at all," Marshall responded. Roosevelt found Marshall's honesty refreshing. The following year, he promoted Marshall to the position of chief of staff of the U.S. Army, even though he was ranked thirty-fourth on the seniority list.[22]

Marshall and Stark had a similar view of the world: They both believed that Germany represented the primary threat to American interests, and they hoped to direct precious military resources to the European theater.

Protecting Britain and defeating Nazi Germany was their top priority. While mindful of the dangers of Japan's aggressive stance in the Pacific, they recognized the nation did not yet have the ability to fight two wars. They desperately needed time to train new recruits; to build ships, planes, and tanks; and to beef up the American capabilities in the Philippines.

While they realized that Japan would likely attack British outposts in the Pacific, they emphasized that the United States was not prepared to fight a two-front war. Marshall and Stark sent FDR a memorandum warning that the U.S. fleet "is inferior to the Japanese Fleet and cannot undertake an unlimited strategic offensive in the Western Pacific. In order to be able to do so, it would have to be strengthened by withdrawing practically all naval vessels from the Atlantic except those assigned to local defense forces." As a result, they argued for delay. "The most essential thing now, from the United States viewpoint, is to gain time," they wrote. "Precipitance of military action on our part should be avoided as long as consistent with national policy."[23]

Even as they advised Roosevelt against war with Japan, Marshall and Stark warned their commanders in the Pacific of its possibility. On November 27, with the negotiations clearly near an end, the War Department sent warnings to Lieutenant General Walter Short, the commander of army forces in Hawaii. The message stated: "Japanese future action unpredictable but hostile action possible at any moment." The navy issued an even stronger statement to Admiral Husband Kimmel: "This dispatch is to be considered a war warning." Stark later testified that he deliberately opened his message with the dramatic statement "to accentuate the extreme gravity of the situation." The message continued: "Negotiations with Japan . . . have ceased, and an aggressive move by Japan is expected within the next few days."[24]

There was ample reason to be concerned. On December 2, Japan's emperor approved a war order, setting the date as December 8 (December 7 in Hawaii and Washington). Tokyo sent a message to its ambassador in Washington to burn their code machines — an ominous order suggesting the diplomatic effort had come to an end. At the same time, American military intelligence started receiving reports of a large Japanese fleet of thirty-five transporters, eight cruisers, and twenty destroyers that were moving south from Indochina toward Thailand. "This was confirmation," Hull noted, "that the long-threatened Japanese movement of expansion by force to the south was under way."[25]

Roosevelt, however, was still not ready to accept a colossal distraction of a war in the Pacific. Against the unanimous advice of his closest advisers, FDR sent a message to the emperor on December 6 in a last-ditch effort to prevent hostilities. He had made a similar appeal to the emperor in 1937 following the attack on the *Panay,* and he was convinced that the move led to the resolution of the issue. He was hoping it would work again. Roosevelt knew that Japan had been at war for nearly a decade and that his peace overture could, at best, delay but not prevent a confrontation.[26] "I address myself to Your Majesty at this moment in the fervent hope that Your majesty may, as I am doing, give thought in this definite emergency to ways of dispelling the dark clouds." The concentration of troops in Indochina, he wrote, created a "deep and far reaching emergency," which threatened peaceful relations with the United States. The only way to dispel "the dark clouds," he wrote, was for Japan to withdraw its forces from Indochina.[27]

That evening Roosevelt entertained thirty-two guests at dinner in the White House.

"This son of man has just sent his final message to the Son of God," he told the party. Roosevelt talked about how when the current crisis blew over, he hoped to take a winter vacation from Washington and travel to Key West to sit in the sunshine. An old friend from New York noted that FDR "looked very worn . . . and after the meat course he was excused and wheeled away. He had an unusually stern expression." The president returned to his study, where he toyed with his stamp collection. He still held out hope that his last-minute appeal would convince the Japanese to call off any further military moves.[28]

But Roosevelt's message had not been transmitted to the emperor. The Japanese leadership had already made the decision for war; aircraft carriers were fast approaching Hawaii. Fearing that FDR's peace overture would complicate their political problems at home, the Japanese military held the message hostage, refusing to pass it on to either the emperor or the American ambassador, Joseph Grew. It arrived ten hours late, at 10:30 p.m. The emperor did not receive it until a few minutes before planes appeared in the skies over Oahu.

3

"THIS MEANS WAR"

Soon after Roosevelt retreated to his study, he was joined by his close friend Harry Hopkins, who would shadow the president for the next twenty-four hours. Like most chief executives, FDR often found the presidency a lonely position that left him surrounded by people who always wanted something from him. Over time, FDR learned to be suspicious of the senior members of his own administration. When he needed to relax, FDR often turned to old friends and relatives who had no connection to government. Hopkins was the exception: By all accounts, he and Roosevelt shared a special bond that endured until the day FDR died.[1]

Harry Hopkins, born in Iowa in 1890, became a social worker in New York City after graduating from Grinnell College. After the onset of the Great Depression, Hopkins took a position as head of New

York State's Temporary Emergency Relief Administration under Governor Franklin D. Roosevelt. Hopkins followed Roosevelt to Washington after the 1932 election and spent the next few years developing ingenious new ways to spend the nation's money. He headed up a series of New Deal alphabet-soup agencies designed to provide work and relief to struggling families: the Federal Emergency Relief Administration (FERA), the Civil Works Administration (CWA), and the Works Progress Administration (WPA).

Over the years, the two men formed a close bond. Hopkins understood Roosevelt's moods. He knew the appropriate time to talk business and when his boss needed to relax. He had an instinctive feel for when he could push FDR and when it was time to back off. His real talent was in turning Roosevelt's vague ideas into concrete programs. Hopkins was not a big thinker or a political visionary. He divided people into two groups: "talkers" and "doers." Hopkins was the consummate "doer." He knew how to move the bureaucracy and help FDR achieve his goals. Above all else, Roosevelt knew that Hopkins would protect his interests and remain totally discreet in the process. As Roosevelt's friend and speechwriter Robert Sherwood noted, "Hopkins made it his job, he made it his religion, to find out just what it was that Roosevelt really wanted and then to see to it that neither hell nor high water, nor even possible vacillations by Roosevelt himself, blocked its achievement."[2]

Although Hopkins won the president's trust and friendship, by 1935 he had alienated powerful members of Congress and found himself at odds with more conservative members of the administration who were pushing Roosevelt to scale back spending. "He was regarded as a sinister figure by all of Franklin D. Roosevelt's enemies and by many of Roosevelt's most loyal friends," Sherwood noted. People resented his enormous power and his privileged access to the president. When questioned by Republican presidential hopeful Wendell Willkie about why he kept Hopkins around, Roosevelt responded, "Someday you may well be sitting here where I am now as President of the United States. And when you are, you'll be looking at that door over there and knowing that practically everybody who walks through it wants something out of you. You'll learn what a lonely job this is, and you'll discover the need for somebody like Harry Hopkins who asks for nothing except to serve you."[3]

In 1937, a few weeks after his wife died, Hopkins was diagnosed with stomach cancer and had a large portion of his intestines removed. The surgery eradicated the cancer, but it also prevented him from properly digesting food, leaving him shockingly thin. FDR jokingly referred to him as "the half man" because of his sickly, frail appearance.[4]

In December 1938, Roosevelt appointed Hopkins secretary of commerce, but Hopkins was too sick to work. He spent months at the Mayo Clinic, but his condition was grave. "The doctors have given Harry up for dead," Roosevelt told friends. Unwilling to let his friend go without a fight, FDR intervened and had Hopkins transferred to Washington, where navy physicians managed to save his life. Hopkins offered the president his resignation, but FDR refused to accept it, saying, "Why you'll be back in your office in a couple of weeks and going great guns!" The recovery was slow, however, and Hopkins remained very sick and largely bedridden for months.[5]

In May 1940, Hopkins mustered the strength to attend dinner at the White House. He looked awful and felt worse. Roosevelt was so concerned that he told him to spend the night. He would call the White House his home for the next three and a half years. "It was Harry Hopkins who gave George S. Kaufman and Moss Hart the idea for that play of theirs, 'The Man Who Came to Dinner,' " quipped Grace Tully. Hopkins lived in the Lincoln Suite, which consisted of a large bedroom with a four-post bed, a small sitting room, and a bath. The room was just two doors down the hall from FDR. His daughter, Diana, moved into a bedroom on the third floor.[6]

With a room down the hall from the president's private study, Hopkins needed no appointment to stroll down and discuss events with Roosevelt. After breakfast, numerous times throughout the day, and often in the evenings after dinner, he would casually saunter into the president's study and talk over the day's news. They enjoyed the same kind of humor, poking fun at other officials and telling off-color jokes. Often in the evening the two men could be heard laughing from inside the president's private study. Most of all, they were both staunch liberals and devoted internationalists.

By the winter of 1941, Hopkins appeared a ghost of a man. A friend once described his physical appearance as being akin to "an ill-fed horse at the end of a hard day." But he refused to let his deteriorating health slow him down. He smoked four packs of Lucky Strikes a day. He also loved the racetrack, always betting at the two-dollar window. He enjoyed the company of women. Frequent nightlong soirees at various clubs and bars earned him the reputation as a playboy. "Our biggest job is to keep Harry from ever feeling completely well," said the White House physician, Admiral Ross T. McIntire. "When he thinks he's restored to health he goes out on the town — and from there to the Mayo Clinic."[7]

Roosevelt trusted Hopkins more than his own State Department. Beginning in 1940, after Hopkins left the Commerce Department, Roosevelt gave him the title of special assistant to the president and used him as a private envoy. Roosevelt trusted Hopkins to lead delicate diplomatic missions, communicate messages, and gather intelligence. In the spring of 1941, FDR sent him as a special envoy to Winston Churchill. FDR wanted to assess British morale and offer assurance that America would be sending aid. Churchill, who, like Roosevelt, appreciated Hopkins's ability to zero in on a problem, nicknamed him "Lord Root of the Matter." Despite fragile health that required frequent stays in the hospital, Hopkins continued in this role of amateur diplomat while cementing his position as Roosevelt's alter ego.

At 9:30 p.m. on December 6, Lieutenant Lester Schulz arrived at the White House with a locked pouch containing a top-secret document. The pouch contained thirteen parts of the fourteen-part Japanese reply to the hard-line U.S. proposal that Hull had presented to Japan in November. The messages had been sent from Tokyo to the Japanese Embassy in Washington, but had been intercepted by American intelligence. The United States had cracked the Japanese diplomatic code, nicknamed "Purple," in August 1940. American officials had been reading the messages before the diplomats received them, which meant that Roosevelt had the advantage of knowing what the Japanese government was doing and saying for the sixteen months before Pearl Harbor. They had not, however, cracked the military code, so while the U.S. government was aware of Japan's diplomatic maneuvering, it remained in the dark about the specific movements of Tokyo's navy.

As Hopkins paced back and forth, Roosevelt read the fifteen typewritten pages carefully for about ten minutes. Most of the document outlined Japan's peaceful intentions in the region and laid blame for the rising tensions on the United States. There was still a critical fourteenth part missing, but the final section of this document announced there was no chance of reaching a diplomatic settlement with the United States "because of American attitudes." As he finished, FDR turned to his trusted adviser. "This means war," he said.

Despite his dramatic comment, FDR most likely did not believe that the message signaled an imminent threat to American bases in the Pacific. It meant that war would come sooner than expected, and it would likely be precipitated by a Japanese attack on British, or possibly Dutch, possessions somewhere in the region.

Hopkins agreed and suggested to FDR that perhaps the United States should launch a preemptive strike. "Since war was undoubtedly going to come at the convenience of the Japanese," Hopkins noted, "it was too bad that we could not strike the first blow and prevent any sort of surprise." Roosevelt, like Lincoln on the eve of the Civil War, understood the political appeal of having the enemy fire the first shot. "No," he said, "we can't do that. We are a democracy and a peaceful people." He raised his voice and said, "But we have a good record." Schulz, who waited in the study until the president finished reading the document, understood Roosevelt's comments to mean that the United States would have to wait. "The impression that I got was that we would have to stand on that record, we could not make the first overt move. We would have to wait until it came."[8]

Roosevelt wanted to alert the navy as quickly as possible. It was important that the navy be on alert, prepared for a possible Japanese move. He tried to reach Admiral Stark, who was attending a revival of Sigmund Romberg's *Student Prince.* Fearing that summoning the admiral from a public theater might cause "undue alarm," Roosevelt waited until shortly before midnight to pass along the warning.

Roosevelt may have been alarmed by the message, but his foreign policy advisers did not share his concern. Stark, who read the message after returning home from the theater, later testified before the Navy Court of Inquiry that he, too, was convinced that war was inevitable. But he believed that the commanders in Hawaii had already been sufficiently warned about the prospect of hostilities, and he saw nothing in the thirteen-part message that suggested an imminent threat to the United States. "I thought she was more likely to strike in the Philippines than elsewhere, so far as United States territory is concerned."[9]

That evening, a messenger also brought the decoded thirteen-part Japanese message to Secretary of the Navy Frank Knox at his Wardman Park home on Connecticut Avenue. While Knox read the pages in silence, Mrs. Knox told the messenger that she was hoping that her exhausted husband could take the next day off and "sleep around the clock." Knox, seeing nothing new in the message, decided to wait until the following morning to discuss it with Stimson and Hull. There was still a missing fourteenth part to the message. Knox hoped that the complete message would be available at that time and they would know Japan's intent.[10]

Aides to Secretary Hull and General Marshall, who also received the thirteen-part message that evening, did not see any reason to disturb their bosses with the new information on a Saturday night. An aide to Hull read the thirteen-part message and concluded it had "little military significance." He promised to show it to the secretary in the morning.[11]

FDR was still in bed on Sunday morning

when he received notice that his military aide, Admiral John Beardall, would be bringing the locked pouch containing the fourteenth part of Japan's diplomatic message. Beardall delivered the pouch to the president at 10:00 a.m. and waited patiently while FDR read it. It contained the missing fourteenth part of the message that began arriving the previous evening. It stated that the chances of achieving peace in the Pacific "through cooperation of the American Government" had "been lost."

The pouch likely also contained a second message that instructed the Japanese ambassador to destroy the code machines at their Washington embassy and to deliver the message to the secretary of state at one o'clock. But if these instructions were included in the package that FDR read, he apparently was not alarmed. After reading the materials, the president turned to the admiral and said, "It looks as though they are breaking off negotiations." It was obvious to FDR that the Japanese were planning to strike, but when? And where? There was nothing that suggested to him that an American installation would be a target.[12]

Roosevelt confronted a dilemma: The Japanese response made clear they were breaking off diplomatic relations and were likely to strike Allied possessions in the Pacific. He assumed that the likely target would be either British Malaya or the Dutch East Indies. Without American intervention, the Japanese could control a vast area that was rich in natural resources that stretched from the Aleutian Islands to India. This aggression would strengthen the Japanese war machine and make them a more formidable enemy for the United States. It would also weaken the British, forcing them to expend precious resources to protect their colonial possessions that could be better used to fight Hitler.

Although a Japanese offensive against British possessions would present a long-term danger to the United States, FDR doubted if he could motivate the nation to go to war to save British imperial land in the Pacific. Congress had only reluctantly agreed to support FDR's efforts to defend Britain. As Sherwood noted, "Why, then, should Americans die for Thailand, or for such outposts of British imperialism as Singapore or Hong Kong or of Dutch imperialism in the East Indies, or for Communism in Vladivostok?"[13]

Even if the president were to muster all of his political skills, a congressional debate over war could drag on for weeks. FDR had been warning the American people about the danger in the Atlantic and the need to support Britain. How could he now convince them to go to war in the Pacific? Much of his rhetoric had been focused on convincing Americans to supply aid to Britain so that American soldiers would not have to fight and die in another foreign war. He was reluctant to abandon that message or to remove the focus from the war in Europe.[14]

The hawkish Stimson and Hull were pondering the same question on Sunday morning at their 10:00 a.m. meeting. "Hull is very certain that the Japs are planning some deviltry and we are all wondering where the blow will strike," Stimson noted in his diary. Like Roosevelt, they were convinced that the likely target would be British, not American. One question persisted: What should the United States do if the Japanese attacked Singapore, Malaysia, or Thailand? Stimson and Hull were convinced that the United States needed to join the British if a fight erupted. But they clearly wondered whether Roosevelt would agree.

The possibility that Japan would strike America or its possessions seemed remote to all. The day before, while holding his daily briefing with civilian aides and military chiefs, Knox had reviewed all the intelligence information. Reports claimed that a large Japanese task force was at sea, apparently headed along the south coast of Indochina. "Gentlemen," Knox asked, "are they going to hit us?' " His advisers were unanimous in their response. "No, Mr. Secretary," declared Admiral Richmond Kelly Turner, who was in charge of war planning for the navy. "They are going to attack the British. They are not ready for us yet." As a naval aide noted, "There was no dissenting voice. Turner's concise statement apparently represented the thinking of the Navy Department."[15]

And so in the hours before the Japanese attacked Pearl Harbor, FDR's main foreign policy advisers were busy developing a strategy for getting him to declare war against Japan if it attacked either a British or a Dutch possession. Knox dictated a memorandum that urged the president to recognize that "any threat to any one of the three of us is a threat to all of us." As Knox later told a congressional committee investigating the attack, his goal was to convince Roosevelt to state that the United States would respond by force if the Japanese attacked Thailand or "British, Dutch, United

States, Free French, or Portuguese territory in the Pacific area."[16]

At the Munitions Building on Independence Avenue in Washington, Colonel Rufus Bratton, an intelligence aide to General Marshall, was not alarmed by the official fourteen-part Japanese response. He was, however, stunned when he read the second cable instructing Japan's ambassadors to present the message to the secretary of state at precisely 1:00 p.m. and to destroy their code machines. He believed that it was an "activating" intercept. The 1:00 p.m. message convinced him that the Japanese were planning to strike near dawn somewhere in the Pacific.[17]

Bratton urgently tried reaching General Marshall, who was out riding his horse. Bratton had to settle for leaving a message with Marshall's orderly. "Please go out at once, get assistance if necessary, and find General Marshall," he pleaded.[18]

Marshall returned to his office at 11:25 a.m. and began carefully poring over the entire fourteen-part message. After finishing, he looked up at his aides and asked whether they saw any significance in the instruction to present the message at 1:00. Bratton said he "thought it probable that the Japanese line of action would be into Thailand but that it might be into any one or more of a number of other areas." Marshall's aides recommended that all American outposts in the Pacific and on the West Coast be notified before the 1:00 p.m. deadline.[19]

General Marshall then called Admiral Stark and told him that he was planning to send a warning message to army posts in the Pacific and the Panama Canal region and asked whether he planned to send one to the navy. Stark told him that he felt that the navy had already been provided sufficient warning of a possible attack, and he felt no reason to send a new one. Marshall then started scribbling out his message: "Japanese are presenting at one pm eastern standard time today what amounts to an ultimatum. Also, they are under orders to destroy their code machine immediately. Just what significance the hour set may have we do not know but be on alert accordingly." While he was writing the message, Stark had a change of mind and called Marshall back, agreeing that naval authorities should be sent the same message. Marshall added to his message: "Inform naval authorities of this communication."[20]

Marshall delivered his handwritten message to Bratton and ordered that it be sent for immediate transmission with top priority given to the Philippines. Since the message had to be typed, it was not sent until 11:58 a.m. The Army Signals Center sent the message first to the Caribbean Defense Command in the Panama Canal Zone. The message to Manila went out at 12:06 and a few minutes later to the Presidio in San Francisco. Because of atmospheric interference, it was not possible to send a message to Hawaii. So the Signal Center opted for a direct teletype through Western Union. The message was clocked at 12:17 p.m. in Washington. The RCA bicycle man picked up General Marshall's message in Honolulu at 7:33 a.m. Since the package was not marked "urgent," the messenger tucked it in his bag for regular delivery. It was not delivered until after the bombs started falling.

Roosevelt's first scheduled appointment on Sunday, December 7, was with the Chinese ambassador, Dr. Hu Shih, at 12.30 p.m. The ambassador had taken the midnight train down from New York for the meeting. They met in the Oval Study. Roosevelt wanted to let the ambassador know that he had sent a private appeal to the Japanese emperor. He read portions of the letter to Dr. Shih and explained that he planned to release the text on Tuesday. As the president read the letter, he highlighted phrases that he deemed especially clever. "I got him there," he said, clearly pleased with himself. "That was a fine, telling phrase. That will be fine for the record." He assured the ambassador that if the emperor did not intervene and restrain the military, war between the United States and Japan would be inevitable. "I think," FDR said, "that something nasty will develop in Burma, or the Dutch East Indies, or possibly even in the Philippines."[21]

After China's ambassador left at 1:10 p.m., Roosevelt and Hopkins sat together eating lunch. Afterward, FDR looked over his stamp collection while Hopkins lounged on the sofa. By this point, Roosevelt suspected that Japan was going to strike, but he was still convinced it would avoid a direct confrontation with the United States and instead nibble around the edges of the European empires in the Pacific. Hopkins recalled numerous conversations with FDR about the subject. He claimed that FDR "really thought that the tactics of the Japanese would be to avoid a conflict with us; that they would not attack either the

Philippines or Hawaii but would move on Thailand, French Indo-China, make further inroads on China itself and attack the Malay Straits."[22]

Secretary of War Stimson also feared that Japan would strike British and Dutch holdings in the Pacific, carefully avoiding a direct confrontation with the United States. If that happened, what would the cautious Roosevelt do? He wrote in his diary, "We should maneuver them into the position of firing the first shot." He never expected the first shot to be delivered in such a devastating manner.[23]

4
"THIS IS NO DRILL!"

At 1:25 p.m. eastern standard time (7:55 a.m. in Hawaii), fighter pilot Mitsuo Fuchida peered down at the U.S. Navy ships berthed at the U.S. Naval base at Pearl Harbor. Fuchida shouted, "To-to-to," the first syllable of the Japanese word for *charge,* into his radio. That was followed by an even more significant transmission: "Tora, tora, tora," meaning *tiger,* the message confirming that the attack caught the Americans by surprise.

The island of Oahu, which housed the American Pacific Fleet, was considered by many military planners to be the strongest military outpost in the world. "Here in Hawaii," said the American commander, Walter Short, "we all live in a citadel." Massive coastal guns surrounded the perimeter, 45,000 army troops protected the fleet and air bases from attack, and squadrons of bombers, scouts, and fighters patrolled the skies. Three aircraft carriers, eight battle-ships, and twenty-nine destroyers provided the anchor for military operations in the Pacific.[1]

The formidable American naval base at Pearl Harbor seemed an unlikely target, but over the past few months, Japan's military leaders had decided that it was essential to cripple the U.S. Navy in order to realize their territorial ambitions in the region.

The attack on Pearl Harbor was the brain-child of Admiral Isoruko Yamamoto, the commander in chief of the Japanese Com-bined Fleet. He was a battle-tested warrior. In 1905, at age twenty-one, he lost the second and third fingers on his left hand during a ferocious battle with the Russians at the Tsushima Strait. After World War I, he traveled to the United States, studied at Harvard, and later served as a naval attaché in Washington. More than most Japanese leaders, he understood the United States and respected its enormous industrial capability. He also demonstrated an ap-preciation for American culture and history. When a junior officer asked him what he should read to improve his English, Yama-moto recommended Carl Sandburg's biog-raphy of Abraham Lincoln. "I like Lincoln," he said. "I think he's great not just as an American, but as a human being."[2]

Although he was not a pilot, Yamamoto had developed great respect for the military capability of airpower. He had also earned a reputation for being a bold thinker who was willing to take risks. In his spare time, he enjoyed high-stakes all-night poker games where he tested his opponents' nerves and patience. "In all games Yamamoto loved to take chances just as he did in naval strategy," an aide recalled. "He had a gambler's heart."[3]

In 1940, Yamamoto devised a daring and pragmatic plan for defeating the United States. He advocated an offensive operation against the American Pacific Fleet in its home port of Pearl Harbor. He believed the American fleet needed to be crippled before Japan could wage war in Asia. The model for his attack was Hitler's successful *Blitzkrieg* strategy in Europe. The goal was to hit the enemy hard with overwhelming force.

Yamamoto understood the risks of going to war against an industrial giant like the United States. In order to gain the upper hand, he realized that Japan would need to strike a decisive blow. As he explained to his navy minister, "We should do our very best . . . to decide the fate of the war on the very first day." A decisive, crippling blow, he believed, would demoralize the American people, making them less likely to support a long, costly war in the Pacific. It would take years for the United States to recover, and by that time it would face a fait accompli, with Japan controlling everything between the Indian and Pacific oceans.[4]

When Yamamoto first raised the idea, it was universally dismissed as impractical: Pearl Harbor was too far away and too well defended. Yamamoto, however, remained convinced that with careful planning, and some luck, Pearl Harbor could be destroyed by a massive stealth air attack. Quietly, the determined admiral began assembling a team of trusted lieutenants to plan the assault. To execute the attack, Yamamoto turned to Commander Minoru Genda, a thirty-six-year-old daredevil pilot who was the famed leader of "Genda's Flying Circus," a team of skilled pilots who entertained audiences with acrobatic aerial performances. Known as "Mad Genda," for his fanaticism, he was also a profound strategic and tactical thinker.[5]

Genda convinced Yamamoto that a successful attack would need to be made at dawn and would require every available carrier in the fleet. He believed that it should include dive-bombing and high-level bombing as well as torpedoes. The element of surprise was essential. They had to strike before the Americans could mobilize their potent ground and air defenses. Perhaps most important, he convinced the admiral to recruit a classmate, Mitsuo Fuchida, to train the pilots and lead them into the attack. The thirty-nine-year old Japanese commander was the grandson of a famous samurai. He wore a toothbrush mustache to express his admiration for Adolf Hitler.

Throughout the summer, Fuchida drilled his pilots, using Kagoshima Bay in Kyushu because it resembled the topography of Pearl Harbor. The biggest challenge was to figure out a way to get torpedoes to work in the shallow forty-five-foot average depth of Pearl Harbor's water. Aerial torpedoes usually needed at least one hundred feet of water to operate successfully. Genda came up with the solution: He added wooden tail fins to the torpedoes so they would remain closer to the water's surface. He also added steel fins to the sixteen-inch armor piercing bombs that would be used to penetrate the thick armor on the American battleships. The fins guaranteed that the bombs would fall tip down, maximizing their explosive impact.[6]

The plan called for the torpedo bombers to strike first, descending to thirty feet above the water line, assaulting the largest battleships. Since the ships were moored in pairs, the bombers would be able to hit only the outside ships. Torpedo bombers would be followed by horizontal or high-level Nakajima B5N2 bombers that were responsible for hitting the remaining battleships. Genda scheduled a final wave of dive-bombers to destroy the main army and navy airfields. The plan also involved using well-placed spies on the island to provide intelligence about ship movements and security procedures.

On November 17, the Japanese armada left their training base in Saeki Bay for their rendezvous point at Hitokappu Bay in the Kuriles, north of Japan's main islands. There it began its relentless drive toward Pearl Harbor. The task force boasted six carriers, 400 warplanes, two battleships, two cruisers, nine destroyers, and a dozen other surface ships. At an average speed of thirteen knots, refueling daily, the attack fleet pursued a 3,500-mile course across the empty expanse of the North Pacific. Included in the fleet's orders was a provision that "in the event an agreement is reached in the negotiations with the United States, the task force will immediately return to Japan." But nobody expected that to happen.

By the time the government issued the attack order — "Climb Mt. Nitaka 1208" — on December 2, the fleet had already traveled half the distance to Pearl Harbor. The reference was to the highest peak in Japan, a fitting metaphor for such an ambitious plan. Moving in wedgelike formation, they were roughly 900 miles north of Hawaii on December 4. At 11:30 a.m. on December 6, the sprawling armada turned south toward Oahu and increased its speed to twenty knots. By 5:50 a.m. the following morning, December 7, the fleet was 220 miles north of Oahu. "I have brought the task force successfully to the point of attack," the commander told Genda. "From now on the burden is on your shoulders."[7]

At 6:00 a.m. the Japanese carriers turned into the wind and launched their first wave of 183 planes. All six carriers launched at the same time. It took fifteen minutes for all the planes to lift into the air for the first assault. Before taking off, each officer tied a *hachimaki* around his head. This traditional white cloth, marked with the symbol of the Rising Sun, signified that they were embarking on an important mission that required courage and determination. Once launched, the bombers assumed their aerial positions. The high-level bombers rose to 9,300 feet, with torpedo bombers to their right and dive-bombers to their left. Zero fighters swarmed around the constellation of bombers, providing protection.[8]

At 7:05, the carriers launched a second wave of 167 aircraft. Military planners would have preferred a single strike with overwhelming force, but because it would take too long to get all the planes into the air, they broke into two separate strike forces. The first wave started its flight toward Oahu as a second wave began launching. It took ninety minutes for all the Japanese assault planes to be airborne.[9]

The Japanese pilots had practiced a careful system of signals for the final approach. If they managed to achieve complete surprise, Fuchida would fire one "black dragon" signal from a pistol. That would allow the slow-moving and vulnerable torpedo planes to attack first. They would be followed by the horizontal bombers and finally the dive-bombers. If Fuchida did not have the element of surprise, he would fire two flares, which would mean the torpedo bombers would engage last while the Americans were focused on the other bombers.[10]

Realizing that he had caught the Americans unprepared, Fuchida fired his single "black dragon" flare. When the fighter-group leader did not respond, Fuchida assumed he had missed the signal, so he fired a second flare. The leader, however, saw both flares and interpreted it as the signal that they had lost the element of surprise.[11]

The tactical miscue failed to slow the advancing planes. Peering through his binoculars, Fuchida could see Battleship Row in the distance. The fleet's aircraft carriers were out to sea that day, but the battleships and destroyers were lined up like sitting ducks. Although disappointed not to see any American carriers in their designated places, he was thrilled by the line of apparently unsuspecting targets in the distance. "What a majestic sight, almost unbelievable!" he thought to himself. He was told there would be nine ships, but he counted only seven (he missed the *Pennsylvania,* which was in drydock).[12]

The first wave of 183 fighters, bombers, and torpedo planes split into two groups. A dozen planes set out for Hickam Field, while the rest headed for the ships on Ford Island. Fighters and dive-bombers swarmed over the airfields at Kaneohe, Hickam, Ewa,

Bellows, and Wheeler. Meanwhile, the main force headed to the primary target at Pearl Harbor.

As Fuchida's aircraft swooped overhead, the brass band on board the USS *Nevada* was playing "The Star-Spangled Banner" in preparation for the standard 8:00 a.m. flag raising. Japanese fighters sprayed the band with machine-gun fire and dropped a torpedo that missed the nearby USS *Arizona.* Soldiers and sailors were so accustomed to military drills and the crackle of gunfire that they were not immediately alarmed by the sounds. It never occurred to anyone that they could be under attack from the Japanese. On board the USS *Arizona,* shocked soldiers stood on deck, watching the Japanese planes dropping bombs and firing machine guns, but it did not register. "This is the best goddamn drill the Army Air Force has ever put on!" remarked one confused sailor.[13]

With bombs exploding around them and machine-gun fire strafing the decks, it soon became clear that the sailors at Pearl Harbor were witnessing the impossible: a full-scale Japanese attack on what most Americans considered an impenetrable fortress. At 7:58 a.m. the command center at Ford Island announced, "Air raid, Pearl Harbor, this is no drill!" A sailor onboard the USS *Oklahoma* issued a more impassioned warning on the ship's public address system: "Man your battle stations! This is no shit!"

Of the one hundred ships at Pearl Harbor that day, the main targets were the eight battleships, seven of which were moored on Battleship Row on Ford Island. Within the first few minutes, all seven of the battleships near Ford Island were hit. Two torpedoes had already rocked the USS *Oklahoma,* which started listing to port and then capsized. Nearby, a bomb fell into the forward magazine of the USS *Arizona,* creating a fireball that soared five hundred feet above the ship. The explosion and fire killed 1,177 crewmen.[14]

For the men onboard the stricken ships, the quiet morning had turned into a living hell. Many were engulfed by the flames that consumed the ships. "There were bodies of men" everywhere, recalled Private First Class James Cory, who was on the deck of the *Arizona* before it sank. "These people were zombies, in essence. They were burned completely white. Their skin was just as white as if you'd taken a bucket of white-wash and painted it white. Their hair was burned off; their eyebrows were burned off . . . and the insoles of their shoes was about the only thing that was left on these bodies."[15]

Flying overhead, Commander Fuchida could not take his eyes off the inferno. "A huge column of dark red smoke rose to 1,000 ft., and a stiff shock wave rocked the plane," he recalled years later. "It was a hateful, mean-looking red flame, the kind that powder produces, and I knew at once that a big magazine had exploded. Terrible indeed."

At the same time, another group of bombers and fighters was crippling the U.S. Air Force with a swift and powerful assault on Navy air bases at Ford Island and Kaneohe Bay, Marine fields at Ewa, and Army Corps fields at Bellows and Wheeler. The Japanese assault also devastated Hickam Field, where most of the Air Force bombers — twenty B-17s, twelve A-20 light bombers, and thirty-two B-18s — sat clustered. Since the army had feared sabotage more than Japanese bombers, it had ordered the planes kept close together so they could easily be patrolled and protected. The move backfired: Lined up wingtip to wingtip, the planes were easy targets for the Japanese pilots.

Admiral Kimmel, at home when the attack started, received a panicked phone call from an aide. "There's a message from the signal tower saying the Japanese are attacking Pearl Harbor and this is no drill," he told the admiral. Kimmel, who had an unobstructed view of Battleship Row from his front lawn, slammed down the receiver and rushed outside, where he was joined by his neighbor Mrs. John Earle. She recalled watching the planes flying over "circling in figure 8's, then bombing the ships, turning and dropping more bombs." She could see the Rising Sun on their wings, "and could have seen the pilots' faces had they leaned out." Kimmel, she noted, stood next to her "in utter disbelief and completely stunned." His face, she observed, was "as white as the uniform he wore."[16]

The first Japanese attack wave broke off the assault around 8:45 a.m. and headed back to their carriers. After a lull of about thirty minutes, the second wave of 167 planes appeared in the sky. While Japan achieved total surprise on the first wave, the second wave encountered heavy antiaircraft fire and inflicted only minor damage. Nearly 90 percent of the damage was done in the first wave.[17]

At the end of the second attack, Fuchida circled above Pearl Harbor to assess the damage his forces had inflicted. He was satisfied with the results. It had taken roughly fifteen deadly minutes for the Japanese attackers to destroy the American Pacific Fleet. But Fuchida realized his forces had missed a number of key targets. They had left the shipyard untouched and the vital oil-storage facilities. There were also a number of American ships still afloat. Another run would be necessary.

When Fuchida returned to the aircraft carrier, a third wave of planes was preparing to launch. Admiral Nagumo, however, decided that the mission had been accomplished and it was time to go home. They were low on fuel, and he knew that the American carriers would be looking for him. At 1:00 p.m. the task force turned toward home.[18]

In 1946, the Joint Congressional Committee investigating the events of December 7 described Pearl Harbor as "the greatest military and naval disaster in our Nation's history." It was an accurate assessment. In a matter of a few minutes, Japanese bombers sank or severely damaged eight battleships, three light cruisers, four destroyers, and 350 airplanes. The Americans suffered 3,566 casualties. Of the 2,388 killed, nearly half — 1,177 men — died on the USS *Arizona,* where they remain entombed today. By

5
"HAVE YOU HEARD THE NEWS?"

As Japanese planes circled above Pearl Harbor, navy officials in Hawaii informed Washington of the attack. Pearl Harbor was not the first crisis of the Roosevelt presidency, but it was the most unexpected and the most challenging. In the critical minutes that followed, FDR reached out to the people he needed and trusted most to develop an appropriate strategy to confront the crisis.

The Naval Station in San Francisco picked up the announcement of the Japanese air raid on Pearl Harbor. The message was relayed to Washington and handed to Frank Knox, who was meeting with Admiral Stark. "My God, this can't be true, this must mean the Philippines," Knox said after reading the bulletin. Stark looked at the message and recognized the origin code — CINC-PAC — which made clear that it was accurate and authentic. "No, sir," said Admiral Stark, "this is Pearl." Knox realized that he needed to reach the president as quickly as possible.[1]

At 1:47 p.m., roughly twenty-seven minutes after the first Japanese planes began their bombing raids in Oahu, the White House operator informed Roosevelt, still in his study, that Knox was on the phone with an urgent message. "Mr. President," Knox said, "they had picked up a radio from Honolulu from the Commander-in-Chief of our forces there advising all our stations that an air raid attack was on and that it was 'no drill.'" It appeared, he said, "as if the Japanese have attacked Pearl Harbor." "NO!" Roosevelt shouted.

After he hung up with Knox, Roosevelt told Harry Hopkins the news. Hopkins was convinced the report was wrong. "I expressed the belief that there must be some mistake and that surely Japan would not attack in Honolulu," he noted in a memorandum he wrote about the events that day. Roosevelt likely hoped that it was a false report, but his instincts told him otherwise. "The President thought the report was probably true and thought it was just the kind of unexpected thing the Japanese would do, and that at the very time they were discussing peace in the Pacific they were plotting to overthrow it," Hopkins observed. But it is unlikely that Roosevelt anticipated the extent of the disaster that was unfolding in Hawaii. Like most military officials, FDR considered Pearl Harbor largely invulnerable to attack.[2]

FDR had only a skeleton crew on hand in the White House when he learned of the attacks. There were few aides, and no support staff, working on Sunday afternoon. With the exception of his war cabinet, most of the White House staff, and many other aides, were away.

Suddenly, the switchboard lit up, initially with calls from Hopkins and FDR trying to contact staff, and then with officials calling the White House for more information. Since it was a Sunday, and expected to be a slow day, there was only one operator on duty, a new recruit named Jesse Gill. The veteran, Louise (Hackie) Hackmeister, who had been the chief operator since 1933, was at home. Hopkins instructed Jesse to track down a handful of trusted aides and tell them to get to the White House. FDR insisted that she get in touch with his senior foreign policy advisers so he could speak with them. In addition to placing these calls, Jesse asked Hackie to come in and help. It was going to be a busy day at the White House switchboard. "I didn't leave my position at the board from 2 p.m. until 11 that night," Hackie told a reporter. "My legs almost collapsed me when I finally got up."[3]

Roosevelt's secretary Grace Tully was relaxing in her apartment at 3000 Connecticut Avenue when she received the call from the White House operator. "The President wants you right away," she said. "There's a car on the way to pick you up. The Japs have just bombed Pearl Harbor." Tully reflected that she was "too stunned" to react to the news. "The President needed me. He had confidence in me. My only objective was to get to the White House as fast as I could." She "dressed like a fireman" and "jumped to like a fireman."[4]

The White House also contacted FDR's son Captain James Roosevelt, who was taking an afternoon nap at his home in Washington. He was told only that the Japanese had attacked Pearl Harbor and that his father wanted to see him right away.

The first phone call the president made was to Secretary of War Henry Stimson. According to Hopkins, FDR made the call at 2:05 p.m. Stimson had been in his office that morning but had gone home for lunch.

When he picked up the phone, he recognized Roosevelt's voice. In "a rather excited voice," FDR asked him, "Have you heard the news?" Stimson was not sure what news FDR was referring to. "Well, I have heard the telegrams which have been coming in about the Japanese advances in the Gulf of Siam." FDR replied, "Oh, no. I don't mean that. They have attacked Hawaii. They are now bombing Hawaii." Stimson quickly finished his lunch and returned to his office.[5]

Given his hawkish stance, and his belief that war with Japan was inevitable, Stimson noted in his diary that he felt a sense of "relief" when he learned of the assault on Pearl Harbor. His "first feeling was of relief that the indecision was over and that a crisis had come in a way which would unite all our people," he wrote.[6]

After hanging up with Stimson, Roosevelt contacted Secretary of State Hull. The secretary was in his office, waiting to receive Ambassador Kichisaburo Nomura and special "peace" envoy Saburo Kurusu. They had called the State Department at noon and requested a 1:00 p.m. meeting, but they were running late because Tokyo had insisted that only staff with high-level security clearance could translate the final message.

Neither of the diplomats knew how to type. Realizing they would not make the 1:00 p.m. deadline, they rescheduled for 1:45 p.m., but showed up twenty minutes late, which gave FDR enough time to reach Hull.[7]

While the Japanese envoys sat in the diplomatic reception room, FDR told Hull about the attack on Pearl Harbor. In his testimony before the Roberts Commission, Hull claimed that there was at that point still some uncertainty about whether the original report was accurate. "There was a report that Pearl Harbor had been attacked," he recalled FDR saying. Hull discussed with the president "whether I would accredit that report as the unquestioned truth of the situation and refuse to admit them or whether in view of the extremely delicate relations I would leave open the one chance in ten or more that the report was not correct." Roosevelt instructed Hull to receive the representatives but not to mention that he knew about the attack. Hopkins recalled Roosevelt saying that Hull should "receive their reply formally and cooly and bow them out."[8]

Hull made the ambassadors wait outside his office until 2:20 p.m. When they entered, Nomura stated that "he had been instructed to deliver at 1:00 p.m." and apologized for being late. When the secretary asked why he had specified 1:00, the ambassador replied that he did not know why. Hull pretended to read the document, even though he had already seen it, and then, in clear violation of FDR's instructions, issued a blistering rebuke. "In all my fifty years of public service," he said, "I have never seen a document that was more crowded with infamous falsehoods and distortions — infamous falsehoods and distortions on a scale so huge that I never imagined until today that any Government on this planet was capable of uttering them." Before they could respond, Hull lifted his hand to silence them and then nodded toward the door. The two ambassadors "then took their leave without making any comment."[9]

Hull assumed that the ambassadors knew of the assault and were part of the conspiracy. In reality, they had not been informed of the plan and learned the news only after they returned to the embassy. Nomura was shocked. For him, it meant that his peace mission had been a failure. And many others in the embassy were extremely worried about the prospect of war between the United States and Japan and far less sanguine than the Japanese military planners about their prospects of victory. As one secretary told his wife, "Oh, it's terrible! Why did they do such a terrible thing? Japan is doomed."[10]

FDR realized that reporters would soon learn of the attack, and he wanted to control the flow of information. He had devoted a great deal of time developing close ties with the press, and he did more than any previous president to manage the news. His trusted partner in that effort was Steve Early, the first full-time White House press secretary.

The two men had met at the 1912 Democratic Convention in Baltimore. Early was working as a wire reporter for United Press International (UPI), and FDR was a Wilson supporter in the New York delegation. The two men struck up a friendship. In 1920, when FDR was running as vice president on Ohio governor James Cox's ticket and needed to create a campaign staff, he hired Early to be his advance man. While Roosevelt spent most of the 1920s fighting to overcome polio, and reemerging as a political figure, Early took a job with Paramount Pictures, where he oversaw the production of Washington newsreels. After FDR won election to the presidency in 1932, Early joined the White House staff. He had planned to stay for only two weeks, but he was still on the job twelve years later when Roosevelt died.

Early had expected a slow news day. On Saturday, he met briefly with reporters, joking that "the President decided you fellows have been so busy lately and Christmas is coming so close that he would give you a day off to do some shopping." A journalist, picking up on the light atmosphere, said, "I suppose he is over at the House writing a declaration of war, isn't he." Early admitted that he was at the White House, but said he was not writing, "he was shaving." He told reporters to take the weekend off. FDR "will stay over the House this morning; and is not coming to the office. No appointments for today and none tomorrow; and I don't assume there will be."[11]

Early took Sunday off and planned to lounge around his house. He was still in his bathrobe, sitting in the second-floor study at his home on Morningside Drive in Northeast Washington, when the special line that connected him directly to the White House started ringing. There were no pleasantries this morning. The first words he heard were, "Have you got a pencil handy?" Early assumed that Roosevelt was playing a practical joke. "Do I need it?" Early replied. Roosevelt was all business. "Yes," FDR responded. "I have a very important statement. It ought to go out verbatim."[12]

The press secretary could tell from the tone of Roosevelt's voice that he was serious. He called out to his wife, Helen, to help him record the message. "The Japanese have attacked Pearl Harbor from the air and all naval and military activities on the island of Oahu, the principal American base in the Hawaiian Islands." Oddly enough, after dictating the statement, Roosevelt asked Early, "Have you any news?" Early was shocked by the question. FDR had just dictated a message that amounted to a declaration of war, and he was asking Early if he had any information to report. He replied, "None to compare to what you have just given me, sir."[13]

As soon as he hung up with Roosevelt, Early called the White House operator and asked her to connect him to the three wire services: the Associated Press (AP), United Press, and International News Service. At 2:22 p.m., Early addressed the three major wire services on a three-way hookup from his home. "This is Steve Early. I am calling from home. I have a statement here which the President has asked me to read." After reading the president's statement, he told them that he was on his way to the White House and would call them with more information as soon as he had it.

Before leaving his house, Early called the news agencies back to report, falsely it turned out, that the Japanese were also bombing Manila. "A second air attack is reported. This one has been made on army and navy bases in Manila." It is unclear why he called back with the second report and where he received the information. The most likely source would have been FDR, but there was no evidence of an assault on Manila at the time or that the president had received such a report. It is likely that Washington officials had trouble reaching Manila in the minutes after learning about Pearl and assumed that the Philippines was also under attack. What was actually taking place in the Philippines would be a source of concern and confusion all day at the White House.[14]

Early then changed his clothes and drove to the White House for what would turn out to be one of the most stressful twenty-four hours of his life.

FDR made one more phone call in the minutes after learning of the assault on

Hawaii. It went to the Chinese ambassador, Hu Shih, who had just left the White House a few hours earlier. "Hi Shih," FDR said, "I just wanted to tell you that the Japanese have bombed Pearl Harbor and Manila." Shih recalled FDR sounding "very much excited and very angry and worked up." He repeated, "It is terrible; simply terrible." Roosevelt concluded the brief conversation by saying, "Since you were the last person I talked to before this happened, I thought I ought to call you up and tell you about it."[15]

6

"I DON'T KNOW HOW SECURE THIS TELEPHONE IS"

By 3:00 p.m., as his team gathered in his cluttered Oval Study on the second floor of the White House, FDR had begun to receive the first official damage reports from Pearl. They made clear that the Japanese had delivered a devastating blow to the Pacific Fleet. More troubling was the evidence that American forces had offered little resistance and appeared to have been taken completely by surprise. FDR quizzed his secretaries of war and navy about how the Japanese could have pulled off such a brazen assault and have succeeded in destroying a military base that most Americans considered impregnable. No one had a good answer to that question. The next question on everyone's mind was: Where would Japan strike next, and what could America do to stop it?

James Roosevelt hurried to the White House, arriving shortly before 2:30 p.m., where he noticed that his father was wearing one of his old sweaters. As he looked closer, he observed his father's "extreme calmness — almost a sad, fatalistic, but courageous acceptance of something he had tried to avert but which he feared might be inevitable." FDR was too busy to engage in conversation. "Hello, Jimmy," FDR said. "It's happened." He instructed Jimmy to stand by in case he needed him.[1]

FDR's main task was to collect as much information as possible. At 2:25 p.m., all he knew was that the Japanese had attacked. But what was the extent of the damage? Perhaps he hoped that some American aircraft had managed to get into the air and repel the invaders. Were some of the ships parked at Pearl Harbor able to respond with antiaircraft fire? Was the air attack the prelude to a land invasion? Roosevelt had many questions, but few answers.

The first official to arrive at the White House was Roosevelt's naval aide Admiral John Beardall. He found Roosevelt and Hopkins together, both working the phones. "Take over the phone to the Navy Department," FDR instructed him. Beardall used the phone in the lobby and started calling his contacts in the navy to find more information. Later, Roosevelt's private secretary,

Grace Tully, relieved him.[2]

The lack of a direct line between the White House and Pearl Harbor made communication difficult. Admiral Claude Bloch at Pearl Harbor had to contact Admiral Stark at the Navy Department, who then forwarded reports to the White House. The first full report came at 2:28 p.m., more than twenty minutes after the initial bulletin. At first, Bloch was vague about the extent of the damage, fearing that the Japanese were listening in on the call and would know what a crippling blow they had delivered. Finally, Stark pressed, "Claude, how about it?" "It's pretty bad," Bloch replied, but he was afraid to provide more details. "I don't know how secure this telephone is," he said. Stark told him to give the numbers anyway. "Go ahead and tell me," Stark said. Bloch proceeded to report that the Japanese had inflicted extensive damage to the fleet and the United States had suffered a significant loss of life. "If any unauthorized person has heard the remarks I have just made to the Chief of Naval Operations," Bloch concluded, "I beg of you not to repeat them in any way. I call on your patriotic duty as an American citizen."[3]

Stark relayed the information to the White House, providing FDR with the first glimpse of the disaster at Pearl. According to Hopkins, the president then instructed Stark to execute the orders that the army and navy had agreed to in the event of an outbreak of hostilities in the Pacific.[4]

A few minutes later, General Marshall called the White House and confirmed the report that Roosevelt had received from the navy. "Mr. President," he said, "I have just talked to a staff Officer in Hawaii. An attack by air, apparently from a carrier, started at eight o'clock their time. It is still in progress. As far as they can tell at the moment at least 50 Japanese bombers involved." Marshall reported that the "hanger [*sic*] at Nicholas and Wheeler Field are in flames." He also mentioned that the Japanese "were machine gunning Hickam field," although he could not confirm the report. "Communication seriously disrupted. Our planes are in the air and as far as they know Navy planes are in the air."[5]

As Roosevelt continued to receive updates, his senior military officials began arriving for their 3:00 p.m. meeting. Stimson and Knox arrived around 3:05 p.m., followed shortly by General Marshall and Hull. Staff members were also filtering into the room: Grace Tully, Steve Early, and appointments secretary Marvin McIntyre. White House physician Ross McIntire rushed over to keep a careful eye on his patient. Naturally, Harry Hopkins remained as Roosevelt's constant shadow.

The president's team sat in soft leather sofas and brocade chairs, while Roosevelt sat at his desk, often answering the phone on the first ring. The day had gone gray; the sunshine that had warmed his bedroom that morning had disappeared, replaced by clouds and dropping temperatures.

Despite the dreadful reports pouring in from Hawaii, there was a sense of relief in the room, mixed with shock and anger. For the past few months, FDR had been struggling with the threat of war in Europe and Asia. Always the skilled politician, he understood the deep public reluctance to get into either war. Perhaps he also recalled his 1940 campaign promise to keep the nation out of "foreign wars." Just a few hours earlier, his advisers had been busy fretting over whether FDR would commit the nation to support the British if Japan attacked its outposts in the Pacific. With one decisive action, the Japanese had made his decision for him. According to Hopkins, "The conference met in not too tense an atmosphere because I think that all of us believed that in the last analysis the enemy was Hitler and that he could never be defeated without force of arms; that sooner or later we were bound to be in the war and that Japan had given us an opportunity. Everybody, however, agreed on the seriousness of the war and that it would be a long, hard struggle."[6]

Roosevelt began the meeting by cross-examining both Knox and Stimson about the attack. According to Grace Tully, FDR questioned them "closely on what had happened, on why they believed it could have happened, on what might happen next and on what they could do to repair to some degree the disaster." No one, most of all someone as knowledgeable of the navy as FDR, could understand why the fleet was taken by surprise.[7]

It was obvious to everyone in the room that the navy had been dealt a crippling blow. Perhaps even more troubling was the fact that the army and army air corps had been rendered helpless as well. According to Hopkins, Roosevelt quizzed Marshall about "the disposition of the troops and particularly the air force." The damage at Pearl had been so complete that the forces that remained were in no position to prevent further Japanese aggression. Japan had free rein in the Pacific and beyond. "It was easy to speculate," Tully recalled, "that a Jap invasion force might be following their air strike at Hawaii — or that the West Coast itself might be marked for similar assault."[8]

The beleaguered general was now focused on the fate of American forces in the Philippines under the command of General Douglas MacArthur. Marshall recognized that the American air bases at Clark Field in Manila would be the next likely target. As the possibility of war with Japan increased, military planners in Washington had shifted resources to the Philippines to serve as a bulwark against Japanese expansion. General MacArthur, whom Roosevelt appointed as commander of U.S. Army Forces in the Far East the previous July, was the chief architect of the strategy. In a series of memorandums, the general assured Washington that he could create an effective fighting force in the Philippines that would be capable of defending the islands against a Japanese assault. "I don't *think* that the Philippines can defend themselves. I *know* they can," he had declared.[9]

MacArthur represented America's best hope for stopping Japan's rampage through the Pacific. The general had continued to provide optimistic reports about progress in building up the island's defensive capabilities. "The Secretary of War and I were highly pleased to receive your report that your command is ready for any eventuality," Marshall had radioed MacArthur a week before Pearl Harbor. Although resources were scarce, Marshall provided the Philippines with thirty-four B-17 bombers, giving MacArthur the largest concentration of American bombers in the world.

On Sunday afternoon, before leaving for his 3:00 p.m. meeting at the White House, Marshall wrote a note to MacArthur. The radiogram was sent at 3:22 p.m. and arrived at MacArthur's headquarters at 5:35 a.m. on December 8 (to the west of the international date line, the Philippines are a day ahead of the United States). The message stated: "Hostilities between Japan and the United States . . . have commenced. . . . Carry out tasks assigned in Rainbow Five." The military strategy called for carrying out "air raids against Japanese forces and installations within tactical operating radius of available bases." At the 3:00 p.m. meeting with Roosevelt, Marshall assured the president that he had ordered MacArthur to execute "all the necessary movement required in event of an outbreak of hostilities with Japan."[10]

According to Hopkins, Marshall "was

clearly impatient to get away" from the meeting in the White House. He was worried about the fate of the Philippines. He had not been able to reach the general, and MacArthur had so far failed to acknowledge receiving the orders. It was not clear in Washington whether MacArthur was busy fighting off a Japanese attack or if there was a communications problem. Either way, Marshall wanted to get back to the War Department to monitor the situation.[11]

Surprisingly, FDR spent a great deal of time at the meeting with his advisers discussing the situation in Latin America. FDR conferred with Hull about "the urgent necessity of keeping all of the South American Republics not only informed but to keep them in line with us." The nations in South America had not yet been pulled into the war, but FDR worried that the Germans and Japanese had been active in the region in an effort to stir up anti-American feeling. He was especially concerned about the strategic importance of the Panama Canal and the nations that bordered it.

Since the days of the Monroe Doctrine, the United States has forged a protective shield around Central America and Latin America. Franklin Roosevelt came to office determined to work hard to develop closer ties with nations in the region. His inaugural address had one line devoted to foreign policy: "In the field of world policy I would dedicate this nation to the policy of the good neighbor." Although the appeal was general, he directed it specifically to Latin America. Over the next few years, the administration had pushed through trade agreements that lowered tariffs by up to 50 percent, allowing for a freer exchange of goods between North and South. Roosevelt also disavowed the use of military intervention in the region, and he followed up his rhetoric with concrete actions.[12]

As war raged across the ocean in Europe, Roosevelt became increasingly focused on Nazi influence in the region. Concern about regional security pushed the administration to negotiate for naval and air bases across the region. The United States sent military advisers to Latin America and invited their officers to study at American military schools. U.S. officials kept blacklists of suspected subversives and pressured governments to fire employees with ties to the Axis powers.[13]

FDR had reason to believe the threat of Nazi subversion in the region was real. Less than two months before Pearl Harbor, Roosevelt told the nation that he had in his possession "a secret map" of Latin America drawn up by Hitler's generals. The map, he said, took the fourteen republics in Latin America and reduced them to "five vassal states . . . bringing the whole continent under their domination." Hitler's plan, he said, represented a threat to "our great life line, the Panama Canal." Although Roosevelt did not know it at the time, the map was bogus, cooked up by British intelligence to help nudge America into the war.[14]

According to Hopkins, there was also a spirited debate about FDR's message to Congress. Roosevelt had decided that he would give a speech before a joint session of Congress the following day. He wanted to keep that dramatic address as brief as possible, followed by a more detailed radio address to the nation later in the week. There is no evidence that he discussed the idea with any of his advisers or asked for their input on the decision. "The President expressed himself very strongly that he was going to submit a precise message and had in mind submitting a longer message later," Hopkins noted in his memorandum.[15]

Hull objected to the president's plan. He insisted that the president give a long, detailed speech that reviewed the whole history of U.S.-Japanese relations. Hopkins estimated that it would take up to thirty minutes for FDR to give the type of speech that Hull recommended. Although Roosevelt understood the appeal of a message that would make the case for war against Japan, he insisted on delivering an address that would be short, succinct, and emotionally powerful. Most of all, it needed to resonate with the millions of Americans who would be listening on radio.

By 1941, radio was competing with newspapers as the public's primary source of information. There were more than 45 million radios in the United States, including 6.5 million in cars. Nearly 90 percent of all homes with electricity had at least one radio, which families listened to on average for more than four and a half hours per day.[16]

FDR had mastered the new medium. He viewed radio as a way to communicate directly with the American people without journalists running interference. Radio, he said, tends "to restore direct contact between the masses and their chosen leaders." He had cultivated a bond with his audience that stretched back to his first "fireside chat" in the opening days of his presidency.

As Steve Early noted, "The President likes to think of the audience as being a few people around his fireside." Although his speeches were carefully scripted, they succeeded in creating a sense of intimacy between the president and the people. "You felt he was talking to you," observed journalist Richard Strout, "not to 50 million others but to you personally."[17]

FDR was remarkably skilled at projecting his personality over radio. He understood the power of brevity and kept most of his addresses under thirty minutes. He spoke slowly and clearly, usually enunciating fewer than one hundred words per minute. Perhaps most important, FDR used words and phrases that conveyed empathy and connected with everyday Americans. He littered his speeches with analogies ("when your neighbor's house is on fire") and with personal appeals ("together we cannot fail") that allowed him to create a personal bond with his listeners. He even paid close attention to the microphone angle and sound. When FDR realized that a space between his front lower teeth produced a noticeable whistling sound on the radio, he ordered a fake tooth. On many occasions he would remember the tooth at the last minute, producing a mad scramble to retrieve it in the seconds before he went on the air.[18]

While FDR's skill and sensitivity to his radio audience played a role in his decision, there were other reasons that argued in favor of a shorter war message. It is possible that a longer statement would have required him to go into too much detail about the damage done and the lives lost. Would a detailed overview of the devastation demoralize the American people? Although it would have been easy to inflame public anger toward Japan, Roosevelt believed that Germany remained the greater threat to America. He had to maintain a delicate balancing act, inspiring Americans to fight against Japan, while not distracting them from the battle in Europe.

Hopkins advised FDR to hold two conferences before the end of the day to build political support for the address: one with the cabinet and one with congressional leaders. While the White House switchboard tracked down the cabinet, FDR and Hopkins discussed which congressional leaders to invite to the meeting.

While the president was meeting with his advisers, Admiral Stark continued to call in with the latest updates from Pearl Harbor. A few times, FDR answered the phone himself, but Grace Tully usually took the calls. She was originally stationed at a phone outside the Oval Study, but when the commotion of aides coming and going became too distracting, she moved into FDR's bedroom. "It was my job to take these fragmentary and shocking reports from him in shorthand, type them up and relay them to the Boss," she reflected.[19]

The news was grim, with each report more depressing than the last. "I could hear the shocked unbelief in Admiral Stark's voice as he talked to me," she said. FDR's military aides hovered over her as she took each call, hoping to overhear what Stark was telling her. They followed her as she rushed into another room to type each message. "The news was shattering," she recalled. "At first," Tully recalled, "the men around the President were incredulous; that changed to angry acceptance as new messages supported and amplified the previous ones." Roosevelt, she observed, "maintained greater outward calm than anybody else but there was rage in his very calmness. With each new message he shook his head grimly and tightened the expression of his mouth."[20]

At around 3:30 FDR received a report that an army cargo ship, seven hundred miles west of San Francisco, had sent a distress signal. The assumption was that a Japanese submarine had attacked it. If true, it meant that Japanese submarines were operating far out in the Pacific. Where were they headed next?[21]

At 3:50 p.m., Tully handed FDR a long report that dimmed any lingering hope that the navy had managed an effective counter-attack and repelled the main Japanese force. "The Japs attacked Honolulu time about eight o'clock this morning," Stark reported. "The first warning was from a submarine that was outside the harbor which was attacked by a destroyer with depth bombs." He reported that a second submarine "was sunk by aircraft." He then proceeded to describe the raid. "They attacked with aircraft, with bombs and torpedoes." He also mistakenly reported, "At least two aircraft were known to have a swastika sign on them."

He noted that the Japanese had attacked in two waves and inflicted "severe" damage. "The *Oklahoma* has capsized in Pearl Harbor. The *Tennessee* is on fire with a bad list, and the Navy yard is attempting to dry-dock her." The report went on to describe the damage to the drydock. Two destroyers were hit. One had blown up. Another was on fire. The *Oglala* was beyond repair. The powerhouse had been hit but was still operational. The Japanese planes had also inflicted heavy damage to the airfields at Ford Island, Hickam, Wheeler, and Kanoehe. "Probably heavy personnel casualties but no figures." He mistakenly reported that the Japanese "have no details of the damage which they have wrought."

Roosevelt was trying to piece together the puzzle. He still did not have a complete picture of the nature of the Japanese attack and the American response. Stark's reports had offered only a glimpse of the damage. For example, the admiral had made no mention of the *Arizona,* which accounted for nearly half of the U.S. fatalities. As a result, FDR not only had no concrete figures on casualties but probably at this point could not have imagined that thousands of Americans had been killed or injured.

It was in this climate of incomplete information — and even in some cases misinformation — that FDR and his advisers sought to understand Japan's intention. Was the attack designed to cripple the American military in anticipation of a land assault on Hawaii? Was the same Japanese armada responsible for the attack continuing eastward for a possible assault on the West Coast of the United States? Was the attack part of a larger initiative designed to destroy key American military and political centers? And what, if any, role had Germany played in the attacks? Given Stark's mistaken mention of swastikas on some of the offending aircraft, Roosevelt must have wondered why Hitler would commit German planes to attack Pearl Harbor. But he likely welcomed the notion that Hitler might have been directly involved in the attack. It would make it easier for him to declare war against Germany.

Threats closer to home also weighed heavily on Roosevelt on Sunday afternoon. He was clearly worried about damaging details of the attack leaking to the press. There was general agreement among FDR's advisers that the government should establish formal censorship of the press. Most newspapers had been practicing self-censorship since the outbreak of World War II in Europe. FDR wanted tighter controls in the aftermath of Pearl Harbor, however. He feared that detailed damage reports would embolden the enemy and demoralize the American public. Within hours of the attack on Sunday afternoon, the Office of Naval

Intelligence started monitoring all radio and telephone traffic from the island. Any communication that provided details of the carnage was immediately shut down. At the same time, the War Department started opening and reading mail coming to the mainland.[22]

In addition to restricting press freedom, Roosevelt took steps to protect the nation from potential sabotage. FDR probably assumed that the Japanese saboteurs played a key role in the successful attacks. Would there be an effort to disrupt the government in Washington? The question was clearly on his mind when he issued orders to guard against possible sabotage to key facilities in Washington. To prevent potential attacks at home, the president ordered Stimson and Knox to place armed guards around all key facilities, especially private munitions factories and all bridges. Always concerned about political symbols and the messages they sent, FDR did not want armed soldiers surrounding the White House.[23]

7
"INFAMY"

The gathering in the Oval Study ended around 4:15 p.m. After his advisers filtered out of the room, Roosevelt turned his attention to crafting his speech. He understood that his address would serve as the centerpiece of his strategy of building support for war. But what would he say? Should he recite a long list of grievances against Japan? Would the public support a simultaneous declaration of war against Germany and Italy? Writing speeches was usually a long, drawn-out process that involved many people and numerous drafts. FDR's speechwriters were out of town and could not be reached, so he had to prepare the most important speech of his presidency on his own.

He was comfortable with the task. Since his days as an editor of the *Harvard Crimson,* FDR had thought of himself as a writer, and he had generally played a major role in drafting many of his most important speeches. He also had a clear idea of what he wanted to say and how he would say it.[1]

At 4:50 p.m., FDR called Grace Tully to his study. "He was alone," Tully observed. On his desk were three neat piles of notes with all the information he had received that afternoon. "The telephone was close at hand." He had exchanged his sweater from earlier in the morning for a gray sack jacket. FDR took a deep drag from a cigarette as she walked into the room. "Sit down, Grace, I'm going before Congress tomorrow. I'd like to dictate my message. It will be short."[2]

He inhaled again and then in a calm voice he began dictating his war message. "Yesterday comma December 7th comma 1941 dash a day which will live in world history dash the United States of America was simultaneously and deliberately attacked by naval and air forces of the Empire of Japan." Tully had transcribed many messages for FDR, but this one was different, she recalled, because "he spoke each word incisively and slowly, carefully specifying each punctuation mark and paragraph." She noted that the "entire message ran under 500 words" and represented "a cold-blooded indictment of Japanese treachery and aggression." It was, she reflected, "delivered to me without hesitation, interruption or second thoughts."

Tully went into the adjacent room, quickly typed the short speech, and handed it back to the president. Roosevelt picked up his pencil and started editing the speech. In the first sentence, he changed "a date which will live in world history" to "a date which will live in infamy." He crossed out "simultaneously" and substituted "suddenly." At the end of the first sentence, he wrote the words "without warning," but crossed them out.

Thus was born one of the most famous lines in presidential oratory: "Yesterday, December 7, 1941 — a date which will live in infamy — the United States of America was suddenly and deliberately attacked by the naval and air forces of the Empire of Japan."[3]

Later that evening, while having dinner with Hopkins and Grace Tully, Roosevelt decided to make additional changes. Apparently, he realized that the address needed some inspiration and some punch. FDR picked up his pencil and scribbled near the end of the speech, "No matter how long it may take us to overcome this premeditated invasion, the American people will in their righteous might win through to absolute victory." Roosevelt showed the draft to Hopkins and asked for his suggestions. Picking up on FDR's addition, Hopkins added an applause line of his own. At the bottom of the page, under the heading "Deity," he wrote, "With confidence in our armed forces — with the unbounding determination of our people — we will gain the inevitable triumph — so help us God." Roosevelt liked the addition and included it in the speech.[4]

While working on his speech, FDR received two updates on the situation in the Pacific. Shortly before 5:30 p.m., he took a call from Hawaii governor Joseph B. Poindexter. The governor told FDR that the Japanese attacks had killed roughly fifty civilians on Oahu and that the island desperately needed food and planes. He then asked FDR's approval to declare martial law, claiming that the main danger came from "local Japs" who might be aiding a future invasion of the island.[5]

During the conversation, Poindexter shrieked as another round of Japanese planes buzzed overhead. Roosevelt turned to Hopkins, "My God, there's another wave of Jap planes over Hawaii right this minute." If the governor heard planes, they would have been American. There was no third wave of bombers. But the information seemed credible at the time, and Early shared the story with reporters in his 5:55 p.m. press briefing. It became part of many standard accounts of the day.[6]

At roughly the same time, the administration concluded that the Japanese had not started bombing the Philippines and that the initial reports had been false. The problem was that both the War and the Navy departments had sent messages to Manila but had not received any response, or even an acknowledgment that the messages had been received. Initially, the assumption was that a Japanese attack had cut off communications with Washington. As Steve Early now told reporters, however, they were inclined to believe the initial reports were wrong. The president, he said, "is disposed to believe and rather to hope that the first report may be erroneous."[7]

In the midst of the crisis, Roosevelt needed to take personal time to deal with his stubborn sinus infection. At 5:30 p.m., Roosevelt was wheeled down to the office of White House physician Ross T. McIntire, with whom he spent a total of seventy minutes that evening. A graduate of Willamette University in Oregon, McIntire had joined the Navy Medical Corps during World War I. In 1925, he was assigned to the U.S. Naval Dispensary in Washington, where he met Admiral Cary Grayson, who had served as Woodrow Wilson's private physician. Grayson was also a close adviser to FDR.[8]

In 1937, when Roosevelt was looking for a White House physician, he turned to Grayson for advice. Grayson recommended McIntire largely because of his specialty. "The president is as strong as a horse," Grayson told McIntire, "with the exception of a chronic sinus condition that makes him susceptible to colds." A heavy smoker, Roosevelt had been plagued with sinus problems for most of his adult life. Eleanor blamed the flare-ups on anxiety and the damp, cold weather in Washington during the winter. The genial McIntire seemed like a reasonable choice since he was trained in both otolaryngology (ear, nose, and throat, or ENT) and ophthalmology (the study of the eye).[9]

Over the next few years, McIntire joined FDR's inner circle. He saw the president on a daily basis. In addition to being a skilled ear, nose, and throat doctor, McIntire was attentive and unassuming — qualities that Roosevelt appreciated in the people around him. "We understand one another beautifully," McIntire told journalist Leon Pearson in April 1941. Roosevelt enjoyed his doctor's company so much that he often invited him along on fishing trips and other vacations.[10]

The doctor never questioned that his job was to keep FDR healthy and to shoot down any suggestions to the contrary. As late as March 1945, just one month before the president died of a cerebral hemorrhage in Warm Springs, McIntire cooperated with publicist George Creel to squelch rumors that FDR was in poor health. He told Creel that FDR's gaunt appearance was the result of "a bad case of the influenza that left in its wake a stubborn irritation of the larynx and bronchial tubes."[11]

McIntire claimed that he "examined" Roosevelt twice a day. He was often among a small group of aides who would gather around his bed in the morning around 8:30 a.m. while the president scanned the papers and ate his breakfast. He believed that this "look-see" provided him with all the information that he needed. "A close but seemingly casual watch told me all I wanted to know," he recalled in his memoirs. "The things that interested me most were the President's color, the tone of his voice, the tilt of his chin, and the way he tackled his orange juice, cereal and eggs." McIntire would return at 5:30 for another "look-see," although he often insisted that Roosevelt "shut up shop" and either go for a swim in the White House pool or rest before dinner.[12]

This, however, was not a typical day, and McIntire's medical intervention involved more than a "look-see." The physician wrote a memoir of his time in the White House, but he failed to discuss exactly how he treated FDR's various ailments. Since Roosevelt's medical records went missing shortly after his death, it is impossible to know for sure what illness Roosevelt suffered from and also what treatments McIntire prescribed.

According to McIntire, Roosevelt called him shortly after he learned of the attack on Pearl Harbor and asked him to stay with him. He arrived before the 3:00 p.m. meeting with the war cabinet and stayed with FDR for the rest of the afternoon. At 5:30, McIntire accompanied FDR to the White House physician's office, which was on the lower level of the mansion. They entered the main office, which looked out on the south grounds of the White House, and wheeled past a desk with fresh-cut flowers and into the examination room. The room contained a dentist chair, a rubdown table, and closets filled with various medications. All of the medications came from the Navy Department's dispensary.[13]

Roosevelt spent from 5:30 until 6:40 p.m. in the office. Given McIntire's circumspection and the lack of medical records, we can only speculate about what took place during his appointment with McIntire. Both FDR and McIntire knew that the president had a long night ahead of him, including two of the most important meetings of his presidency: one with the cabinet, the other with congressional leaders. He would need to make sure that the tenor of his voice reflected the focused anger and vitality of the American people. It was McIntire's job to make sure FDR was up to the task.

Because there were no antibiotics to treat the underlying sinus infection, McIntire was forced to rely on daily treatments to relieve the symptoms. The therapeutic goal was to diminish the swelling of nasal mucosa and thereby increase the patient's ability to breathe. The key was to reduce the swelling without producing dryness or crusting. McIntire had a few options available to him. He could have used cotton swabs to manually clear Roosevelt's sinuses. Attorney

General Francis Biddle observed McIntire performing the procedure when he went to see the president a few days after Pearl Harbor. "He was swabbing out F.D.R.'s nose," Biddle noted.[14]

It is also likely that McIntire "flushed" or irrigated the sinuses. This could be accomplished by inserting a curved hollow needle up the nose and into his sinuses. The needle would be connected to a machine that would pump saline solution into the sinus cavity. Oftentimes, the same machine would have the capability of then sucking out the fluid along with the pus and mucus.

But in the 1930s and 1940s, it was also common for physicians to use cocaine as part of these treatments. "They most likely used cocaine," observed Dr. Jordan S. Josephson, the director of the New York Nasal and Sinus Center. "Cocaine was the drug of choice for any ENT treating a nasal problem." The physician would apply the diluted cocaine solution directly to the sinuses using cotton swabs. The cocaine would shrink the tissue, offering immediate relief, while also numbing the area, preparing it for the insertion of the needle for flushing. "Cocaine is a very good constrictor," reflected Dr. Murray Grossan, a prominent ENT who recalled that cocaine was still being used when he started his residency in the 1950s. "It was not that unusual for an ethical doctor to use a one or two percent cocaine solution. In those days that was quite common."[15]

As late as 1959, standard textbooks on otolaryngology recommended that physicians apply "1 per cent ephedrine sulfate, or 1 per cent ephedrine sulfate and a 1 per cent cocaine hydrochloride" solution for "temporary relief" of nasal swelling. As recently as 1975, after reviewing the medical literature on the subject, the *Western Journal of Medicine* noted that "cocaine remains a vital instrument in the otolaryngologist's armamentarium." Many doctors still use cocaine today for sinus surgery.[16]

Beginning in the nineteenth century, cocaine became widely available in the United States and was used for a variety of medical ailments. Physicians used the drug as a local anesthesia, and manufacturers sold a host of over-the-counter panaceas that included it. Sigmund Freud called it a "magical" drug. Cocaine was also the active ingredient in Coca-Cola, originally sold as a cure for headaches. (In the 1890s, the new Coca-Cola Company sold the drink as both a "sovereign remedy" and a pleasurable drink.)[17] Cocaine fell out of favor in the twentieth century as social reformers campaigned against it, and by the time Roosevelt was elected president, cocaine had been banned in the United States. It survived only as a surgical anesthetic and as a treatment for ear, nose, and throat problems.

Even if McIntire did use a cocaine solution as part of his regimen, it remains unclear whether it would have had any impact on FDR's behavior. The effect would depend on the strength of the solution, and there does not appear to have been a common standard for treatment in 1941. Dr. Josephson believes the cocaine would have been powerful enough to produce a brief sense of euphoria and a temporary burst of energy. Dr. Grossan stated that most patients would probably have no reaction, but a few could "get a jack" from the treatment. Dr. Robert Lofgren, who graduated medical school in the 1950s and practiced for many years at Massachusetts's Eye and Ear Hospital, believes that the solution would likely have been too diluted to have any measurable impact.[18]

Even if McIntire had used a strong dose of the drug, the cocaine effect would have been short-lived, providing FDR with only a temporary respite from the grim news of the day. The draining of the sinuses, however, would have provided him with noticeable and sustained relief and helped prepare him for the long evening ahead.[19]

It is likely, though not certain, that FDR was getting treated on a regular basis, including the day of the Pearl Harbor attacks, with a diluted form of cocaine. But if he was, he almost certainly did not know it. The medical literature at the time instructed physicians not to tell their patients that they were using the drug. "The habit-forming properties . . . of this drug are well-known and must be ever guarded against," one medical textbook at the time explained. "Patients are never informed as to the nature or name of the drug used because in itself this may act suggestively." Eleanor worried about the daily nasal treatments her husband received. "I always worried about this constant treatment for I felt while it might help temporarily, in the long run it must cause irritation," she reflected. FDR, however, never seemed to question the treatments or to inquire about his medical condition.[20]

8

"GET TO THE WHITE HOUSE FASTASYOUCAN"

While the president remained secluded in the White House, word of the attack was spreading across the nation. The major radio stations announced the news within minutes of receiving Steve Early's phone call, and the major newspapers rushed "extra" editions to press. Initially, information about the attack spread slowly, and most Americans did not panic. By evening, however, a wave of fear swept the nation, especially on the West Coast and in Hawaii.

At 2:25 p.m., less than thirty minutes after Secretary Knox first advised FDR of the attack, United Press International flashed a bulletin: "Washington — White House announces Japanese have attacked Pearl Harbor." About sixty seconds later Mutual radio station WOR interrupted the broadcast of the Dodgers-Giants football game with the same flash. NBC read the announcement at

2:28 p.m.

At 2:31 CBS's John Daly broke into the regular broadcast with the first live coverage of the events. "The Japanese have attacked Pearl Harbor, Hawaii, by air, President Roosevelt has just announced. The attack was also made on naval and military activities on the principal island of Oahu." CBS switched to its Washington bureau chief, Albert Warner, who speculated that the attack meant that Roosevelt would be asking Congress for a declaration of war and that Congress would support it. At 2:39, Warner, repeating the false report filed by Steve Early, announced that "a second air attack has been reported on Army and Navy bases in Manila."[1]

The network then reached its London correspondent, Robert Trout, hoping that he could provide the British perspective on the flash, but the news had not yet reached government officials. CBS managed to reach its Manila stringer, but it quickly lost the connection. CBS, however, was able to set up a telephone connection with KGMB, its Honolulu affiliate, which confirmed that the raid was still in progress.[2]

As soon as the story broke, reporters rushed to the White House for more information. The White House press office was small and informal, as there were only about a dozen full-time reporters assigned to the White House in 1941. The three wire services — the United Press, Associated Press, and International News Service — were the main sources of information. Reporters from the major New York, Chicago, Philadelphia, and Washington papers joined them.

Roosevelt had developed a personal relationship with many of the White House reporters. He called them by their first names, joked with them, and invited them for private teas. A few correspondents joined the family for holiday meals. Carrying over a tradition that he started as governor of New York, FDR held regular Sunday-evening dinners where the journalists felt like "neighbors invited in for potluck." After dinner, they retreated to the second floor to watch a movie and the newsreels for the day.[3]

In the past, FDR had told the correspondents that he would not make news on Sunday, so they could plan on having the day off. Early had told the press corps the same thing the day before. And so on December 7, the press office was closed, and there were no reporters present when the flash came about Pearl Harbor.

Merriman Smith, the veteran UPI reporter assigned to the White House on December 7, was planning on spending a quiet day at home. He was in the bathroom when his wife knocked on the door at 2:25 p.m. "You know what the radio just said." "No," he responded. "What?" "It said the Japanese bombed Hawaii." Smith recalled that he "nearly knocked" his wife to the ground as he rushed from the bathroom to get to the telephone. He got to the receiver just as his office was calling him. His editor bellowed into the phone: "Japs just bombed Pearl Harbor. Get to the White House fastasyoucan." He rushed outside, where he flagged down a motorcycle policeman who escorted him to the White House.[4]

Smith arrived in time for the first of many press briefings that day. There were only six reporters present at it. The others were still scrambling to get to the White House. After they gathered in the pressroom, a policeman stuck his head in and announced, "Mr. Early will see you." The reporters pushed into Early's private office and found him sitting behind his desk. His secretary, Ruth Jane Rumelt, sat next to him with a notepad. "So far as is known now, the attacks on Hawaii and Manila were made wholly without warning — when both nations were at peace and were delivered within an hour or so of the time that the Japanese Ambassador and the special envoy, Mr. Kurusu, had gone to the State Department and handed to the Secretary of State Japan's reply to the Secretary's memorandum of Nov. 26." He went on to say that the president "directed the Army and Navy to execute all previously prepared orders looking to the defense of the United States." He closed by announcing that the president was meeting with military advisers and making efforts to inform congressional leaders.[5]

Smith recalled that for the rest of the day "there occurred the maddest scramble, the most rapid succession of world-shaking stories in the memory of the oldest old-timer in the newspaper business around Washington." To put the day in some perspective, he noted that in four hours, he managed four flashes and eight bulletin stories. "Men spend an entire lifetime in press association work without ever handling one flash story. I had four in four hours."[6]

Early provided reporters with regular updates as more journalists filed into the cramped pressroom. After each announcement, reporters who did not have direct lines dashed for the two telephone booths designated for their use. At 4:09 p.m., NBC had successfully installed a microphone and became the first network to broadcast live from the pressroom at the White House. CBS followed with its broadcast two hours later.

As reporters were about to leave his office following a 4:30 briefing, Early asked "if there is any one of you reporting for Japanese agencies." If there was, he said, "I am giving you no information and I have asked the Secret Service to take up the credentials of Japanese correspondents." Reporters asked him if their Japanese counterparts would be arrested. Early answered obliquely, "That is an activity of the Department of Justice."[7]

By 5:00 there were nearly one hundred reporters, radiomen, and newsreel and still photographers in the pressroom. Newspapers, eager to feed the public's hunger for information, were printing extra editions. "The world wanted the news of Pearl Harbor and new details when they were available," Smith recalled.[8]

Yet despite the press corps' frenzy of activity — all the major radio stations reported news of the attack within thirty minutes — the information spread slowly. Twenty-three years later, when President John F. Kennedy was assassinated, 92 percent of the public knew what had happened within two hours of the shooting. Within five hours, nearly every American — 99.8 percent — knew that Kennedy was assassinated. There were no comparable studies done in 1941 documenting how the news of Pearl Harbor spread, but anecdotal evidence suggests that it leaked out gradually over the course of the afternoon.[9]

Only a small number of Americans were listening to the radio when the first Pearl Harbor announcements were made. In the 1940s, it was typical for middle-class Americans to eat dinner around 1:00 p.m. on Sunday. Many families living in the East and Midwest were gathered around the dinner table or relaxing after a big meal. Most of the nation was also experiencing nice weather on December 7. More people than usual were outside, going for afternoon drives in the country, walking in the park, attending football games, or catching a matinee at the local movie theater.

Despite the enormity of the news, many organizations chose not to release it. At Washington's Griffith Stadium, management chose not to make an announcement to the 27,102 fans attending the Redskins game with the Philadelphia Eagles. Among those in attendance was a young ensign named John F. Kennedy. The owner later explained, "No announcement of hostilities was made because it is against the policy of the Redskins management to broadcast non-sports news over the stadium's public address system."[10]

But the crowd must have sensed that something important had happened by the succession of important people who were being summoned by the public address system. About halfway through the first quarter, the speakers blared, "Admiral W. H. P. Bland is asked to report to his office at once!" Bland was the chief of the Bureau of Ordnance of the navy. A few minutes later came another announcement: "The Resident Commissioner of the Philippines, Mr. Joaquim Elizalde, is urged to report to his office immediately!" The reports continued throughout the game, but most fans were focused on the goalposts, not the public address system. They stayed until the very end and watched the Redskins win in dramatic fashion. Not until after they left the stadium did most learn about the attack.[11]

In Chicago, the first flash came just as many locals were digesting their traditional dinner of roast beef and mashed potatoes.

156

According to one reporter, the city "was just getting ready for a good after dinner belch when the war news came." Those who were at home with the radio on canceled their afternoon plans and listened for updates. Others would learn about the news only later. Theater owners made the decision not to interrupt crowded matinee showings. Moviegoers learned the news only when they stepped outside and heard the newsboys shouting inaccurately, "U.S. Declares War on Japan."[12]

In Southern California, the thermometer climbed near eighty degrees, with bright sunshine overhead. Many people were taking advantage of the nice weather by spending time out of the house and away from the radio. Much of the conversation in coffee shops, in restaurants, and on the sidewalks that late morning was about how the UCLA Bruins had managed to play the superior USC Trojans to a 7–7 tie the day before. There was no dramatic moment when everyone heard the news. Instead, it spread over a series of hours. "There was no hue and cry on the public streets where the outdoor loving were bound for their Sunday pleasures," noted reporter Sidney James. The news "moved through backyard gardens, across golf courses, into bars . . .

and finally to the beaches of the fateful Pacific."[13]

Radio broke the story, but it was the telephone that helped spread it over the course of the afternoon. Phone lines across the nation jammed as people called family members and friends to share the news. Because there were no direct-dial phones in 1941, every call had to be placed manually by switchboard operators. A deluge of calls quickly overwhelmed them. There were one-hour delays on all calls into Chicago. In San Francisco, the rush of calls crashed the phone system. No one was able to get calls through to Hawaii or the Philippines, although it was unclear on Sunday whether that was because of military censorship or overwhelming demand. Western Union reported a flood of cables to Honolulu and Manila.[14]

In addition to radio and telephone, the other major source of news was daily newspapers. Major newspapers called in reporters to cover the story and produce "extra" Sunday-afternoon editions. The *Atlanta Journal* came out with an extra at 4:40 p.m. The city's other leading paper, the *Constitution,* followed with its own "extra" a few minutes later. In Chicago, the *Herald American* hit the streets two hours after the news was announced on the radio. At the *Los Angeles Times* office, the AP reporter heard the flash warning at 11:30. It produced an afternoon edition that rolled off the press at 2:10 p.m. with four-inch block letters crying "WAR." On a Sunday, the typical *Times* circulation was 25,000 copies. By that evening, it had sold 150,000 papers.[15]

Newsboys standing on street corners hawking the "extras" made a small fortune on December 7. "We sold the three-cent paper for twenty-five cents and higher, whatever the market could handle," recalled a precocious thirteen-year-old.[16]

Perhaps because most Americans were not aware of the extent of the damage inflicted, or the number of casualties, they seemed to take the attack in stride. Oddly enough, many radio networks reported that their phone lines were jammed with callers. Most of the calls, however, were not from people asking for more information about the attack on Pearl Harbor, about the potential for sabotage, or about the imminent declaration of war. Instead, they simply wanted to know when their favorite shows, which were now being preempted by news, would be rebroadcast.[17]

A reporter for the *Kansas City Times* reported that the city maintained "a business-as-usual calm" in the hours after the story broke. The main reason, he speculated, was that most people did not learn of the attack until the newspaper boys started shouting the headline on Sunday evening as they pushed late editions on street corners. "Although bulletins had been flashed on the radio, many persons apparently were engaged in Sunday afternoon pursuits that had prevented their learning previously of the news." The custodian of the Liberty Memorial, dedicated to the fallen soldiers of World War I, reported a typical Sunday crowd of 3,000 visitors that day. He recalled only one person mentioning the attack. Local theaters made the announcement, but most people responded by settling in and watching the movie.[18]

The fairly calm public response was due in part to the prevailing belief that Japan represented little threat to America. Most Americans clung to widely held notions of Japan as a third-rate military power that was no match for the United States. Before the attack, Gallup asked if the United States would win a war with Japan, and 92 percent said yes. Only 1 percent said no. When asked if the U.S. Navy was "strong enough to defeat the Japanese Navy," 80 percent said yes, and only 4 percent said no.[19]

After surveying people on the street on the afternoon of December 7, one reporter noted, "Whether rightly or wrongly, people seem to believe all the so-called experts' claims that Japan has only two bath tubs in the navy, no money, no oil and all Japanese fliers are so cross-eyed they couldn't hit lake [*sic*] Michigan with a bomb." A service-station attendant told the *Los Angeles Times,* "We should be able to clean up on those fellows in six weeks or less."[20]

There was so little hard information available that most people reached their own conclusions about the extent of the damage. Given their views of Japanese inferiority, and the confidence in the impregnable Pearl Harbor, Americans remained optimistic. A restaurant chef told the *Los Angeles Times,* "The Japanese must know what they're up to. But from early reports it seems they didn't accomplish any major objective. Once we start fighting it won't last long." An upholsterer agreed: "Lord help those Japanese when our planes begin dropping bombs on some of those paper and wood cities. They'll start an inferno that will spread over all Japan. It won't last long."[21]

Most Americans did not make an immediate connection between the attack in Hawaii and the war in Europe. In most of the interviews conducted on Sunday, people spoke only about the likelihood and necessity of America's going to war against Japan. Few seemed to recognize that the attack made America part of a worldwide struggle that would involve war on two fronts. Some Americans assumed the story was a hoax. With Orson Welles's famous 1938 "War of the Worlds" broadcast of an invasion from Mars still fresh in their memories, many people were determined not to be fooled again. When a New Jersey reporter stopped a man walking his dog and asked him for his reaction to the news about Pearl Harbor, he responded, "Ha! You're not going to catch me on another of your pranks." In Los Angeles, a reporter for the *Times* stopped at a local restaurant on his way to do a story from an army base and found that no one had heard the news, and when told, they assumed it was a joke. Most pretended not to hear and went on eating. He noticed that most of the drivers on the road seemed equally oblivious to the news. "It's a peaceful Sunday drive for them, with nothing worse than a traffic snarl to worry about," he observed. Even the guards who greeted him at the army post were unaware that the nation would soon be at war.[22]

■ ■ ■ ■

By early evening, however, the initial calm and confidence that greeted the news gave way to fear. As day turned into evening and the newsboys' cries of "war extra" filled the streets of cities across America, the reality of war became impossible to ignore. Front-page headlines screamed the news. "WAR!" covered the top of the late edition of the *Philadelphia Record.* The *New York Times* was more restrained: "JAPAN WARS ON U.S. AND BRITAIN."[23]

The anxiety was greatest in Hawaii, where many people wondered whether the assault on Pearl was a prelude to a land invasion. Shortly after the attack, military authorities took to the airwaves to provide civilians with instructions. "Stay off the streets, get your car off the street, do not use the telephone except in cases of extreme emergency, seek shelter, boil all water in case of contamination." Shortly afterward came a call for all doctors, police officers, nurses, disaster squads, and Pearl Harbor workers to report to their stations. Officials told plantation owners to plow open fields in order to prevent Japanese planes from landing. At 4:30 p.m. the governor announced that he had imposed martial law on the island.

Many people defied the warnings to stay off the streets, as they gathered on street corners and in drugstores and taverns to share the latest rumors. There were numerous unconfirmed reports of Japanese paratroopers dispersed over the island. One radio report claimed the Japanese had landed at Diamond Head. Another said that Waikiki Beach had been overrun with Japanese troops. There were also false reports that the entire north shore of Oahu was occupied and that both Pearl Harbor and Schofield Barracks were in Japanese hands. "Long lines had formed at all grocery stores and there was a mad rush as semi-hysterical people tried to buy everything on the shelves," noted an observer. "Bakeries were short of flour and yeast and the meat markets were down to their last hamburger."[24]

There were rumors that Japanese pilots who had been shot down carried American money in their pockets and tokens for using the public transportation system in Oahu. One pilot who was supposedly shot down was more than six feet tall — too tall to be Japanese. Since his body was burned beyond recognition, the word spread that he was German.[25]

Many of the rumors were picked up by

the wire services and rushed into extra editions of newspapers across the country. The *Oakland Tribune* ran a large headline in its second extra on Sunday evening announcing "Parachute Troops Seen over Harbor."

The military repeated the rumors, giving them an air of credibility. Throughout the day, officials reported sightings of Japanese saboteurs wearing "working-blue coveralls with red circles on breasts," troop landings, and enemy aircraft dropping parachutes over Honolulu. A report at 11:40 local time stated, "Parachute Troops have landed on north shore & have been identified as wearing blue coveralls with RED DISC ON LEFT SHOULDER." At 12:05, military officials told of a "hostile force" that was "attempting to swim ashore," but being repelled by U.S. troops. At 2:30 p.m., the navy stated that one or two hundred parachutists had landed at Barbers Point. A few minutes later came a call that a force of enemy planes had flown over the island and been repelled by navy forces.[26]

By late afternoon, the military had investigated many of the supposed sightings and proven them false. At 4:00 p.m., the 27th Infantry stated that "all reports of enemy activity in Honolulu area have been investigated and found false." But even as the old claims were being discredited, new ones came flooding in. As late as 10:00 p.m., there were reports that bombs had been dropped at Pearl Harbor and enemy troops had landed in northern Oahu.[27]

Though false, the information became part of official intelligence estimates about Japan's capability and intent. On Sunday evening, under the heading of "Summary of Enemy Situation," military officials reported "four or five transports," one battleship, and three aircraft carriers off the coast of Hawaii. There were "numerous reports that parachutists landed throughout the island," along with a "few individual attempts at sabotage." The intelligence estimate predicted that Japan was planning a full-scale invasion that evening. "It is not improbable that the enemy will attempt to demolish Pearl Harbor and our entire air force prior to attempting a landing in force. Small landing parties may attempt to force landings on favorable beaches tonight during darkness."[28]

In response to these false reports, General Short sent an alert to army commanders in Hawaii that the Japanese were attempting to invade and occupy Oahu. Soldiers took up defensive positions along the Oahu shoreline and prepared for the onslaught.

Not wanting to provide a potential Japanese air raid with easy shooting targets, the army ordered a complete blackout for that night. It also forced all cars off the road, except those authorized by the police. Any cars that went on the road had to go to the local police station and have their headlights painted blue. People were ordered to stay in their homes. All stores, bars, and restaurants were closed, and the sale of alcohol was banned.[29]

Anxiety levels were also high on the West Coast, where public officials assumed that the same Japanese armada that launched the attack on Pearl was now approaching the mainland. Lieutenant General John De-Witt ordered troops to stand guard every fifty yards along the beach near San Francisco and look for signs of Japanese submarines. In San Francisco, streetlamps were turned off. Air raid sirens sounded. A panicky General DeWitt told newsmen that Japanese aircraft had been spotted in the skies over the city. "I don't think there's any doubt the planes came from a carrier," he said.[30]

Worry was not limited to the West Coast and Hawaii. In New York, Mayor La Guardia declared the attack the direct result of the "Nazi technique of mass murder."

People knowledgeable about world affairs, he declared, know that Nazi "thugs and gangsters" had orchestrated the attack. He warned residents that they should not feel secure just because they were on the eastern seaboard.[31]

During his 3:00 p.m. meeting with his foreign policy advisers, FDR had made it clear that he wanted censorship of the press. But it took a few days for formal procedures to be put into place. In the meantime, the administration kept a tight control on information. Press secretary Steve Early instructed government departments, including the War Department, that all information to the press had to come from the White House. He made clear there would be no further updating of casualty figures beyond the 104 dead and "slightly over 300 wounded" that had already been announced. During the day, he held regular briefings with reporters, updating them on the president's activities, but carefully avoiding any discussion of specific casualty figures or damage reports.[32]

The administration could control the flow of information, but it could not stop the spread of rumors or prevent people from asking questions. At his press briefings on

Sunday, reporters quizzed Early about the damage at Pearl Harbor, pointing out that they were hearing many different, and often conflicting, stories. At 5:15 p.m., for example, NBC reported that 350 men were killed at Hickam Field alone. Early, however, refused any comment.[33]

CBS radio broadcaster Eric Sevareid, whose calm and reasoned coverage of the crisis in Europe had made his one of the most recognized and respected voices in America, was now sitting in the White House pressroom covering America's entry into the conflict. He told his listeners on Sunday evening that credible but unconfirmed reports were floating around that the damage at Pearl was extensive and far more severe than the White House acknowledged. "Now there is one report which I must give you which is not at all confirmed — a report which is rather widely believed here and which has just come in," he said in his soft, unassuming voice. "And that is that the destruction at Hawaii was indeed very heavy, more heavy than we really had anticipated. For this report says that two capital ships of ours have been sunk, that another capital ship has been badly damaged, and the same report from the source says that the airfield hangars there in Hawaii were completely flattened out and that a great many planes have been damaged." Sevareid went on to remind listeners again that the report was "unconfirmed," but said that "it has come in from a fairly reliable source and many reporters here indeed believe it."[34]

According to Robert Sherwood, every reporter had a source telling him that the damage was much worse than the administration was reporting. But even before the government censorship rules went into effect, most papers continued their policy of self-censorship. The White House had already made the case that revealing information about the extent of the damage at Pearl Harbor would potentially aid the Japanese. In the hours and days after the attack, no newspaper wanted to appear to be aiding the enemy by publishing unconfirmed rumors. They needed official confirmation from Washington — something that the Roosevelt White House refused to provide.

Politicians were less circumspect. "The jittery conduct of some of the most eminent of our Government officials was downright disgraceful," Sherwood noted. "They were telephoning the White House, shouting that the President must tell the people the full extent of this unmitigated disaster — that our nation had gone back to Valley Forge — that our West Coast was now indefensible and we must prepare to establish our battle lines in the Rocky Mountains or on the left bank of the Mississippi or God knows where."[35]

The fires were still burning in Pearl as the recriminations in Washington commenced. Reporters covering the State Department overheard Foreign Service officers asking, "Where were the patrols? How could they have let an aircraft carrier get so near the Islands[?] The carrier must have got within two hundred miles. Are they playboys or sailors?" Edmund Starling, the head of the White House Secret Service detail at the time of the attack, noted in his duty log for December 7: "Understand one admiral on duty at Pearl Harbor. All of the others out at parties."[36]

Congressman John Dingell of Michigan demanded that the top five army and navy leaders, including Admiral Kimmel and General Short, be court-martialed. "Hundreds of our boys have paid with their lives for the seeming deficiency of their superiors," he told reporters the following day. "The Army and Navy in Hawaii obviously

Two views of FDR's Oval Study. He would conduct all of the nation's business from this room in the twenty-four hours after Pearl Harbor. (*Courtesy of the Franklin D. Roosevelt Presidential Library and Museum, Hyde Park, New York*)

FDR at his desk with Grace Tully, Stephen Early, and Marguerite "Missy" LeHand. The picture was taken on May 22, 1941, less than two weeks before LeHand would suffer a debilitating stroke. (*Courtesy of the Franklin D. Roosevelt Presidential Library and Museum, Hyde Park, New York*)

This picture, taken in February 1941, is one of only three photos showing FDR in a wheelchair. The White House carefully choreographed FDR's public appearances, including his address to Congress on December 8, 1941, to disguise his disability. (*Courtesy of the Franklin D. Roosevelt Presidential Library and Museum, Hyde Park, New York*)

Harry Hopkins with FDR in the Oval Study in June 1942. Hopkins was FDR's constant shadow in the hours after the attack on Pearl Harbor. (*Courtesy of the Franklin D. Roosevelt Presidential Library and Museum, Hyde Park, New York*)

Two photos taken by the Navy on December 7, 1941, reveal the damage inflicted by the Japanese on Pearl Harbor. Smoke and flames fill the sky as the magazine exploded on the destroyer USS SHAW (top). The battleship USS ARIZONA sinking after being struck by a Japanese bomb (bottom). (*Courtesy of Department of Defense. Department of the Navy. Fourteenth Naval District. Pearl Harbor Naval Shipyard. Office of the Commandant*)

FDR delivers his address to Congress on December 8, 1941. On the right is his son, James Roosevelt. In the background are Vice President Henry A. Wallace (left) and Speaker of the House Sam Rayburn. (© *Corbis*)

FDR signing the declaration of war against Japan on Monday afternoon, December 8, 1941. (*Courtesy of the Franklin D. Roosevelt Presidential Library and Museum, Hyde Park, New York*)

FDR signs the joint resolution declaring that the United States is at war with Germany and Italy on December 11, 1941. (*Courtesy of the Franklin D. Roosevelt Presidential Library and Museum, Hyde Park, New York*)

9

"DO YOU THINK WE OUGHT TO HAVE SOLDIERS AROUND THE WHITE HOUSE?"

Japan's successful surprise assault on Pearl Harbor forced the Secret Service to reevaluate its plan for protecting the president. For the first time since the Civil War, political leaders faced the threat of an assault on the symbols of American political power. If the Japanese could pull off a surprise attack on a secure naval base at Pearl Harbor, then no place was safe, not even the White House.

The immediate task of protecting the president fell to Mike Reilly, who had been assigned to the White House detail since 1935. On the morning of December 7, he was second in command of the president's security detail, reporting to Colonel Edmund Starling. By the end of the day, Secret Service chief Frank Wilson had promoted Reilly to supervising agent. He believed the colonel, who was sixty-four years old and in poor health, lacked the energy to respond to the new security environment. "I decided that the need for a young and very active man to head the Detail was urgent," Wilson reflected.[1]

Reilly did not wait for his promotion to assume control. As soon as he heard the news of the attack on Pearl Harbor, he told the White House operator, "Start calling in all the Secret Service men who are off duty. Don't tell 'em why, just call 'em in. All the White House police, too." He then called Ed Kelly, Washington's chief of police, and asked him to send sixteen uniformed police officers over to the White House.[2]

Shortly after 2:00 p.m., Reilly placed a call to Frank Wilson, who was at home and about to sit down for dinner. When the phone rang, his wife answered and was told "Get the Chief on the phone, quick." When Wilson grabbed the receiver, he heard Reilly's excited voice. "Chief," he said, "the Japs have bombarded Pearl Harbor."[3]

Wilson recalled that he was "stunned to silence" by the news, but quickly regained his voice and instructed Reilly to start calling every Secret Service agent and White House policeman and have them report to duty — a task that Reilly had already completed.[4]

■ ■ ■ ■

Although we are now used to heavily guarded government buildings, prior to World War II the White House had been open and casual. Visitors, for example, could have picnics on the grounds during daylight hours. The guards protected only the house, not the surrounding grounds. There were no guardhouses at any of the four entrances to the building. On most days, a lone policeman stood at each entrance to control traffic. Every day, thousands of visitors came through the White House's formal rooms. There were no bag checks or metal detectors. Reporters covering the president found the same lax rules. "The gates were wide open and no one had heard of a White House pass," recalled Merriman Smith.[5]

But when war broke out in Europe, the Secret Service reevaluated White House security. A 1940 report had noted that the White House lacked enough guards to provide adequate security in the event of an emergency. Prior to Pearl Harbor, the Secret Service had 25 men — policemen plus agents — assigned to the presidential protection team when FDR was at the White House. In the event of an emergency, those who guarded the president had access to twenty riot guns and three submachine guns, which were held in locked cases around the grounds. In addition, the existing guard could be supplemented with 73 city and U.S. park patrolmen, 43 U.S. infantryman, and 55 off-duty White House guards. Although these forces were adequate for normal times, they were insufficient during a time of war.[6]

The report also observed that the regular Secret Service force included "only four men in the South Grounds to take care of any situation which might arise after an alarm has been given and until assistance arrives." These men were "the first and only line of defense outside the White House on the South Grounds." Between 1937 and 1940, twenty people had climbed the White House fence. None had meant any harm to the president, and all were quickly apprehended. The Secret Service speculated about what could happen if someone who intended to kill the president had jumped the fence and then "sneaked from tree to bush . . . until he was within throwing distance of the White House with a grenade or a bottle of nitro glycerine." The report had recommended the strategic positioning of four police posts along the fence that surrounded the White House. These outposts would allow the guards to view people as they approached the grounds and to catch them before they could navigate the fence. The report also called for the hiring of 15 additional officers to staff the booths.[7]

Most of these recommendations were considered too expensive and impractical — until the attack on Pearl Harbor. Almost immediately, Chief Wilson dramatically increased the number of agents assigned to protecting FDR. "My greatest fear," he reflected later, "was that a Nazi undercover agent or saboteur might be willing to sacrifice his own life if he could assassinate our President. I immediately decided to intensify to a high degree the protection extended to him." A detail of army soldiers was assigned to guard the outer ring along the perimeter. Sentries with machine guns were placed on the roof of the White House and surrounding buildings. Washington police officers formed the second line of defense inside the fence. The beefed-up Secret Service formed an airtight seal around FDR.[8]

In a long memorandum written on December 11, 1941, Mike Reilly spelled out the changes initiated in presidential protection after Pearl Harbor. Prior to December 8, Reilly wrote, there had been between 17 and 22 White House policemen and 4 to 6 agents assigned to the White House. "Since December 8th on each tour of duty, there have been 22 to 28 White House Policemen, 20 Metropolitan Policemen or 20 Uniformed Secret Service Guards; two Metropolitan Detective Sergeants and from 8 to 15 Secret Service Agents." In addition, a "squad of four soldiers in an Army reconnaissance car equipped with two 50 caliber machine guns" patrolled the avenues around the White House. It was decided that at least 119 "protective personnel" would be on duty at the White House at all times.[9]

Wilson made sure that no potential assassin could gain entry to the grounds. By Sunday night, temporary sentry gates were set up to channel visitors to the grounds. According to Reilly, the Bureau of Engraving and Printing prepared "a radically changed design" of the White House identification card. Everyone who entered the White House was now forced to show identification. Even Cordell Hull, who regularly shuttled back and forth between the White House and the State Department, was now required to show his credentials. For the first time, reporters were photographed, fingerprinted, and issued passes, which they were forced to show every time they entered the grounds. Only cars carrying officials with appointments with the president were permitted on the White House grounds.[10]

The Secret Service also worried about the threat of an air attack. Reilly assigned a detail of firemen between the Treasury Building and the White House who could respond in the event of a fire caused by an incendiary bomb. He insisted on a complete "blackout" of the White House grounds, fearing that the bright lights would make for an easy target for enemy bombers. He provided all agents with flashlights equipped with blue bulbs. At the same time, he sent Henrietta Nesbitt, head of housekeeping, to purchase black cloth to block light from the windows. The president's residence on the second floor was equipped first, followed by the lower floors and then the offices. When the first set of blackout curtains was not thick enough, Nesbitt purchased a second layer. Her staff covered every window, including those in the basement. Skylights and bathroom windows were painted black. The staff also dimmed the lights around the White House to make it a less inviting target and placed a ban on picture taking that evening. "We're not going to have the White House lit up tonight. Absolutely no pictures of the cabinet," said Early.[11]

Guards issued everyone in the White House a gas mask, including Roosevelt. "Gas masks were provided and fitted for the Boss," recalled Tully, "and for every other individual in the White House." According to Wilson, the president's mask "was tied to his wheel chair so that it would be ready for immediate use at all times." The president refused to test his mask. "He felt it would look silly," recalled Merriman Smith. According to Smith, press secretary Early did not want the public to know about the gas masks, perhaps fearing that it would raise fears of a possible Japanese attack using poison gas.[12]

The Secret Service also worried about homemade bombs. Prior to the attacks, the guards had sent all packages received at the White House to the mail room, where they were examined for bombs. In its 1940 report, the Secret Service had pointed out that the president's office, "while on the floor above, is on the same side of the building, and not more than 35 feet east of the mail room." They had recommended using an outside facility to examine the mail.[13]

The Secret Service got its wish after December 7. The White House established a mail and package room a few blocks away, where all packages had to be cleared before being sent to the executive mansion. Every package sent to the president was first tested for a timing device by an instrument called a detector, which amplified the sound of a clock. If no obvious problems were discovered, the package would be X-rayed. If the guards saw anything suspicious, they would soak the package in oil, which, in Reilly's words, "gums up the machinery." The agents would then place the oil-soaked package in a bomb carrier, where it would be detonated at a safe location outside the city.

On one occasion, a few weeks after December 7, the X-ray revealed a solid black mass surrounded by wires. In the middle was an object that looked like a stick of dynamite. It had come from England in a diplomatic pouch, but no one in the British Embassy had any knowledge of it. The Secret Service decided the safest step would be to carry the package out of the city, dig a hole, and blow it up. After the destruction, they peered in to the hole and were surprised to discover that the potential bomb was a stack of a dozen records sent to FDR by Winston Churchill.[14]

Also in the 1940 report, the Secret Service had suggested that old furniture and other unnecessary articles, along with combustible materials such as paint and carpets, be removed from the White House to prevent fires. The agents pointed out that the White House's internal structure was composed largely of wood, making it a potential firetrap. Given FDR's affection for his comfortable furniture, it is no surprise that the recommendation was never implemented. After Pearl Harbor, the Secret Service instead had to settle for placing a bucket of sand and a shovel in every room to help put out fires.[15]

It wasn't just the phalanx of additional guards that transformed the White House the evening after the Pearl Harbor attacks. The interior was transformed dramatically as well, as an army of engineers, electricians, and technicians descended on the White House. Engineers installed an emergency backup power plant to supply current in the event of a power failure. Interestingly, FDR's bedroom and the Oval Study, and not the Oval Office, were the only rooms hooked into the emergency system. Apparently, the decision was made to protect the rooms where FDR spent most of his time.

The communications system was also upgraded: Technicians installed a more elaborate phone system that would connect the White House switchboard with the U.S. Park Police and the army reserve stationed in the Treasury Building. All of the major offices in the White House were now tied into the switchboard, and new call boxes were installed at key points around the White House grounds. The army signal corps loaned the Secret Service two-way radio units. "These units," Reilly noted, "will provide two-way communication between all sentry posts and from each sentry post to a central station either at the White House or at any place the President may be."

In addition, the outside of the White House was fortified. That night, construction teams installed temporary barriers at each of the entrances to the White House to prevent a car or truck from crashing the gates. They would soon be replaced with permanent barriers, designed, in Reilly's words, to be able to stop a "7-ton truck traveling at 40 miles per hour for a distance of three city blocks." He noted that agents installed a device "to guard against the presence of radium which may be used in an attempt to injure the President."[16]

By Sunday evening, Washington had been transformed into an armed fortress.

Machine-gun-carrying guards surrounded the White House and Munitions Building. The entire city's police force was also called to duty. All leaves and vacations were canceled. The police were issued specific orders to "pay special attention to all bridges, power stations, pumping stations and public utilities, to prevent acts of sabotage or interference with normal operations, to be especially alert for any suspicious persons loitering in or about such places." Hundreds of armed guards stood watch around bridges, power stations, and other vulnerable areas. Thirty-eight police officers were assigned to guard the city's water supply.[17]

The added security failed to satisfy Secretary of the Treasury Morgenthau, whose agency oversaw the Secret Service.

Morgenthau, a tall, ungainly man who spoke with a high-pitched voice, was deeply suspicious and nervous on the best of days. Two reporters described him as "a born worrier and inclined to be suspicious." His dour demeanor and slow speech earned him the nickname "Henry the Morgue."

The attack on Pearl Harbor seemed to put Morgenthau over the edge. He could not understand how the Japanese could have pulled off such a surprise attack. The navy "is supposed to be on the alert," he complained to aides that evening, "and how this thing could have happened — all the explanations I have heard just don't make sense, and Stimson says they don't make sense to him either."[18]

Morgenthau worried about every possibility in the hours after the attack on Pearl Harbor. On the afternoon of December 7, when the Treasury secretary met with the Secret Service to discuss the new protective measures for the president, Mike Reilly recalled Morgenthau peering out of the White House windows, looking for Japanese airplanes. Since he lived in downtown Washington, Morgenthau worried about his family's safety in the event of a Japanese attack. On Sunday afternoon, he called a local drapery shop and insisted that his house be equipped with blackout curtains within twenty-four hours.[19]

On Sunday evening at 6:35 p.m., Morgenthau met in his office with Chief Wilson and Assistant Secretary Herbert E. Gaston to discuss the additional steps that had been taken to protect the president. As usual, Morgenthau had a secretary taking notes. Wilson assured his boss that the White House guard had been doubled and additional guards had been added to the protection force. But Morgenthau was not satisfied. "Do you think," he asked, "we ought to have soldiers around the White House?" Wilson delicately dismissed the idea. "Well, personally we have got 80 first class men over there and we have 20 high class agents who are up on their toes, and I think they can handle the situation in pretty good shape." Morgenthau was not convinced and asked what security procedures the Wilson administration had used during the First World War. When told that army soldiers had patrolled the White House, Morgenthau quickly supported the idea. "That's what I would like," he declared. The Japanese had already taken the government by surprise, he noted. "How do you know what trick they might pull from within?" Morgenthau made clear that he wanted one hundred soldiers carrying machine guns and patrolling the White House at all times.

In order to expand protection, Morgenthau needed FDR's permission. It would be a tough sell, especially since the president had already made clear earlier that afternoon that he did not want armed guards patrolling the White House. At 6:40 p.m., Roosevelt came on the line, and Morgenthau pressed the issue of soldiers. Once again, Roosevelt demurred. Although he understood the need for added security, he still worried about turning the White House into an armed fortress. "As long as you have one about every hundred feet around the fence, it's all right," he instructed Morgenthau. FDR also stated that he wanted to "block off both Executive Avenues" and recommended placing "barricades between the White House and the treasury and also on the one [block] between the White House and State Department."[20]

Perhaps upset that the president did not grant his request for army patrols, Morgenthau decided to conduct his own inspection of White House security that evening. He was shocked by what he found. "I just made an inspection . . . and in the whole rear of the White House only three men," he complained to the Secret Service. And the agents hardly seemed trained to handle an emergency. "I asked one man to take out his gun. He started tugging away . . . and after about two minutes got the gun out." The inspection provided Morgenthau with little assurance that the Secret Service was capable of protecting the president. "Anybody could take a five ton truck with 20 men and they could take the White House without any trouble."[21]

Morgenthau, however, was not the only official inspecting the added security arrangements that evening. Around 2:00 a.m. on the morning of December 8, Secret Service chief Frank Wilson decided to conduct his own review. He found the agents on the White House detail were "on their toes." He was shocked, though, to find a police officer, the one on duty closest to the president's bedroom, resting comfortably in a chair, "snugly wrapped in a blanket." Wilson noted that the officer was "so nearly asleep that I was not even challenged as I approached."[22]

In the days that followed, a host of security experts descended on the White House and made recommendations for making it safer. With images of the London blitz in mind, they were especially concerned with the possibility of an attack from the air. The army's bomb experts advised the Secret Service that the White House was especially vulnerable to a bomb blast. According to Reilly, they concluded that "the mortar of the original part of the White House was made from ground oyster and clam shells and the entire White House would immediately crumble in the event of a direct or near hit."[23]

Security experts introduced a number of possible solutions, some more practical than others. Some, for example, suggested that the White House be painted black to make it less visible. Another idea mentioned was to move the seat of government farther inland and away from the coast. There was even a discussion about changing the direction of the Potomac and Anacostia rivers. It was not as crazy as it sounded. As Reilly pointed out, "No camouflage of the White House is practical while the confluence of these rivers remains a mile from the mansion. A pilot would find it quite simple to hit the White House by flying up either river and getting his 'fix' at the confluence."[24]

Since no one previously had seriously considered the possibility of enemy planes dropping bombs on the nation's capital, the Secret Service had to develop new strategies for protecting the president. They created ten safe houses in the Washington, D.C., area where they could take FDR in the event of an attack. If necessary, a plane stood ready to whisk him away from D.C.

The Secret Service also proposed a number of alterations to the White House to make it more resistant to an air assault. On December 15, they provided Morgenthau with a list of suggested changes, which included covering the skylights with six inches of sand topped with a layer of tin. They also wanted to cover the roof with sandbags and have machine guns installed. The west colonnade, which the president passed through on his way to the Oval Office, would be equipped with movable steel barricades. The Secret Service also recommended that bulletproof glass, along with roll-down steel curtains, be installed in all of the windows of rooms used by the first family, especially FDR's Oval Study. In addition, the guards proposed that all of the outer doors have "light and air or gas locks" so that the house could be quickly sealed.[25]

Roosevelt objected to most of the added security measures, and only a few were implemented. FDR understood the symbolic value of the White House and likely worried about the psychological impact on the public if they saw pictures of the grounds surrounded by heavily armed guards, or if word leaked that elaborate new security measures were being put into place. The Secret Service did add bulletproof glass halfway up the windows of the Oval Office directly behind the president's desk, and a concrete "bomb barrier" was poured along the west wall of the Executive Office Building. Most of the other suggestions, however, remained on the drawing board for the rest of FDR's presidency.

The Secret Service did, however, implement some significant changes. For both Morgenthau and the Secret Service, constructing a bomb shelter beneath the White House was a top priority. Since no shelter existed, they decided to use a large vault under the Treasury Department as a temporary refuge. The vault, which was used to store contraband opium and currency, was supported by walls constructed of heavy armored plates and reinforced with concrete. "The shelter had an office and a bedroom for the President and a relatively large outer office planned for use by the staff," Tully recalled. "Bunks were built along the walls of this larger room and emergency telephone facilities were also crowded in."[26]

A few days after Pearl Harbor, the government started construction of a tunnel to connect the shelter, located in the basement of the Treasury Building, to the White House. Security experts recommended building a zigzag path from the White House to the vault, pointing out that a straight tunnel would leave the president vulnerable to flying debris. "The tunnel was 761 feet long, about 7 feet wide and 7 feet high, and of a zigzag design intended to lessen danger from concussion in the event of a direct or close bomb hit," recalled Wilson. The shelter itself was stocked with twenty-four cases of Poland water, two hundred pounds of food, twelve beds, twenty-four blankets, twelve first-aid kits, and a portable toilet.[27]

Once again, FDR remained dubious. Although construction went forward, the president opposed the idea of a bomb shelter and never visited it. "Henry, I will not go down into the shelter unless you allow me to play poker with all the gold in your vaults," he joked with Morgenthau.[28]

The Secret Service also began exploring additional protective measures, including the creation of a traveling speaking rostrum that would screen the president from a bomb blast or an assailant with a gun. A few months after the Pearl Harbor attack, the Secret Service contracted with a company to create a steel protective shield that would be hidden inside a standard rostrum. In the event of an emergency, an agent could press a button that would extend a six-foot, three-inch steel shield that would encase the president. "It is semi-circular in shape to afford full protection from all frontal angles," the service reported.[29]

The agency also set up a new alarm system to alert agents when FDR moved around the White House. It had become standard practice for the usher to sound three alarms to notify the staff that the president was moving from the mansion to the executive offices. Those charged with protecting the president now set up their own system to track FDR's movements. "Whenever the Supervisor is notified the President is about to leave his quarters, or his office in the West Wing," instructed a Secret Service guide, he was now required to inform all White House police officers and agents on duty.[30]

Although FDR bristled at most of the added security measures, he did see the new focus on security as an opportunity to expand the White House, a project he had been contemplating for some time. Remarkably, while processing the original reports about the Japanese assault, and laying the groundwork for America's entry into World War II, FDR had the wherewithal to plan future construction projects. According to White House architect Lorenzo Winslow, FDR called him on the afternoon of December 7 and told him to start planning to construct new buildings. "Mr. Roosevelt called me, and I went down to the White House that evening," he told a reporter in 1961. "He wanted to discuss more office space for the expansion he knew would be needed." FDR said that steps should be taken at once to provide space in temporary buildings on the South Lawn of the White House, Winslow reflected in his memoirs, "and he gave me a detailed list of the people who would be housed in the quarters." The next morning, before going to Congress to deliver his war message, FDR summoned Winslow to his bedroom and suggested that instead of designing temporary buildings, he should create a permanent East Wing. "It has always been interesting to me that he should have been concerned with this while he must have been thinking of so many other things," Winslow recalled.[31]

FDR had wanted to build a new East Wing for three years to accommodate his growing White House staff. At the time, the East Wing looked much as it had when his cousin Theodore Roosevelt had built it in 1902. Until 1941, it served as the social entrance to the White House and contained guard stations, a colonnaded corridor, and a long cloakroom. Despite the enormous new burdens of war that had been thrust upon him, FDR found the time to offer specific design ideas for the new addition. Picking up on FDR's suggestions, Winslow drew up plans by the end of the month. The army decided to add to his design by calling for the construction of a permanent air-raid shelter under the new wing.

Construction on the new wing commenced within months, and the first occupants moved in during the spring of 1942. Although construction was not completed until after the war, the new wing quickly filled up with executive-branch offices. Roosevelt also replaced the old cloakroom with a movie theater. A secure bomb shelter sat beneath the East Wing, complete with seven-foot-thick concrete walls laced with steel. The shelter consisted of one large room with a presidential private area in the middle that contained a bedroom and bathroom.

If there was a direct security threat to the president, the assumption was that alien residents from Germany, Italy, or Japan would be the likely perpetrators. Within hours of the attack on Pearl Harbor, Washington moved to round up potential suspects. The fear of domestic terrorism would lead to one of the most serious violations of civil liberties in American history and leave a dark stain on FDR's leadership.

Reporters noticed that Solicitor-General Charles Fahy had slipped into the White House at around 7:00 p.m. When he tried to leave, they cornered him to find out what he had been doing. Reluctantly, he admitted that he had a brief meeting with the president. When pressed, he whispered, "My visit had to do with the aliens — the Japanese — living in the United States."[32]

Fahy was referring to the roughly 92,000 Japanese Americans living in the United States in December 1941. The first-generation immigrants, known as Issei, had mostly arrived before 1907. Although they were longtime U.S. residents, the federal government had prevented them from becoming naturalized citizens. Their children, the Nisei, were born in the United States and therefore claimed full citizenship. A much smaller group, the Kibei, were American born but raised and educated in Japan. Roughly, about 90 percent of all Japanese Americans were clustered on the West Coast, around San Francisco and Los Angeles. The Japanese also made up about 30 percent of the territory of Hawaii's total population.

As tensions between the two countries increased in the late 1930s, FDR had grown worried about the loyalty of the Japanese community within U.S. borders. He and his military advisers had watched as a "fifth column" of German spies aided Hitler's lightning-fast conquest of Europe. There must be similar networks in the United States, he assumed. At the urging of his military advisers, FDR approved steps to investigate and neutralize potential subversive activity among Japanese residents in Hawaii.

Although the administration worried to some extent about German and Italian spies, the Japanese came under much closer scrutiny. FDR had long harbored negative attitudes toward Japanese Americans. Early in his career, he called both the Issei and the Nisei a "menace" and "chronic irritation" to their white neighbors. During the 1920s, he opposed Japanese immigration to America. Unlike many nativists, Roosevelt did not consider Japanese racially inferior, and he deplored racial prejudice. Like most Americans, however, he believed the Japanese were incapable of assimilating into mainstream society and therefore potentially more dangerous than German and Italian Americans.[33]

In 1940, Congress had acted on those general fears by passing the Alien Registration Act. The law required all resident aliens over the age of fourteen to register with the government. Each year they had to go to their local post office, where they were fingerprinted, photographed, and instructed to provide authorities with accurate and up-to-date information about where they lived and worked. To keep track of the resident aliens, the Justice Department set up an Aliens Division, which worked closely with the FBI and military intelligence, to establish detailed Custodial Detention Lists, also known as "ABC Lists," of perceived security threats.[34]

In the months leading up to the attack on Pearl Harbor, both the attorney general and the FBI had assured FDR of the loyalty of the Japanese community in America. The only spies they could identify were paid agents of the Japanese government. Roosevelt was unconvinced and, in typical fashion, assigned a special agent to bypass traditional channels and report directly to him. On November 7, exactly a month before Pearl Harbor, his representative, Curtis B. Munson, reported, "There is no Japanese 'problem' on the Coast. There will be no armed uprising of Japanese."[35]

There was no evidence that the Japanese community was involved in subversive activity and overwhelming evidence that they were in fact loyal to the United States. Yet in their brief ten-minute meeting on the evening of December 7, FDR instructed Fahy to implement Emergency Proclamation 2525, which authorized the FBI to arrest any aliens in the continental United States whom it deemed "dangerous to public peace and safety." He gave little thought to the matter and approved the request without debate or discussion. He promised to formally sign the proclamation the following day.[36]

Even before FDR approved the new security measures, FBI agents and local police had formed task forces to find those listed by the Aliens Division as dangerous. By late Sunday afternoon, FBI agents had fanned out throughout Southern California, raiding private homes to detain suspicious Japanese. According to the *Los Angeles Times,* nearly two hundred were arrested in the hours after the attack. The *Times* reported that thousands more would likely be detained after the formal declaration of war.[37]

In the New York metropolitan region, a special task force of one hundred FBI agents, along with city police and detectives, scoured the city, shutting down Japanese businesses and arresting Japanese nationals on their target list. Those arrested were taken to Ellis Island, where they were held indefinitely until they received further instructions from Washington. Estimates suggest that a few hundred were detained. New York mayor Fiorello La Guardia directed Japanese nationals to stay in their homes. The police closed the Nippon Club on West Ninety-third Street. Police escorted the twelve members at the club to their respective homes. Additionally, New York City policemen visited every Japanese restaurant in the city. They allowed diners to finish their meals before closing the restaurants and escorting the owners and staff to their homes.[38]

Also on December 7, the Treasury Department under Morgenthau started waging economic warfare against Japanese-owned businesses in the United States. The government invoked a "total embargo" on shipments of every kind to Japan and its occupied territories, making it illegal for an American to transact business with Japan. On Sunday evening, Morgenthau sent some 4,000 agents to forcibly sever all economic ties between Japan and the United States. Treasury agents also visited and assumed control of every Japanese bank in the United

States. The government froze the assets of Japanese nationals, preventing them from withdrawing money from their bank accounts to buy food and other necessities. (At the urging of the first lady, the Treasury Department later allowed each family to withdraw one hundred dollars per month for living expenses.)[39]

What began as a relatively modest security program prior to Pearl Harbor quickly morphed into a massive violation of civil liberties. Stories circulated about plots among Japanese residents to aid an enemy landing on the coast of California. Deeply embedded racism reinforced the fear of sabotage. Newspapers vilified Japanese residents, calling them "mad dogs, yellow vermin and nips." Business interests saw an opportunity to eradicate competition from Japanese farmers. The entire political establishment of California clamored for action against Japanese residents.

The Japanese living on the West Coast were obvious and easy targets. There were too many German and Italian aliens to arrest them all, and they exercised considerable political clout, especially in the Midwest and East. There were also too many Japanese Americans in Hawaii to be moved. Those of Japanese descent on the West

Coast thus became the chief available targets for American frustration and hostility. "These people were not convicted of any crime," Eleanor wrote years later, "but emotions ran too high, too many people wanted to wreak vengeance on Oriental looking people. There was no time to investigate families or to adhere strictly to the American rule that a man is innocent until he is proven guilty."[40]

Roosevelt, preoccupied with the military and diplomatic demands of fighting a global war, and largely indifferent to violations of civil liberties, would eventually give in to the pressure. According to Stimson, he and Roosevelt discussed the possibility of evacuating the Japanese from the West Coast on February 11, 1942. FDR expressed no opinion. He considered it a military matter, and he left it up to the War Department to develop a policy. Stimson, in turn, handed the issue off to Assistant Secretary John J. McCloy, who was responsible for domestic security. McCloy believed that he was given "carte blanche" by the president "to do what we want" with the Japanese.[41]

On March 21, 1942, Roosevelt signed Executive Order 9066, authorizing the forced evacuation of Japanese residents on the West Coast. More than 100,000 people, many of them American citizens, were told to dispose of their property however they could before being rounded up and taken to government "relocation" centers scattered throughout the West. Attorney General Francis Biddle, who opposed the measure, claimed FDR showed no regret in signing it into law. "I do not think he was much concerned with the gravity or implications of this step," he wrote. "He was never theoretical about things. What must be done to defend the country must be done. The military might be wrong. But they were fighting the war. Nor do I think that the constitutional difficulty plagued him — the Constitution has never greatly bothered any wartime President."[42]

Roosevelt may have viewed the evacuation as a matter of military necessity, but his decision was shaped by both prejudice and indifference. He considered the egregious violation of civil liberties a trivial issue, especially when compared with the larger strategic goal of fighting and winning a global war. In 1982, a government commission reviewing the internment criticized the Roosevelt administration for "race prejudice, war hysteria, and a failure of political leadership." Unfortunately, it was a fair assessment.

10

"WE ARE ALL IN THE SAME BOAT NOW"

On Sunday evening, Winston Churchill was having dinner with the American ambassador to Britain, John G. "Gil" Winant, along with diplomat Averell Harriman and his wife, Pamela. "The Prime Minister seemed tired and depressed," Harriman recalled. "He didn't have much to say throughout dinner and was immersed in his thoughts, with his head in his hands part of the time."[1]

There was plenty of reason for gloom. For most of the year, as Nazi bombs rained down on London, Churchill's top priority was to convince Roosevelt to enter the war. To his dismay, he had managed to wrangle old ships and other material but few commitments from the frustratingly elusive Roosevelt.

The two men had started a correspondence in September 1939 when Churchill joined the cabinet as the first lord of the admiralty. Churchill sent a series of letters about the problems confronting the British navy. On May 10, 1940 — the day that Hitler invaded Belgium, the Netherlands, Luxembourg, and France — Churchill became prime minister, and the correspondence became more frequent, and more urgent. On May 15, he promised to fight alone, but if the United States did not intervene, he warned Roosevelt, "You may have a completely subjugated, Nazified Europe established with astounding swiftness, and the weight may be more than we can bear."[2]

Roosevelt was not sure about his new counterpart. Although they came from similar social backgrounds and possessed a flair for the dramatic, Churchill was a political conservative who dreamed of preserving the British Empire. His love of alcohol, and capacity for consuming it, was legendary. "I suppose Churchill was the best man England had," FDR told his cabinet on hearing the news that he was the new prime minister, "even if he was drunk half of his time."[3]

In January 1941, Roosevelt had sent Harry Hopkins to London as his personal emissary to get a better sense of Churchill. "I suppose you could say — but not out loud — that I've come to try to find a way to be a catalytic agent between two prima donnas," Hopkins told CBS correspondent Edward R. Murrow, who was in London at the time. Hopkins spent twelve evenings with Churchill, traveled with him to military posts, and came away inspired by Churchill's determination and statesmanship. "People here are amazing from Churchill down," he wrote FDR, "and if courage alone can win — the result will be inevitable. But they need our help desperately."[4]

The frail, businesslike Hopkins was a big hit with Churchill as well. Interior Secretary Harold Ickes noted, "Apparently the first thing that Churchill asks for when he gets awake in the morning is Harry Hopkins, and Harry is the last one he sees at night." Hopkins lobbied for more aid, but Roosevelt remained cautious. While declaring that America "must become the great arsenal of democracy," he refused to give Churchill what he needed most — a declaration of war against Germany and American troops on European soil.

Over the next few months, Churchill continued to write as many as two or three letters a week to Roosevelt, describing Britain's plight and pleading for American intervention. His radio addresses, which were broadcast in the United States, were extremely popular. By 1941, Churchill ranked second only to FDR as the "favorite personality" on U.S. radio. Although his words inspired Americans, they seemed to make little difference in Washington. British ambassador Lord Halifax observed that trying to pin down the Roosevelt administration on a clear policy toward Britain was like "a disorderly day's rabbit-shooting."[5]

At the end of 1940, Roosevelt suggested that he and Churchill meet "to talk over the problem of the defeat of Germany." Churchill accepted, and in August 1941, they met at Placentia Bay in Newfoundland — the first of many conferences between the two leaders. "I've just got to see Churchill myself in order to explain things to him," FDR told Henry Morgenthau. Both men came away with renewed respect and affection for each other. After an informal lunch, Roosevelt noted in a letter, "[Churchill] is a tremendously vital person & in many ways is an English Mayor La Guardia. . . . I like him — & lunching alone broke the ice both ways."[6]

Roosevelt's main reason for calling the meeting was to issue a declaration of war aims, which he hoped would educate the public about the European conflict and prepare them for the possibility of American intervention. The statement would also ease American anxieties that the United States might be forming an alliance that included the Soviet Union. Before the meeting ended, the two leaders issued the Atlantic Charter. The declaration pledged both nations to honor the principles of self-determination, free trade, nonaggression, and freedom of the seas, promising a postwar world in which all people "may live out their lives in freedom from fear and want."[7]

But Churchill continued to press Roosevelt for a declaration of war against Germany. Roosevelt dodged, promising "to wage war, but not declare it." He pledged the navy to protect British convoys as far east as Iceland while he looked for an "incident" to justify a more aggressive posture. Despite the good feelings between the two national leaders, Roosevelt's position remained the same: support Britain in every way short of war. FDR was acutely aware that the public, while favoring a tough line with Japan, wanted to stay out of a war in Europe. For now, he had no intention of challenging public attitudes.[8]

By December, British prospects seemed bleak. Churchill expected Germany to eventually defeat Russia, although the struggle was taking longer than expected. Once Hitler had vanquished Russia, he would turn the full force of his military on England. At the same time, Japan was making threatening moves in the Pacific. He now faced the prospect of a spring offensive from the Germans and a war with Japan in the East.

There was a general sense in Britain that the war was already lost. An American diplomat who traveled to Scotland reported back to the embassy that most people he met believed that "the British are now losing the war." The only way Hitler could be defeated was by a massive offensive on the ground. The simple reality was that the British lacked the manpower and the matériel to launch such an offensive without direct American intervention. British merchant ships carrying food and supplies were being sunk faster than they could be replaced. His field marshal in Africa cabled Churchill on November 4: "I am struck by the growth of the impression here and elsewhere that the war is going to end in stalemate and thus fatally for us."[9]

As a flood of intelligence poured in that winter indicating that the Japanese were planning a major offensive, Churchill worried they would bypass American possessions and strike only at the British. At lunch on December 7, he asked Ambassador Winant bluntly, "If they declare war on us, will you declare war on them?" He did not get the answer he wanted. "I can't answer that, Prime Minister. Only the Congress has the right to declare war under the United States constitution." Churchill sat in silence. His empire stood on the brink of destruction, and the best his American counterpart could offer was a civics lesson.[10]

Just before 9:00 on the evening of December 7, an aide handed Churchill a fifteen-dollar radio that had been presented to him as a gift from Harry Hopkins. Operating like a music box, it started playing when the lid was opened. Churchill used the radio to tune into the 9:00 p.m. broadcast of the *BBC News,* which he never missed. A few minutes into the broadcast came a bulletin announcing the Japanese attack. "President Roosevelt has announced that the Japanese have bombed the Hawaiian base of the United States fleet at Pearl Harbor."[11]

There was initially some confusion among those gathered around the dinner table. Harriman repeated the announcement in shock. "My God," he exclaimed, "they've attacked Pearl Harbor." Another guest, however, assuming the announcement was wrong, said, "Oh, no, it was Pearl River." Churchill's butler settled the dispute. "Yes, yes, we've heard it too. They've attacked the Americans at Pearl Harbor."[12]

Churchill jumped up, slammed down the lid on the radio, and announced, "We will declare war on Japan." The Japanese had already attacked Malaya, but the news had not yet reached the prime minister. Winant tried to calm the prime minister down. "Good God," he said, "you can't declare war on a radio announcement." He suggested they call Roosevelt to get the latest information and to learn whether a declaration of war would follow.[13]

A few minutes later, the two men went to the war room at Chequers. Ambassador Winant placed a call to the White House and soon had Roosevelt on the line. "I've got someone with me who wants to speak with you," Winant said. "Who's that," FDR asked. "You'll find out when he speaks." Churchill, who was listening on an extension, broke into the conversation. "Mr. President, what's this about Japan," he asked. "It's quite true," Roosevelt answered. "They have attacked us at Pearl Harbor. We are all in the same boat now." He told Churchill that he would go before Congress and ask for a declaration of war the next day. Churchill was thrilled that the United States had finally entered the war. "This certainly simplifies things," the prime minister responded. For the first time, he believed the Allies could now win. "To have the United States at our side," he wrote later, "was to me the greatest joy. Now at this very moment I knew the United States was in the war, up to the neck and in to the death. So we had won after all! . . . Hitler's fate was sealed. Mussolini's fate was sealed. As for the Japanese, they would be ground to powder."[14]

Later that evening, Churchill recalled what the British foreign secretary had told him about the United States during World War I. He had compared the United States to a giant boiler. "Once the fire is lighted under it there is no limit to the power it can generate." The British leader said that night he "slept the sleep of the saved and the thankful."[15]

Despite his optimistic statements, Churchill still worried that Roosevelt would choose to fight only in the Pacific. If the Americans moved in this direction, it would pull essential resources away from the Atlantic theater, denying Churchill the men that he needed both to stop Hitler's planned invasion and to start an offensive operation to retake Europe.[16]

American reporters in London were surprised that the British public showed little reaction to the news that evening. "Regarding the Jap war, I feel sure London reaction is much less intense than you'd imagine," Jeffrey Mark cabled his editors in New York late on December 7. "It is important to realize that to Britishers, Hawaii is not a naval base but a South Sea island with a Hollywood ukulele and hula hula trimmings." While the British thought it was good that the Americans were finally part of the conflict, that feeling was "qualified by the thought that America will now attend to her own defense needs frantically and tend to neglect British and Russian lease-lend." They also worried that the U.S. Navy would abandon its Atlantic patrols and relocate to the Pacific.[17]

Despite the underlying anxiety about how America would respond to the attack, Churchill and the British people could take considerable comfort from knowing that they now had a powerful ally in their once lonely struggle against fascism.

Adolf Hitler was at the Wolf's Lair, an underground bunker nestled in the forest

213

about 450 miles northeast of Berlin, when he heard the news of the Pearl Harbor attack. After a late dinner, he gathered with a handful of minions. Although he refused to acknowledge it, his troops were stymied on the eastern front, bogged down by unexpectedly strong Russian resistance and a typically brutal Russian winter. The previous summer, Hitler had launched Operation Barbarossa — his assault on his former ally, the Soviet Union. By the beginning of December 1941, German troops had advanced to Istra, a suburb only 15 miles west of Moscow. But the frigid temperatures and Stalin's patriotic appeals to a shell-shocked nation had slowed the German advance. Fighting the killing cold and the stiffening Russian resistance, the invaders' losses mounted. On December 5, as the Japanese sailed toward Pearl Harbor, the Soviet army launched a massive counterattack along a 560-mile front.

For the past few years, the Nazis had encouraged Japan to attack British and Dutch possessions in Asia, while trying to avoid a direct confrontation with the United States. Hitler's strategy was to keep the United States neutral for as long as possible. He calculated that Roosevelt would not be able to convince the American public to enter the war unless they were attacked. By late November, however, as it became clear that negotiations between Japan and the United States were deadlocked, Germany switched positions. A few days before the attack, the German foreign minister assured Japan that Germany would intervene on its side if it decided to declare war on the United States. He prepared a draft of an agreement that was still unsigned when the bombs started falling on Pearl Harbor.[18]

While Hitler expected a Japanese move against the United States, he did not know the place or the time. Around midnight on December 7, the German leader was discussing the eastern front and how the German people were supporting the troops by contributing warm clothing to the cause. Suddenly, his press officer burst into the room with a bulletin. They had picked up an American broadcast indicating that the Japanese had attacked at Pearl Harbor. Hitler was elated by the news. Leaping to his feet, he shouted, "The turning point!" As he rushed from the room, he told an aide, "We can't lose the war at all. We now have an ally which has never been conquered in three thousand years." He called for champagne and invited all the officers for the celebration.[19]

Hitler was elated because he believed that a U.S. war with Japan would relieve pressure on him in the Atlantic. America's policy of providing escorts to British ships while clinging to a policy of neutrality had made life difficult for German U-boat commanders. "How can a commander know when he should fire his torpedoes and when he shouldn't?" He added that it was impossible for a U-boat commander to "read through a whole book before he fires a torpedo in order to discover if the ship is a British or an American one!"[20]

The successful Japanese attack, Hitler believed, would destroy "the myth of American superiority." American military capability, he declared, was overrated. Shortly after the attack, Hitler said he did not "see much future for the Americans." He dismissed the nation as a "decayed country," for which he felt nothing but "hatred and deep repugnance." America, he claimed, was "half Judaized" and half "Negrified." "How can one expect a state like that to hold together — a country where everything is built on the dollar?"[21]

Italian leader and fellow fascist Benito Mussolini also welcomed the Japanese attack that brought the Americans into the war. Like Hitler, "Il Duce" believed that

Roosevelt was too weak, and the Americans too soft, to wage a successful war. He too doubted that "a country of Negros and Jews" could create an effective fighting force. He also believed that American industrial capabilities were overstated. Most of all, he simply could not understand how a man incapable of walking could lead a nation during war. "Never in history has a people been ruled by a paralytic," he contemptuously said of FDR. "There have been bald kings, fat kings, handsome kings, and even stupid ones, but never a king who when he wants to go to the toilet or to dinner must be assisted by other men."[22]

Though for different reasons, both Churchill and Hitler were elated by the news of the Japanese attack. The reception was less enthusiastic among some of Roosevelt's critics at home. There was a large "America First" rally scheduled in Pittsburgh that afternoon at 3:00 p.m. at Soldiers and Sailors Memorial Hall. The committee, formed by a group of students at Yale University in the fall of 1940, was the largest, most powerful isolationist group in the country. "Our first duty is to keep America out of foreign wars," its founding document stated. "Our entry would only destroy democracy, not save it." The group held large rallies, organized letter-writing campaigns, and attracted the support of such luminaries as aviator Charles Lindbergh and dozens of elected officials. By December 7, 1941, there were 450 chapters with around 800,000 members, mostly based in the Midwest.[23]

Organizers billed the gathering as the "greatest mass rally" of those opposed to the administration's policies and bragged about the featured speaker, North Dakota senator Gerald P. Nye. The organization issued a press release saying that Nye's appearance "is our answer to the local warmongers who would send other men's sons to die on foreign battlefields." By 3:00 p.m., a crowd of 1,500 had gathered in a hall decorated with red-white-and-blue bunting and dozens of "Defend America First" signs. Before Nye was scheduled to speak, a local reporter, Robert Hagy, had seen the AP wire announcing the strikes on Pearl. Wanting to get Nye's reaction, Hagy found the senator backstage and shoved the Teletype describing the Japanese attack at him. "It sounds fishy to me," Nye said. "Can't we have some details? Is it sabotage or is it open attack? I'm amazed that the President should announce an attack without giving details." He compared the announcement with the way Roosevelt described the USS *Greer* incident, suggesting that it was just another FDR deception.[24]

The news had already been broadcast over the radio, but apparently few in the audience had heard it. A series of speakers rose to the podium to denounce Roosevelt. Among them, a state senator called Roosevelt "the chief warmonger in the U.S." Sitting in the back row was a plainclothes member of the Pittsburgh Reserve, Colonel Enrique Urrutia Jr. He knew of the attack and grew increasingly agitated by the partisan jabs. At one point, he stood up and asked whether this was the appropriate time to be making these comments. "Can this meeting be called after what has happened in the last few hours?" he shouted. "Do you know that Japan has attacked Manila, that Japan has attacked Hawaii?"[25]

The head of the America First chapter claimed that Urrutia was "speaking in broken English" and that it "was very difficult to understand what he was trying to say." Many in the crowd, however, seemed to understand him perfectly. They booed him, called him a "warmonger," and shouted, "Throw him out!" Some started to get physical. When an angry group of men moved toward Urrutia, the police intervened and rescued him. "I came to listen," Urrutia told a reporter afterward. "I thought this was a patriots meeting, but this is a traitors meeting."[26]

After the incident, Nye strutted to the platform as if nothing had happened. For nearly forty-five minutes he gave his standard isolationist speech. "Whose war is this?" he asked. The crowd chanted, "Roosevelt's." During his speech, Hagy received word from his editor that Japan had declared war on the United States. He wanted to get Nye's reaction, so he wrote on a piece of paper, "The Japanese Imperial Government at Tokyo today at 4 p.m. announced a state of war with the U.S. and Great Britain." He walked onto the platform and handed it to Nye. The senator paused to look at it and then proceeded with his rant for another thirty minutes.[27]

Finally, at 5:45 p.m., Nye reluctantly acknowledged the news. "I have before me the worst news that I have encountered in the last 20 years." He then proceeded to read the note to the crowd. "I can't somehow believe this," he concluded.

Later that night a defeated and dejected Nye spoke before a crowd of six hundred people at the First Baptist Church. He reviewed the events that led to the war while accusing Roosevelt of "doing his utmost to promote trouble with Japan." Resigned to the reality of war, he could not resist taking one more swipe at Roosevelt. "We have been maneuvered into this by the President," he insisted, "but the only thing now is to declare war and to jump into it with everything we have and bring it to a victorious conclusion."[28]

11
"I WILL GO DOWN IN DISGRACE"

At 6:40, FDR returned to his study, where he tried to enjoy a quiet dinner with Harry Hopkins and Grace Tully. The White House kitchen set up trays of food. The president ate at his desk, and Tully and Hopkins sat on the leather sofas, resting their trays on folding card tables. Roosevelt did not want to talk about Pearl Harbor, but it was difficult to ignore. "For the life of me I can't remember what we ate but I do remember the Boss was happy to have a few quiet minutes before the evening meetings," Tully recalled.[1]

The attack on Pearl Harbor represented the opening salvo in a breathtaking Japanese offensive. Three hours after the assault on Pearl Harbor, Japanese planes appeared in the skies above the island of Guam. Attacks on Thailand followed. At 3:00 p.m., Japan launched its first attacks against Singapore. Forty minutes later, Japanese planes bombed Khota Baru in British Malaya. Before the day was over, Japanese forces would assault Hong Kong, the Midway Islands, Wake Island, and the Philippines.[2]

By early evening, Roosevelt still did not have a full picture of the breadth of Japanese aggression. It is difficult to know precisely when FDR learned about the various offensives, but in the original draft of his speech, which he dictated around 5:00 p.m., FDR referenced only the attacks on Pearl Harbor and Malaya. Right after returning from his medical treatment with McIntire, FDR received a report from the Navy Department that Guam was under attack.[3]

More bad news was coming, but for now FDR seemed overwhelmed by the potential consequences of Pearl Harbor. Over dinner, FDR shared his private fears about the day's events with Tully and Hopkins. With the Pearl Harbor fleet destroyed, there was nothing stopping Japan's navy from invading and capturing the Hawaiian Islands. Perhaps more frightening, he acknowledged that Japan could invade Los Angeles or San Francisco. Given the poor state of American readiness, he speculated that an invading army could advance as far east as Chicago.

It was also not clear to Roosevelt that evening how the attack would play out politically. He planned to keep tight control of information about the destruction and casualties, but eventually this information would leak. Would the nation blame him for the disaster? White House butler Alonzo Fields recalled overhearing Roosevelt say, "My God, how did it happen? I will go down in disgrace."[4]

While reports of other Japanese offensives were coming in, FDR was most interested in getting updates from Admiral Stark about Pearl Harbor. According to Hopkins, "Stark continued to get further and always more dismal news about the attack on Hawaii."[5]

It seems likely that Stark passed along information that he received during a 7:10 update from Admiral Bloch. "Here in the harbor, as nearly as I can ascertain there are six battleships out of business," Bloch said as a stenographer took careful notes. "Six battleships, and three of them, at least, look like they are salvage jobs." Bloch provided a detailed description of the damage suffered by each of the ships. "The *Nevada* was hit by a torpedo and set on fire. . . . The *Oklahoma* was hit by three torpedoes . . . and she was capsized." The *Tennessee* was "partially capsized." The *California* "was set on fire and she is burning." The *Arizona* "was hit by torpedoes or aerial bombs and she . . . is capsized." The *West Virginia* "is still afloat and all right, but pretty badly damaged by fire." The *Helena* had "a crack under her water line and her fire rooms are flooded." Crews pumped so much water into the *Raleigh* to put out a fire that "she is in bad shape."[6]

Bloch said that all available planes, along with two task forces, had "gone out to look for these fellows" who had attacked Pearl. But he cautioned that the army had lost a lot of pursuit planes. "They lost one squadron, I heard." He noted that Guam was under attack by two squadrons of Japanese fighters, and there were unconfirmed reports of parachute troops landing on the island. When he told Stark that the United States had sunk three enemy submarines, including one inside the harbor, Stark responded, "The submarine sunk in the harbor, is it German?" Block responded that he did not "know what it is as yet."[7]

Both men seemed to believe that the Japanese ships were still off the coast of Hawaii and possibly preparing for a land invasion the following morning. "I prophesized that there might be a raid in the morning," Stark said. Bloch, who was "expecting attacks on Wake and Midway," summed up the situation: "It's a pretty bad mess here. Of course they came in with no warning at all. They did their job very efficiently."[8]

It is likely that Roosevelt also received an update on the Philippines at some point during his dinner. The army finally got General MacArthur on the line at 7:00 p.m. in Washington (about 8:00 a.m., December 8, in Manila). The general acknowledged receiving the reports that Japan had attacked Pearl Harbor. In Washington, General Leonard Gerow, calling on behalf of Marshall, warned MacArthur of the possibility of an imminent Japanese offensive. "Report immediately any Japanese operations or any indications," he said. "I wouldn't be surprised if you got an attack there in the near future." To underscore the point, Gerow repeated the last sentence. MacArthur assured the general that he was prepared and asked him to pass along a message to Marshall that "our tails are up in the air."[9]

Although it must have been reassuring that Manila had not been attacked, there was little doubt in Washington that the islands were going to be targeted at some point. (Indeed, although they did not know it at the time, the Japanese had been planning a dawn attack that morning but had been stymied by heavy fog on Formosa, from which the planes were to have been launched.) MacArthur's air force commander had placed his forces on alert as soon as he learned about the attack on Pearl Harbor, and he requested permission to launch a preemptive strike against Japanese positions in Formosa. MacArthur, however, vetoed the idea, saying, "We couldn't attack until we were attacked."[10]

Shortly after 10:00 a.m. on the morning of December 8, the skies over Formosa cleared, allowing Japan's military commanders to launch their force of 108 bombers and 84 Zeros. By 11:30 a.m., radar crews in the Philippines started tracking a large echo approaching Luzon from the north. Before noon, MacArthur received the first reports that Japanese bombers had assaulted Baguio in northern Luzon, along with Iba, Tuguegarao, and Tarlac. Finally, a stunned and apparently disoriented MacArthur gave permission to attack Formosa. But the order came too late. At 12:20 p.m., while crews were fueling the planes and loading them with bombs, a fleet of Japanese fighters and bombers appeared overhead.

Over the next hour, Japanese fighters strafed buildings and planes while bombers dropped their deadly cargo. When the attack ended, nearly 100 American aircraft had been destroyed, including a dozen B-17 bombers. More than 80 men were killed and another 150 wounded. For the second time in less than twenty-four hours, Japan found another surprised and unprepared American military outpost ripe for destruction.[11]

Reports of a Japanese move against the Philippines would start trickling into the White House late on Sunday evening, but FDR would not learn the full extent of the military disaster until the following morning.

In addition to getting information from military officials around the world, White House staff were listening to reports on the radio and checking with other news sources. At 6:11 p.m., the Associated Press, citing a source in Tokyo, stated there was one Japanese aircraft carrier near Hawaii. That was followed by repeated claims of invading Japanese troops. At 8:35 p.m., the army stated that troops were landing on the west coast of Oahu. There were also claims that two enemy aircraft carriers had been sunk: one in the Pacific, the other off the coast of an unspecified Latin American country.

These stories were mixed with accurate accounts of Japanese planes over Wake Island and Guam, along with a 5:20 p.m.

announcement that Japan declared that a state of war existed with the United States and Great Britain. At 8:06, military intelligence confirmed the assault on Singapore and heavy fighting at Kota Bharu near British Malay. Later that evening, Roosevelt complained about the conflicting information that he was receiving and how difficult it was to sort fact from fiction.[12]

Roosevelt liked telling the story about the time the poet Carl Sandburg came to visit him. Sandburg, who was writing his magisterial biography of Abraham Lincoln, asked FDR what window Lincoln had looked out to see the smoke of Confederate cannons across the Potomac. Roosevelt did not know, but he invited Sandburg to tour the second floor and decide for himself. Sandburg stopped at the center window of the Oval Study and, according to FDR, "stood there silently for about ten minutes." FDR, not wanting to disturb him, shuffled some papers. "Yes," Sandburg finally said, "that's the one — the center window." When Roosevelt asked how he knew for sure, the poet responded, "I felt it."[13]

If Roosevelt looked out the three large windows of his study, he would have seen the same sweep of the Potomac that Abraham Lincoln saw on the eve of the Civil War and that Woodrow Wilson stared out at in the days leading up to World War I. FDR seemed mindful of the lessons of both wars in the months leading up to December 7. Like Lincoln, while viewing war as inevitable, he understood the moral and psychological advantage of having the enemy fire the first shot. He had not anticipated that the first shot would cripple the Pacific Fleet, but he now planned to mold public outrage to his war goals. He was determined to avoid the mistake that Wilson made, turning his war into a crusade for democracy, only to have the initial idealism and enthusiasm turn to despair and disillusion when the realities of battle settled in.

FDR walked a delicate line in the hours after Pearl Harbor: He needed to use the attack to justify declaring war against Japan, but he wanted to avoid providing the public with details of the devastation. Perhaps Roosevelt worried that the specifics would demoralize the nation, allowing his enemies to blame his administration for the glaring security lapse. It is also likely that FDR feared that arousing too much passion would undermine his larger strategic goals. He wanted to transform anger at Japan's actions in the Pacific into a mandate to enter the war against Germany in Europe.

Whatever steps he decided to take, the president realized that he needed to remain mindful of public opinion. FDR, who possessed an instinctive feel for the national mood, probably appreciated the crosscurrents that engulfed the nation that evening.

While strong undercurrents of anxiety and fear gripped Hawaii and the West Coast, the hundreds of telegrams that poured into the White House that evening revealed the outrage and resolve of a nation prepared to follow his leadership. Governors, mayors, local city councils, civic organizations, and ordinary citizens took the time to send telegrams to the White House expressing their outrage at the attacks and their unqualified support for any response he ordered. For the first time since the early days of the New Deal, FDR confronted a unified nation devoid of political differences and desperately looking for him to take charge.

The governors, Democrats and Republicans, of nearly every state sent messages of support to the White House. "There is imperative need for courageous unified action by the American people," wrote his vanquished 1936 election opponent, Alf Landon. "Please command me in any way I can be of service." Kentucky governor Keen

Johnson wrote that the people of his state believed it was an "outrage" that Japan responded to the president's peace overtures by launching a brutal surprise attack. "As governor of Kentucky I assure you people of this state are prepared to follow your leadership and make any sacrifice you regard necessary to meet emergency." The governor of Alabama, Frank M. Dixon, echoed the sentiment of most elected officials when he wrote, "In this crisis you can be assured that the people of Alabama are behind you and that you will have their united support in whatever decisions you may reach for the good of the nation."[14]

Touching letters from private citizens also flooded into the White House. A mother from Lancaster, California, told the president of the great sacrifice she was willing to offer to the war effort. "I have very little to offer," she wrote, but she was willing to part with "the only thing I have on this earth . . . one son, whom I love excessively." She noted that as war seemed imminent, he now "belongs to America."[15]

Many people living in the Washington, D.C., area chose a more visible demonstration of their support. By the evening of December 7, a large crowd had gathered outside the White House. "The night was chilly and a cold damp wind swept in from the Potomac," observed Merriman Smith, "but the shivering crowds remained." They broke into a spontaneous rendition of "God Bless America" and "My Country 'Tis of Thee." "The words and music were faltering at first," Smith noted, "but swelled up strong." Smith wondered if FDR "could hear those unrehearsed songs coming spontaneously and from the hearts of the little people across his back lawn."[16]

12
"DEADLY CALM"

At 6:30 on Sunday evening, as FDR was being wheeled up from his doctor's appointment back to his study for dinner, Eleanor Roosevelt was entering the NBC studios in Washington. Two months earlier, in October 1941, Eleanor had agreed to host a regular Sunday-evening radio show sponsored by the Pan-American Coffee Bureau. The show provided her with a forum to discuss issues impacting American women. The first lady could have used the attack on Pearl Harbor as an excuse to cancel her scheduled appearance on December 7. Instead, she decided to use the occasion to speak to the American public. She crafted her own remarks, and there is no evidence that she cleared them with her husband, or with anyone else in the White House.

On the day of the Pearl Harbor attacks, Eleanor Roosevelt had resolutely gone about her schedule. She had organized a large lunch party with thirty-one guests in the White House Blue Room for 1:00 p.m. One of the guests, Mrs. Charles Hamlin, recalled that "Eleanor was quite a little late in joining us and she seemed a bit flustered as she told us she was so sorry but the news from Japan was very bad" and that her husband would not be able to join them. "It was while we were at that luncheon that the bombardment of Pearl Harbour took place," she reflected, although no one was aware of it at the time.[1]

At 2:40 p.m., after saying good-bye to her guests, Eleanor made her way back upstairs to her sitting room on the second floor. As she passed by Franklin's study, she saw all of the commotion and knew that something awful had happened. "All the secretaries were there, two telephones were in use, the senior military aides were on their way with messages. I said nothing because the words I heard over the telephone were quite sufficient to tell me that finally the blow had fallen and we had been attacked." Realizing that FDR was too busy, she decided not to interrupt him.[2]

Later that afternoon when she peeked into his office, she noticed his "deadly calm." It was a calm she had witnessed before, a part of his character that had developed over years of struggle against a body that had betrayed him. The roots of Roosevelt's emotional strength trace back to his childhood, but his struggle to return to public life after being diagnosed with polio added a new dimension to his character. It is impossible to appreciate FDR's calm and deliberate leadership on December 7, 1941, without understanding how his background shaped his temperament. Polio would also transform the relationship between Franklin and Eleanor, allowing them to forge a unique private and public partnership that would shape the times in which they lived.

By December 1941, Eleanor Roosevelt had emerged as an independent and strong-minded player in the White House. Since the days of Martha Washington, first ladies were expected to limit themselves to social and ceremonial affairs. "The President's wife must be a silent partner," stated the *New York Times Magazine* in 1932. "The unwritten law is that the First Lady gives no interviews, makes no public statements."

That was before Eleanor Roosevelt. She became the first presidential spouse to write a regular newspaper column, to serve as a radio commentator, to hold regular press conferences, and to testify before Congress. Because FDR had limited mobility, he sent Eleanor out to serve as his eyes and ears. She investigated the horrible living conditions of West Virginia coal miners and examined the impact of segregation on blacks in the South. When she returned from her trips, she would brief her husband on what she had witnessed and prod him to action.

In 1940, FDR was seeking an unprecedented third term, but he was reluctant to go before the Democratic Convention in Chicago and ask for it. Instead, he asked Eleanor to go. Despite her reluctance, she agreed and delivered one of the most memorable convention speeches in history. "This is no ordinary time," she said. The angry, sometimes belligerent crowd, which was threatening to reject FDR's selection of liberal Henry Wallace as vice president, turned quiet. "No time for weighing anything except what we can best do for the country as a whole." The crowd burst into applause and overwhelmingly supported FDR and his choice of Wallace as his running mate. One newspaper headline read, "Mrs. Roosevelt Stills the Tumult of 50,000."[3]

Eleanor's route to power, however, had

been paved with pain that stretched back to a difficult, and loveless, childhood. Anna Eleanor Roosevelt was born on October 11, 1884. Her alcoholic father, Elliott, adored her but was largely absent from her life, while her self-centered and vain mother, Anna, was emotionally distant and verbally abusive. Eleanor viewed herself as an ugly duckling, although as a child she was quite attractive. Shy, socially awkward, and unable to win the affection of her mother, young Eleanor was filled with insecurity. She seemed old even as a child, which was why Anna nicknamed her daughter "Granny."[4]

It was not until after the premature deaths of her parents, and her escape from home, that Eleanor started to emerge from her shell. Anna died of diphtheria in 1892 when Eleanor was only eight. Six months later, Eleanor's three-year-old brother, Elliott Jr., also succumbed to diphtheria. Less than two years later, her father died. "Their daughter was just ten years old, an orphan and already hurt by life," said her son James. Over the next few years, Eleanor's stern grandmother raised her. When Eleanor turned fifteen, her grandmother sent her to a boarding school in England. It was there that she found herself and her voice. It was also the first time she felt appreciated for her passion and her intellect.[5]

Growing up as members of a large extended family, Eleanor and Franklin had met as children, but their relationship blossomed after they attended a horse show at Madison Square Garden in 1903. He was a twenty-year-old Harvard undergraduate at the time; she was eighteen years old and had just moved back to New York after three years of boarding school. A few weeks later, they joined other family members to watch her cousin Theodore welcome guests to the East Room of the White House. They continued dating while Franklin completed his degree at Harvard. "He was young and gay and good-looking," she recalled, "and I was shy and awkward and thrilled when he asked me to dance." The future president proposed to Eleanor shortly after he graduated in 1904. They married on St. Patrick's Day, 1905, at a friend's house in Manhattan. The current president, Theodore Roosevelt, gave away the bride.

On first appearance, they were an odd couple. Franklin was tall, athletic, and handsome. Eleanor was too tall, too lanky, and plain. He was charming, warm, and outgoing. She was insecure and painfully shy. As a relative remembered, she "took everything — most of all herself — so tremendously seriously." Eleanor had lived a monastic life, rarely encountering other men. FDR, by comparison, enjoyed the company of attractive women, and they responded to his good looks and charm. "Nothing is more pleasing to the eye than a good-looking lady, nothing more refreshing to the spirit than the company of one, nothing more flattering to the ego than the affection of one," FDR used to quip.[6]

Eleanor, however, charmed him with her sincerity and intelligence. "A more sophisticated woman would have scared the daylights out of him," recalled his son Elliott. The future first lady remembered Franklin telling her that he believed she could help him to be successful. Her response was, "Why me? I am plain. I have little to bring you." The fact that she was the favorite niece of cousin Theodore, who happened to be the president of the United States, no doubt added to her appeal, as did the fact that she sat on a sizable trust fund that was even larger than Franklin's.[7]

For the first few years of their marriage, Eleanor focused on raising a family. She gave birth to her first child fourteen months after the wedding and to five more over the next nine years. (One died in infancy.) Eleanor struggled with her new role as wife and mother. Having been raised with servants, she did not, for example, know how to cook or clean. Her husband offered little emotional support. These were difficult years for Eleanor and for their marriage.[8]

In 1918, after returning from Europe to visit the war front, FDR became violently ill. He had to be carried off the ship and transported home in an ambulance. Eleanor was unpacking his suitcases when she came across a bundle of love letters from the dark-haired and attractive twenty-two-year-old Lucy Mercer. Eleanor had hired Mercer to work as her part-time social secretary, but Lucy soon caught Franklin's eye. Eleanor had been suspicious that her husband was having an affair, but the letters confirmed it. "The bottom dropped out of my own particular world and I faced myself, my surroundings, my world honestly for the first time," she reflected later.[9]

Eleanor believed that Franklin had betrayed her trust. She told him that she would grant him a divorce. But FDR understood that a divorce would have ended his political ambitions. From that point forward, Eleanor and Franklin's relationship was more a merger than a marriage, based in mutual self-interest, not bonds of intimacy. James Roosevelt described it as an "armed truce." "I have the memory of an elephant," she once said. "I can forgive, but I cannot forget." As part of the arrangement, FDR promised never to see Lucy Mercer again — a promise he would later break. He accepted Eleanor's demand that they sleep in separate bedrooms, an arrangement they maintained even in the White House. Eleanor occupied a separate suite of rooms in the southwest corner of the mansion.[10]

Eleanor emerged from the Mercer affair a new woman: more secure, more independent, more self-confident. She and Franklin led separate personal lives, but they would form a remarkable public partnership. "After the affair she was less subservient to father," reflected James. "She demanded respect from then on." "I knew more about the human heart," she confessed later. "I became a more tolerant person . . . but I think more determined to try for certain ultimate objectives." It marked the beginning of her evolution from a private to a public person. She emerged from FDR's shadow, willing to strike out on her own, to pursue the issues that mattered most to her.[11]

It was not until late on the afternoon of December 7 that Eleanor had a chance to talk with FDR. She described him as looking "very strained and tired." But she observed another quality: his "deadly calm." As she reflected later, "His reaction to any great event was always to be calm. If it was something that was bad, he just became almost like an iceberg, and there was never the slightest emotion that was allowed to show."[12]

The "deadly calm" that Eleanor noticed had many sources. No doubt, FDR felt some degree of relief that the uncertainty of America's involvement in the war had come to a dramatic, and tragic, end. "I thought that in spite of his anxiety Franklin was in a way more serene than he had appeared in a long time," she observed. "I think it was steadying to know finally that the die was cast. One could no longer do anything but face the fact that this country was in a war."[13]

The roots of the "deadly calm" traced back to FDR's childhood. Franklin Delano Roosevelt was born on January 30, 1882, in Hyde Park, New York. His patrician family provided him with all the comforts of wealth. Growing up on a serene Hudson River estate, the young FDR forged fond memories that would endure for a lifetime. "All that is in me goes back to the Hudson," Roosevelt liked to say. His childhood memories of a time when he was athletic, and when the world seemed to revolve around him, would provide a psychological retreat in times of crisis. He would return there in his mind many times to find solace and strength. Later in life, he would fall asleep imagining himself as a child sledding down the hill behind his Hyde Park home.[14]

He lived in a world of privilege where anything seemed possible. He summered in Europe, often with royalty. Raised with private tutors and governesses, he attended the finest schools — Groton, Harvard. In 1887, when Franklin was five, he was introduced to President Grover Cleveland. The beleaguered Cleveland placed his hand on FDR's head as he left. "My little man," he said, "I am making a strange wish for you. It is that you may never be president of the United States." At nineteen, his distant cousin Theodore became president.[15]

Franklin's domineering mother, Sara, nicknamed "the Duchess" because of her imperious style, created an ideal environment for young Franklin. Shortly after FDR became president, the *Ladies' Home Journal* observed that "much of the President's strength in facing incredible obstacles [was] planted in a childhood presided over by a mother whose broad viewpoint encompasses the art of living."[16]

He was her only child, and she smothered him with affection and insulated him from the struggles of ordinary life. She controlled every aspect of his childhood. Although servants surrounded Franklin, Sara insisted on bathing and dressing him herself. He was eight years old when he took a bath by himself for the first time. Throughout Franklin's life, Sara provided her only child with financial security and deep affection. She kept a detailed diary of his activities until he was in his twenties. His daughter Anna said of Sara, "Granny was a martinet, but she gave father the assurance he needed to prevail over adversity. Seldom has a young child been more constantly attended and incessantly approved by his mother."[17]

Sara nurtured and protected young Franklin, enabling him to grow up in an idealized world. There were certain rules to being a Roosevelt, however. He was not permitted to show emotion or weakness of any kind. Sara taught her son to hide his feelings behind a veil of pleasantness. The Roosevelts placed a high priority on being upbeat and sunny, even if it meant ignoring inconvenient facts.

In 1890, when Franklin was eight, his father, who was twenty-six years older than Sara and already middle-aged, suffered a heart attack. It was a major blow to Franklin. James had been his active companion, teaching him to ride horses, sail, and swim. Every afternoon, his father took him for an inspection of their estate, teaching him about the management of the land, pointing out the different types of trees and plants. If FDR was shaken by his father's illness, he never revealed it. Instead, he conspired with his mother to ignore his father's declining health.[18]

During the summer, the family traveled to Europe so that James could enjoy the baths of Bad Nauheim in Germany that were supposed to have curative powers. The family made the trips in the hopes of prolonging James's life, but they treated them like vacations. The family's letters reveal no hint of illness or expressions of concern about James and his health.[19]

While James would remain in poor health for the next decade, Franklin and Sara conspired to insulate him from bad news that might disturb him and stress his already damaged heart. When a steel rod sliced Franklin's forehead, for example, he hid so that his father would not see the wound. When a friend accidentally knocked out his front tooth with a stick, FDR deliberately kept his mouth closed so his father could not view the damage.[20]

In December 1900, during FDR's freshman year at Harvard, James suffered a series of heart attacks. FDR rushed home to New York to be by his side. On December 8, exactly forty-one years before he stood before Congress and delivered his war message, FDR watched as James took his last breath. "All is over," Sara wrote in her diary. James left Franklin a significant trust that would remain the main source of his income throughout his life.

After the death of her husband, Franklin became the sole focus of Sara's smothering attention. She took an apartment in Boston to be near him while he was at Harvard. She also opposed his marriage to Eleanor and tried to convince him to call it off. FDR refused, instead allowing Eleanor to compete with his mother for his affection. Sara's wedding present to the couple was a new townhouse in New York City. The only catch was that she would live in the adjacent house, with doors connecting the two residences.

The last time that Eleanor had seen that "deadly calm" expression on her husband's face was in August 1921. The family was at their vacation home at Campobello, a rockbound island in the Canadian waters off the coast of Maine. FDR felt achy but went sailing anyway and trekked two miles with the children to swim at a freshwater lake. After returning to the house, he sat on the porch and read the mail. He was too exhausted to change out of his wet bathing suit. "I'd never felt quite that way before," he said later. The next morning, he stood up for a few minutes and then collapsed on his bed. He would never stand again. He was thirty-nine years old.[21]

Louis Howe, FDR's close friend and political adviser, who was staying with the Roosevelts, summoned the local doctor to examine FDR. He diagnosed him as suffering from nothing more than a cold. When FDR's condition worsened, Howe contacted the famous Philadelphia surgeon William Keen, who was vacationing on a nearby island. Keen told them that a blood clot had settled in FDR's spine, causing "temporary" paralysis of the legs. He recommended vigorous massage. Over the next few days, Howe and Eleanor massaged FDR's lifeless muscles, hoping to stimulate a response. Because of the misdiagnosis, their efforts not only inflicted needless pain, but may have caused more damage to the fragile nerves and made recovery less likely.

For nearly two weeks, FDR lay in bed in terrible pain, his legs so sensitive he could not bear the weight of the sheets that covered them. By this point, massage was out of the question. His hands and arms became paralyzed. His fever soared, and he lost control of his bodily functions. Eleanor and Howe kept a round-the-clock vigil by his bed. She bathed him and turned him over to prevent bedsores. She administered catheters and enemas. She even had to brush his teeth.

Howe was convinced that FDR had been misdiagnosed. Through family connections, he discovered Dr. Robert Williamson Lovett, an orthopedic surgeon from Newport and a leading authority on infantile paralysis, also known as polio. Lovett arrived on August 25. He found his patient in bed, paralyzed from the waist down, with a temperature of one hundred degrees. Lovett made his diagnosis quickly and firmly: FDR was suffering from infantile paralysis. Lovett broke the news to the family. "I told them very frankly that no one could tell where they stood, that the case was evidently not of the severest type, that complete recovery or partial recovery to any point was possible. . . . [I]t looked to me as if some of the important muscles might be on the edge where they could be influenced either way — toward recovery, or turn into completely paralyzed muscles."[22]

Roosevelt now faced the greatest challenge of his life. He was thirty-nine years old, disabled, and a failed vice presidential candidate. He had always fancied himself an outdoorsman and an athlete, but now he could not walk. "He was not accustomed to being confined indoors to bed," James reflected. He had rarely been sick, and now he could not even stand. "It had to come as a dreadful blow to him." His illness could easily have spelled the end of his political ambitions.[23]

His mother's solution was retirement at Hyde Park, where FDR could become the country gentleman she always wanted him to be. Franklin had different ideas. In the weeks and months that followed, he revealed a steely determination and strength of character that surprised even those who knew him best. His privileged childhood had protected him from adversity, but it also denied him the opportunity to challenge himself. He had learned to avoid confrontation and unpleasant news, but there was no avoiding the fact that he could not walk. Winning the battle against polio, observed biographer Geoffrey Ward, "would demand of him qualities not conspicuously displayed so far in his largely charmed life: patience, application, recognition of his own limitations, a willingness to fail in front of others and try again."[24]

Although the doctors had given him a grim diagnosis, FDR seemed relieved to have an unambiguous diagnosis. He now knew the challenges that he confronted, and he never lost confidence that he would prevail. "I remember when he was told that he had Polio, he seemed really relieved that he knew the worst that could happen to him," Eleanor reflected. He immediately started developing a strategy for conquering his illness, even though his physicians told him there was no cure. According to James, "He never admitted that this was the way it was going to be from then on. It was temporary, a test he could meet, a fight he was determined to win."[25]

Just like his mother taught him, FDR refused to show weakness. Eleanor knew that he was experiencing fear, but he never showed it. On the contrary, Roosevelt seemed to work even harder to appear sunny and happy. James recalled that he started to cry when he saw his father propped up on pillows for the first time. His father "just laughed and slapped me on the back and told me how 'grand' I looked. Soon he dropped to the floor and was roughhousing with me." He was constantly providing them with upbeat, but false, reports of his progress. "By golly, I can really feel those muscles coming back," he would say to them.[26]

In the years after he was diagnosed with polio, as he fought to return to political life, Roosevelt worked hard to develop a method of appearing to walk. FDR told his physical therapist that his goal was to "walk without crutches. I'll walk into a room without scaring everybody half to death. I'll stand easily enough in front of people so that they'll forget I'm a cripple."[27]

His solution was to develop a tripod method. He would use steel braces to lock his legs into a rigid position and then lean heavily on the arm of one of his sons with one hand while using a crutch under his other arm. The key was for his son to keep his arm as rigid as a parallel bar and held at a ninety-degree angle. He used his son's arm as a second crutch, and the steel braces allowed him to place all of his body weight on his lifeless legs and remain erect. In this position, FDR could "walk" by throwing his body weight forward, swinging one leg at a time while keeping his upper body stabilized.[28]

He used the new method for the first time at the 1924 Democratic Convention at Madison Square Garden in New York City. FDR had wanted to make a dramatic return to politics, and Governor Al Smith, a leading candidate, asked him to give the nomination speech on his behalf. It was only three years after his illness, and Roosevelt feared that it was too soon. But he accepted the invitation and decided that he could not use a wheelchair. With a crutch under his right arm, FDR gripped James's arm and moved slowly toward the stage. He was able to propel his body forward by pivoting and throwing his shoulders from side to side. "As we walked — struggled, really — down the aisle to the rear of the platform, he leaned heavily on my arm, gripping me so hard it hurt," James recalled. "His hands were wet. His breathing was labored. Leaning on me with one arm, working a crutch with the other, his legs locked stiffly in their braces, he went on his awkward way." To disguise the stiffness of his movements and not "scare everybody half to death," as FDR said, he and James engaged in loud banter, pretending to laugh to hide the obvious discomfort.[29]

Standing at the podium, his head thrown back and his shoulders held high in his trademark posture, FDR launched into the speech that would define his return to politics. "He has a personality that carries to every hearer not only the sincerity but the righteousness of what he says," Roosevelt declared, his rich tenor voice filling the Garden. "He is the 'Happy Warrior' of the political battlefield . . . Alfred E. Smith." FDR's speech, which set off an hourlong demonstration, failed to gain the nomination for Smith. But it provided Roosevelt with the psychological boost he needed. "I did it!" he exclaimed to a friend that evening.[30]

FDR's return to politics was a dramatic success, but he was determined to improve his method of walking. One day at Warm Springs, he came up with an idea. He would walk holding on to a man's arm and substitute a less conspicuous cane for the crutch. In 1928, Al Smith planned to be the party's nominee, and he wanted Roosevelt to present the nomination speech. As FDR made his way to the platform, this time holding on to Elliott's arm and using only a cane, the 15,000 delegates roared their approval. Everything about his manner — his optimism, broad smile, and relaxed confidence — contradicted the impression that he was an invalid. Invoking again the image of the "Happy Warrior," he brought the convention to its feet. As expected, Smith won nomination on the first ballot.

FDR also never gave up hope of finding a cure. He consulted with physicians, but he also pursued unconventional therapy. He would spend his afternoons practicing walking with his legs strapped into fourteen pounds of painful steel braces. Somehow, he believed that he could force his lifeless legs to move. "I have faithfully followed out the walking and am really getting so that both legs take it quite naturally, and I can stay on my feet for an hour without feeling tired," he wrote his physician.[31]

Roosevelt looked to water for a cure. "The water got me into this fix," he used to say, "and the water will get me out." He spent part of three winters between 1924 and 1926 living on a used houseboat, the *Laroo-*

coo, in Florida, where he hoped that the sun and fresh air would speed his recovery.[32]

Like his father, Roosevelt believed in the healing power of baths. He discovered Warm Springs in the fall of 1924 after hearing rumors that the eighty-six-degree natural spring waters that bubbled up from the ground held special healing powers. After swimming in the waters for the first time, he wrote his mother about his discovery. "I feel that a great 'cure' for infantile paralysis and kindred diseases could well be established here." He spent a considerable amount of his own money fixing up the resort property and turning it into a rehabilitation center for other sufferers of polio. He took a personal interest in the plight of other polio victims, developed an interest in physiotherapy, and soon began referring to himself as "Old Doctor Roosevelt."[33]

Many biographers have observed that polio expanded FDR's horizons, making him more empathetic with those who suffered. "There had been a plowing up of his nature," Labor Secretary Frances Perkins observed. "The man emerged completely warmhearted, with new humility of spirit and a firmer understanding of philosophical concepts." Once easily dismissed as superficial, ambitious, and shallow, FDR responded to polio in a way that added new depth to his character. It intensified his ability to set priorities and to focus. "Polio," Franklin Jr. said, "taught Father to concentrate on the things he was physically able to do and not waste time thinking about the things he could not."[34]

When asked how polio had changed him, Roosevelt responded, "If you spent two years in bed trying to wiggle your big toe, after that anything else would seem easy!" "Having handled that, he probably thought there wasn't anything he couldn't deal with," said Henry Morgenthau. "Once you've conquered that kind of illness, anything's possible."[35]

There is no question that FDR's long struggle with polio made him a more resilient and ambitious leader. But it may also have contributed to another quality that became central to his character and his handling of the attack on Pearl Harbor: his propensity for deception.

Although his battle with polio was central to understanding FDR's character, he was determined to prevent the public from ever knowing the extent of his paralysis. The grand deception began almost immediately. Howe needed to move Roosevelt from

Campobello to New York without the press knowing the severity of his illness. To avoid having reporters see Roosevelt being carried on a stretcher, Howe brought him by boat to a secluded dock and loaded him on a private train car. He then propped him up so that local residents and reporters would see him in his familiar and reassuring position: smiling and waving from the window. He must have still been in tremendous pain, but appearances were more important. The next day, the *New York Times* ran a story quoting FDR's physician, who assured readers that "he definitely will not be crippled."[36]

Roosevelt developed effective ways to disguise his disability. At state dinners, he was always wheeled into the room and seated before his guests arrived. When traveling by train, he spoke from the rear car, where he could support himself with a metal rail or reinforced podium. He would ride in the back of an open automobile to greet voters. He had ramps specially constructed to allow the car to maneuver up to the podium. He even painted his steel braces black so they would match the color of his pants and shoes.[37]

Although he was the most photographed man of his times, of the thirty-five thousand photographs of him at the Franklin D. Roosevelt Presidential Library, only three show him seated in his wheelchair. There are no photographs, or newsreels, that show the time-consuming task of lifting him from his car into a chair, or of his strenuous, and awkward, effort to walk. An amateur filmmaker, Dr. Harold Rosenthal, captured the only moving images of Roosevelt "walking" in August 1933, when FDR attended an event at Vassar College. Reporters who wrote about Roosevelt rarely mentioned that he had no use of his legs.[38]

Although most Americans knew that Roosevelt was once inflicted by polio, they were not aware of the extent of his paralysis. In cartoons, he is often depicted as walking, running, jumping, and even boxing. When J. B. West was hired as the chief White House usher in 1941, he was shocked when he saw FDR for the first time. "It was only then that I realized that Franklin D. Roosevelt was really paralyzed," he recalled. "Everybody knew that the president had been stricken with infantile paralysis, and his recovery was legend, but few people were aware how completely the disease had handicapped him."[39]

FDR's upbringing, and his struggle with polio, had taught him how to hide his feelings and to be deceptive when necessary. He knew how to deflect attention and to disguise uncomfortable realities. Those qualities would be on full display on the evening of December 7 as FDR met with congressional leaders to discuss the attack on Pearl Harbor.

Temperamentally, Eleanor did not share her husband's cool, calm way of dealing with crises. She pointed out that it was much harder for her. "I can be calm and quiet, but it takes all the discipline I have acquired in life to keep on talking and smiling and to concentrate on the conversation addressed to me. I want to be left alone while I store up fortitude for what I fear may be a blow of fate."[40]

It may have been harder for her to stay calm, but Eleanor shared her husband's activist spirit. On the afternoon of the Pearl Harbor attacks, while FDR prepared to meet with his cabinet, Eleanor was in her study, writing remarks for her regularly scheduled weekly radio address. It revealed a great deal about her stature as first lady that the first Roosevelt the nation would hear from was not Franklin, but Eleanor.

Shortly after 6:30 p.m., she sat down in front of the microphone and addressed the nation. "I am speaking to you tonight at a very serious moment in our history," she told her listeners. "The Cabinet is convening and the leaders in the Congress are meeting with the President. The State Department and Army and Navy officials have been with the President all afternoon." She claimed that the Japanese ambassador was talking to the president "at the very time that Japan's airships were bombing our citizens." No doubt, Eleanor had seen the Chinese ambassador meeting with her husband and confused him for being Japanese. It was a mistake that many Americans would make over the next few weeks and months.

She stated that Congress would have a full report the next day. Although she never mentioned that the president would be asking for a declaration of war, she hinted at it, saying the nation would "be ready for action." For months, there had been anticipation that the enemy would strike. "That is all over now and there is no more uncertainty. We know that we are ready to face it now." The first lady expressed confidence that the nation would pull through the crisis. "Whatever is asked of us, I am sure we can accomplish it: we are the free and unconquerable people of the USA."[41]

13
"1861"

Like most members of the cabinet, Labor Secretary Frances Perkins was away from Washington on December 7. She had traveled to New York, where she had isolated herself in a hotel room to finish writing an important report. White House operators tracked her down in the afternoon and told her she was required to attend an emergency meeting at 8:00 p.m. Initially, the harried operators did not say what the meeting was about. "What's the matter, Hacky," she asked the operator, "why the cabinet meeting tonight?' "Just the war, what's in the paper," the operator said hastily before hanging up to make her next call.[1]

Perkins called for a plane reservation and then rushed to the airport. Although she was a member of the president's inner circle, she still knew little about what had taken place. On the way to the airport, she asked the taxi driver what he knew. "They said on the radio there was shooting somewhere," he said.

At the airport, Perkins met Vice President Henry Wallace, who was in New York, and Postmaster General Frank Walker. They were also in the dark. No one had expected a Japanese attack. On the short plane ride to Washington, the three officials speculated about what might have happened. Since they were on a commercial flight, and surrounded by other passengers, the three administration members spoke in hushed tones. They recalled that FDR had discussed with them a few days earlier that a large Japanese fleet was at sea, but the speculation at the time was that it was headed for Singapore. Roosevelt had also raised the possibility that the fleet was moving north to cut the Russian supply lines. They, however, were not aware of any imminent direct threat to the United States.[2]

Upon arrival in Washington, Perkins, Wallace, and Walker went together directly to the White House, where they were ushered to FDR's private second-floor study. Roosevelt sat silently behind his desk. He nodded when they walked in, but Perkins noticed "there was none of the usual cordial, personal greeting." He "could not muster a smile." She described him as "calm, not agitated." Attorney General Francis Biddle, who had arrived at the last minute from Cleveland, described FDR as "deeply shaken, graver than I had ever seen him."[3]

According to a memorandum that Hopkins wrote about the day's events, the cabinet met "promptly" at 8:30 p.m. "All members were present," he noted. "They formed a ring completely around the President, who sat at his desk." Hopkins described FDR's mood as "very solemn." According to Perkins, Early sat near the president and showed him the latest dispatches. Knox and Stimson, both looking tired and tense, were scanning the same dispatches. "New information kept coming in every few minutes," she recalled.[4]

Roosevelt put down the papers, looked up at the cabinet, and began addressing them in a low voice. He began by declaring this meeting the most important cabinet meeting since 1861 — a reference to the critical early days of the Civil War. "You all know what's happened," he said quietly. A cabinet member spoke up. "Mr. President, several of us have just arrived by plane. We don't know anything except a scare headline, 'Japs Attack Pearl Harbor.' Could you tell us more?"[5]

"The attack began at one o'clock," Roosevelt explained. "We don't know very much yet." According to a detailed diary entry by Agriculture Secretary Claude Wickard, FDR placed blame for the attack on Germany. There was, FDR said, "no question but that the Japanese had been told by the Germans a few weeks ago that they were winning the war and that they would soon dominate Africa as well as Europe. They were going to isolate England and were also going to completely dominate the situation in the Far East. The Japs had been told if they wanted to be cut in on the spoils they would have to come in the war now." Roosevelt told the group that he believed Japan's motive behind the attack was to aid Germany by bringing "about the transfer of American naval vessels from the Atlantic to the Pacific." He was determined to prevent this from happening.[6]

Roosevelt's forced effort to link the Japanese attack to Hitler's ambitions in Europe revealed a great deal about his thinking on Sunday evening. Roosevelt viewed the attack on Pearl Harbor as an extension of the war in Europe. He could not accept that the Japanese were capable of executing such a dramatic and devastating strike without the direct training and supervision of German military planners. The initial report that two of the planes used in the attack had swastikas painted on them no doubt reinforced this perception. For the past decade, Japan had made abundantly clear that its territorial ambitions in the Pacific were separate from events in Europe. FDR, however, insisted on seeing the Japanese as German puppets. In part, this misjudgment reflected his indifference to events in the Pacific and his refusal to understand the underlying reasons for Japan's actions. At the same time, however, it served his larger strategic goal of keeping the nation focused on the war in Europe.

The president provided his team with an up-to-date report on the damage that had been inflicted but warned them to keep the information confidential. He told them that he was not going to be as open with the congressional leaders, who were already gathering outside the room, and would not share the detailed damage reports with them. He also planned to be vague about the message that would be delivered the next day.

He proceeded to tell his cabinet that both Guam and Wake Island were under attack and would soon fall into enemy hands. At Pearl Harbor, a large number of aircraft had been destroyed, and six of seven battleships had been damaged — some very severely. According to Perkins, "the President could hardly bring himself to describe the devastation."[7]

As the president recited the damage reports, Wickard noticed that Knox "had lost his air of bravado" and that Stimson "was very sober." According to Perkins, FDR twice asked Knox during the cabinet meeting, "Find out, for God's sake, why those ships were tied up in rows."[8]

The cabinet was horrified by the reports of destruction. Wickard said he "was shocked at the news," and "so were other members of the Cabinet." Many members could not understand how Japan could have caught the U.S. Army and Navy forces on the island so unprepared. "It seems to me extraordinary," Biddle observed, "that we should have been so unprepared as apparently is the situation." Unwilling to accept that the military commanders had been grossly negligent, they assumed that the Japanese bombers had employed some brilliant new tactical maneuver. Biddle noted that it "is supposed that the Japanese airplanes flew at a great height of 25,000 feet perhaps, and dropped suddenly so that they might not be intercepted by pursuit planes."[9]

Frances Perkins remarked that while FDR was clearly in anguish over the loss of life in Hawaii, his "surprise was not as great as the surprise of the rest of us." She sensed a feeling of relief that "all conflicts which have harassed him for so many weeks or months, were ended." The change in his demeanor was striking. "A great change had come over the President since we had seen him on Friday," she recalled. "Then he had been tense, worried, trying to be optimistic as usual, but it was evident that he was carrying an awful burden of decision." It was not clear what the United States would do if the Japanese struck British ports. "But one was conscious that night of December 7, 1941, that in spite of the terrible blow to his pride, to his faith in the navy and its ships, and to his confidence in the American intelligence service, and in spite of the horror that war had actually been brought to us, he had, nevertheless, a much calmer air. His terrible moral problem had been resolved by the event," Perkins recalled.[10]

After Roosevelt had briefed the cabinet on the attacks, a spirited debate arose over the message that Roosevelt planned to present to Congress the next day. The president read the brief draft that he had dictated to

Tully earlier that afternoon. "The message was short," Wickard noted, "and merely stated how Japan had attacked while still carrying on peace negotiations. It ended by stating that he was asking Congress to declare that a state of war had existed since Japan's attack."[11]

Since talking with Roosevelt about his war message that afternoon, Hull became even more convinced that FDR needed to give a longer address to Congress. He enlisted Henry Stimson for support. Hull said that "he thought the most important war in 500 years deserved more than a short statement." Stimson jumped in, adding that "Germany had inspired and planned this whole affair and that the President should so state in his message." Hull pressed Roosevelt for a detailed address that would establish the history of "Japan's lawless conduct" and connect the attack on Pearl Harbor to the Nazis. Stimson agreed. "I pointed out," he recorded in his diary, "that we knew from the interceptions and other evidence that Germany had pushed Japan into this and that Germany was the real actor, and I advocated the view that we should ask for a declaration of war against Germany also."[12]

Stimson complained that the president's

message "was not one of broad statesmanship. It really represented only the justified indignation of the country at Japan's treachery in this surprise attack and not the full measure of the grievances we have against her as a confirmed law breaker and aggressor. I was afraid that to base it wholly on indignation at the surprise attack would look weak."[13]

Roosevelt had clearly made up his mind to keep his address brief and focus solely on the Japanese attack at Pearl Harbor. "Secretary Hull had seemed to think it should have been a longer statement," Biddle noted, "but the President thought not as a matter of timing in journalism." There were also important strategic considerations. He likely feared that giving a longer message would require providing more details about the destruction at Pearl Harbor. More important, he understood better than his seasoned foreign policy team that focusing too much attention on the Pacific would limit his ability to lead the nation to war in Europe. Finally, he rejected the pleas to include Germany and Italy in the declaration because he was acutely sensitive to public opinion, and polls continued to show a conflict with Japan was more popular than one with Germany. "I seem to be conscious of a still lingering distinction in some quarters of the public between war with Japan and war with Germany," FDR told British ambassador Halifax the following day. FDR likely believed that Hitler would solve his problem for him soon enough by declaring war on the United States.[14]

Stimson remained unconvinced and "urged on him the importance of a declaration of war against Germany before the indignation of the people was over." Roosevelt replied that he planned to keep his address to Congress brief and then present a full case to the American people in a radio address two days later. Stimson relented but noted in his diary that "the feeling among the cabinet was quite strong in support of Hull's view that the message should be broader."[15]

As the meeting came to an end, Wickard could not help but admire Roosevelt's poise and strength. "Through it all the president was calm and deliberate. I could not help but admire his clear statements of the situation. He evidently realizes the seriousness of the situation and perhaps gets much comfort out of the fact that today's action will unite the American people. I don't know anybody in the United States who can come close to measuring up to his foresight and acumen in this critical hour." Biddle made a similar observation: "The President is his usual calm self, but most of us were deeply shocked at the terrific loss."[16]

While Roosevelt was meeting with his cabinet, the White House switchboard received a call from Marguerite "Missy" Le-Hand. It was a reminder that, even in a time of crisis, presidents have delicate private moments.

Eleanor had recruited the blue-eyed Le-Hand to work for her husband in 1921. Over the next few years, she made herself indispensable and became a fixture at his side. Between 1925 and 1928, FDR spent 116 of 208 weeks away from home, trying to regain use of his legs. Eleanor was with him for only 4 of those weeks. Missy was with him for 110 — all but 6 weeks.

Missy provided FDR with the warmth and affection that Eleanor could not. She knew everything about him: his likes and dislikes, his mood swings, his favorite food and drinks. She knew when to press a point and when to back off. To everyone else, he was Mr. Roosevelt, the Boss, or, later, Mr. President. To Missy, he was simply "F. D." — an endearing and informal name no one else would use. Raymond Moley noted,

"Missy was as close to being a wife as he ever had — or could have." They spent most weekends together and often dined together alone. She sat with him while he worked on his stamp collection. She laughed at his jokes and pretended to enjoy his stories, which he repeated many times, as if she was always hearing them for the first time.[17]

Oddly enough, Eleanor was never suspicious of Missy. When FDR was governor, Eleanor gave her the larger bedroom next to her husband's, while she took a smaller room down the hall. She realized that Missy freed FDR from the routines of daily life so he could concentrate on the world of politics. Those were the tasks Eleanor was unwilling to perform.[18]

After FDR became president, LeHand carried the formal job title of secretary. Informally, she was his surrogate wife, living in an apartment on the third floor of the White House. She was forty-three years old and had spent half of her life at FDR's side. The work and strain took their toll, however. "The president would work night after night, and she was always there working with him," a friend recalled. "He could take it, but I think her strength just didn't hold out." She collapsed after dinner on June 4, 1941. Two weeks later, at the age of forty-three, she suffered a massive stroke that paralyzed her left side and rendered her unable to speak coherently.[19]

Missy was transferred from the White House to a hospital in Georgetown, where Eleanor and Franklin visited with her often. According to historian Dories Kearns Goodwin, the visits were painful for FDR. "All his life, he had steeled himself to ignore illness and unpleasantness of any kind." For now, he could not ignore Missy's suffering. FDR ordered that she be provided with round-the-clock care. He paid every expense, talked with doctors about her condition, and made provisions for her to be taken care of in the event of his death. Five months after Missy's stroke, FDR rewrote his will, leaving half of his estate "for the account of my friend Marguerite LeHand" to cover all expenses for "medical care and treatment during her lifetime." "I owed her that much," Franklin told his son James. "She served me so well for so long and asked for so little in return."[20]

A few months before the Japanese attack on Pearl Harbor, FDR had Missy transferred to Warm Springs, where he hoped she would benefit from the therapeutic baths and careful supervision. She was showing signs of recovery in the weeks before Pearl Harbor. On November 14, her physician wrote Admiral McIntire that "she is steadily improving. She is up daily in a wheelchair and goes out into the sun. She seems to be enjoying it a great deal." McIntire also noticed a "definite improvement" in her most recent electrocardiograph.[21]

Tully, who had in LeHand's absence assumed the role of the president's secretary, wrote a note to FDR, informing him of Missy's call. "Missy telephoned and wanted to talk with you. She is thinking about you and much disturbed about the news. She would like you to call her tonight. I told her you would if the conference broke up at a reasonable hour — otherwise you would call her in the morning."[22]

FDR did not return the phone call that evening, or the next day. Missy sat in her wheelchair in Warm Springs waiting for the call and was devastated when it never came. She had once complained that the man she loved and devoted her life to "was really incapable of a personal friendship with anyone." His indifference now marked the end of her brief recovery and coincided with a downward spiral in her spirits and physical condition. Two weeks later, over the Christmas holidays, Missy tried to commit suicide. She survived, and over the next few

14

"WHERE WERE OUR FORCES — ASLEEP?"

Tom Connally, the powerful chairman of the Senate Foreign Relations Committee, seemed cast for the role of southern statesman. A colleague once said that the two-hundred-pound white-haired senator was "the only man in the United States Senate who could wear a Roman Toga and not look like a fat man in a nightgown." Although an early supporter of FDR's New Deal, Connally broke with the president in 1937, following his aborted scheme to pack the Supreme Court. His outspoken opposition to FDR's plan made him persona non grata at the White House for years afterward, even though he remained an internationalist who championed greater aid to the Allies. Connally's banishment from the White House was about to end, but not in the way that he had hoped.[1]

The Texas senator was taking advantage of the unseasonably warm weather on

Sunday afternoon. After having lunch at the home of Interior Secretary Harold Ickes, Connally decided to go for a relaxing drive around Maryland. When he reached Rockville, he turned on the car radio and heard the ominous report: "Japanese bombers have attacked Pearl Harbor. . . . Heavy casualties are reported at Hickam Field and Pearl Harbor has been attacked by the Japanese without warning." Connally rushed home, where he found a message from the White House, summoning him to an urgent meeting with the president at 9:00 p.m.[2]

He arrived at the White House a few minutes early and was ushered to the Red Room on the second floor. An odd collection of congressional leaders had already assembled there — a mix of Democrats and Republicans, liberals and conservatives, internationalists and isolationists whom FDR had handpicked for the meeting. Connally noticed Senate Majority Leader Alben Barkley of Kentucky, along with most of the ranking members of the Senate Foreign Relations Committee, including California Republican senator and isolationist leader Hiram Johnson, Oregon Republican Charles McNary, and Republican Warren R. Austin of Vermont, ranking minority member of the Foreign Relations Committee. Fellow

Texan and Speaker of the House Sam Rayburn led the House delegation, which included most key leaders. House Majority Leader John McCormack could not get to Washington in time, so Tennessee Democrat Jere Cooper took his place. The others from the House included House Minority Leader Joseph Martin of Massachusetts; Sol Bloom, a New York Democrat and chairman of the House Foreign Affairs Committee; and Majority Whip Lister Hill of Alabama.

Also missing from the assembled leaders was the ranking member of the House Foreign Affairs Committee, Hamilton Fish, an outspoken isolationist Republican who had angrily condemned FDR's Lend-Lease proposal. Roosevelt detested the man, and, according to Hopkins, "the President will not have him in the White House." Although he was a logical choice for the meeting, Hopkins and Roosevelt had drawn up a list that managed to exclude Fish. In his place, they invited the next most senior member of the committee, Charles Eaton of New Jersey.[3]

The cabinet meeting was not yet over, so the congressmen waited outside the doors and held what one reporter called "an indignation meeting." They discussed the many rumors floating around Washington:

parachute troops landing in Hawaii, battleships sunk, the Japanese "capture" of Wake and Midway islands. The "Japs" would pay for the attack, Connally proclaimed between puffs on a thick cigar. After a few minutes, a buzzer sounded signaling the end of the cabinet meeting, the door opened, and Grace Tully emerged, announcing that the congressmen could enter. As some of the cabinet members left the room, Connally noted their "shocked expressions." The congressional leaders filled the cabinet's freshly vacated chairs, still arranged in a semicircle around FDR. Seated near the president were Hopkins, Knox, Stimson, and Vice President Wallace.[4]

The president was deadly serious, his tone grave. Numerous dispatches had formed a small pile on his desk. According to one report, Roosevelt passed out fine Cuban cigars. Roosevelt provided the leaders with background on the negotiations with Japan that continued until a few hours before the attack. He expressed outrage over the Japanese ambassador's decision to deliver the final part of their answer after the attack on Pearl Harbor had commenced. Indignantly, Roosevelt called it "an act which is almost without parallel in relationships between nations."[5]

Roosevelt created the impression that he was bringing the congressional leaders into his confidence by sharing secret information. In reality, he was being deceptive. FDR knew that anything he said to the assembled lawmakers would quickly make it into the press. He insisted on maintaining tight control of the information coming from Hawaii, and, at this point, he did not want members of Congress shocking the nation with details of the destruction at Pearl.

FDR overstated the navy's preparedness and slightly understated the damage, but overall he painted a fair picture of the devastation. He told the congressional leaders that the navy had been on alert when the Japanese bombers attacked. Admiral Bloch had given him a detailed, though incomplete, breakdown of the damage reports a few hours earlier. Roosevelt, however, did not want to get into specifics with the congressional leaders. "It looks as if out of eight battleships, three have been sunk, and possibly a fourth," he said. "Two destroyers were blown up while they were in drydock. Two of the battleships are badly damaged. Several other smaller vessels have been sunk or destroyed." He honestly confessed to have "no word" on the navy casualties, but warned they "will undoubtedly be very heavy." He also estimated that the army suffered three hundred casualties. He asked that the congressional leaders not discuss the details with the press. "Now I think that is all there is in the way of information, but it has been suggested that the Army and Navy losses, and the . . . rather definite statements that I have made about these ships, could not be spoken outside, because we must remember that detailed military information is of value to an enemy. I think that is a matter of discretion, which all of you will accept."[6]

After outlining the damage in Hawaii, Roosevelt told his audience that the Japanese navy was still on the move. Guam was being bombed and had probably fallen to the Japanese. Wake Island had been attacked, and there were reports that ports in the Philippines were being bombed. But he seemed skeptical about the information coming from the Philippines. "Those are merely reports," he said, making clear they had not been confirmed. The Japanese had likely taken possession of the Chinese city of Shanghai, where two hundred marines were stationed. Japan had demanded that the marines surrender, but Roosevelt was still unclear about their status. "We are not certain yet whether they have been gotten out or not. Probably not," FDR remarked.[7]

Even though Roosevelt placed the best possible spin on the day's tragic events, the congressmen were still stunned. "The effect on the Congressmen was tremendous," noted Stimson. "They sat in dead silence and even after the recital was over they had very few words."[8]

According to Connally, when Roosevelt finished discussing the day's tragic events, he looked down toward the floor, crushed his cigarette in the ashtray on his desk, and said, "I guess that's all." But Connally, stunned and angry, wanted some answers to obvious questions: How could it have happened? What damage did we inflict on the Japanese? "The President indicated he didn't know but went on to say we had no information to indicate that we had severely damaged the japs," Connally recalled FDR saying. "We think we got some of their submarines, but we don't know" was all the president could offer.[9]

Connally persisted, asking if the United States shot down any of their planes. "We did get, we think, a number of their Japanese planes," FDR said. Roosevelt, however, had been receiving conflicting and often contradictory reports all day, and he was unwilling to get into specifics until he had some hard evidence. Perhaps he also did not want the congressmen to know just how feeble the American response had been. "We know some Japanese planes were shot down, but there again — I have seen so much of this in the other war. One fellow says he has got fifteen of their planes, and you pick up the telephone and somebody else says five. So I don't know what the report on that is, except that somewhere Japanese planes have been knocked down on the Island." By pointing out the rumors that two of the planes used in the raid had swastikas on them, Roosevelt apparently tried to deflect anger away from the military's failure to anticipate and respond to the attacks. "There is a rumor that two of the planes — Japanese planes have a rising sun painted on them — but two of the planes were seen with swastikas on them," he said. At this point, Connally exploded: "Where were our forces — asleep? Where were our patrols?"[10]

At that moment, a new dispatch arrived on Roosevelt's desk, sent from General MacArthur twenty minutes earlier. In it, he announced that Japan had attacked the Philippines. "All possible action being taken here to speed defense," MacArthur assured the president in the minutes before his bomber force was about to be wiped out.

Roosevelt received an update on the two hundred American marines in China. The news was not good. Vastly outnumbered and outgunned, the marines had been forced to surrender. Roosevelt did not dwell on the report. Instead, he moved to end the discussion. "That takes care of that," FDR said. "You have got the rest of it."[11]

The congressional leaders were clearly shocked by the news about Pearl Harbor, but for FDR the real purpose of the meeting was to ask them to invite him to address a joint session of Congress the next day. Congressional leaders wanted to know what he was going to say, and if he would be asking for a declaration of war. If there was a declaration, would it be against Japan or include Germany and Italy as well? Roosevelt had already written his speech and read a draft to the cabinet a few minutes earlier, but he did not want to share his speech with the congressional leaders. He claimed that he had not yet prepared his remarks and had not decided what to say. As Hopkins noted, Roosevelt "knew that he was going to ask for a declaration of war but he also knew that if he stated it to the conference that it would be all over town in five minutes, because it is perfectly foolish ever to ask a large group of congressmen or senators to keep a secret." FDR asked if Congress would be ready to receive him at 12:30 p.m. the following day — twenty-three hours after he first received word of the attack. They agreed.[12]

The discussion then switched back to the situation in the Pacific. Roosevelt needed to harness the outrage over the attack at Pearl to unify the nation for total war. Yet he was always mindful that the first priority was to defeat Germany, not Japan. There were some intelligence reports suggesting that Hitler would quickly declare war against the United States, and the announcement could come before he gave his address to Congress the next day. Regardless, FDR wanted to prepare congressional leaders, and the nation itself, for the prospect of a two-front war, with the Pacific theater playing a secondary role until the Allies achieved victory in Europe. In discussing war strategy, Roosevelt stressed that the struggle for the Pacific would not be determined by decisive battles. Instead, it would be a long, drawn-out struggle designed to strangle the Japanese war machine. The war with Japan, he said, "would be won primarily by the starvation and exhaustion of Japan — starvation and exhaustion." He pointed out that Japan had no naval bases. "And the old axiom used to be that a fleet loses five percent of its efficiency for every thousand miles it gets away from base," he noted. "That is a rule of thumb." As Wickard recalled, FDR "pointed out that it would be necessary to strangle Japan rather than whip her and that it took longer. He once spoke about two or three years being required."[13]

The conference ran until 11:00 p.m. After the congressional leaders left, Secretary of State Cordell Hull lingered for a few minutes. Although Roosevelt had twice rejected Hull's advice about giving a longer speech to Congress, the secretary refused to drop the argument. For reinforcement, he asked Undersecretary of State Sumner Welles to accompany him. Hull knew that FDR respected Welles and often turned to him for advice. Perhaps he thought that by bringing him along, he could help sway FDR to his position.

The strategy failed. According to Hopkins, who witnessed the scene, Roosevelt had no intention of accepting Hull's advice, but he was also tired of listening to him. So Roosevelt did what he did best: He pretended to accept the recommendations if only to mollify the secretary of state and get him out of the room. "Hull's message was a long-winded dissertation on the history of

Japanese relations leading up to the blow this morning," Hopkins recorded. "The President was very patient with them and I think in order to get them out of the room perhaps led them to believe he would give serious consideration to their draft."[14]

When the congressional leaders left the room, Roosevelt dictated a short message for the press, stating that he would address a joint session of the House and Senate at 12:30 p.m. the next day. "It should be emphasized that the message to Congress has not yet been written and its tenor will, of course, depend on further information received between 11 o'clock tonight and noon tomorrow. Further news is coming in all the time."

Reporters confronted the congressional leaders as they left the meeting. Standing on the White House steps, Connally said, "The President will address a joint session of Congress at 12:30 pm tomorrow. That is all I can say." Speaker Rayburn, when asked whether the president would request a declaration of war, responded, "I don't know. He didn't say." He added, however, that Congress would fully support such a move. "I think that is one thing on which there would be unity." Reporters asked Joseph Martin if there was any discussion about abandoning partisanship. "This is a serious moment," he said. "We were not talking about politics. Of course there will be none."[15]

Even Republicans and former isolationists realized there would be little opposition to granting Roosevelt the powers he needed to wage war. "It doesn't make much difference what he asks," a Republican leader of the House told the *Wall Street Journal*. "If it's even remotely connected with the war, we'll have to give it to him. And if it isn't properly connected with the war, he'll find a way to connect it anyway." "The Republicans," said Senator McNary, the Senate minority leader, "will all go along, in my opinion, with whatever is done."[16]

On Sunday night, reporters had little concrete information about what the president was going to say about the attack, though a declaration of war seemed inevitable to most. The question was whether it would include Germany and Italy along with Japan. The *Pittsburgh Post Gazette* noted, "It was evident tonight that a resolution recognizing war between the United States and Japan would be ratified overwhelmingly. Whether Congress would follow as readily in a declaration of war on

Germany and Italy was not clear."[17]

Later that evening, FDR met privately with legendary newsman Edward R. Murrow, who had just returned to the United States after three years stationed in London. Since becoming the chief of CBS's news staff abroad in 1937, Murrow had reported twice every day from England. His reports of the nightly bombings, and of the resilience of the British people, helped bridge the gap between the two nations and allowed Roosevelt to build support for aid to the Allies. Librarian of Congress Archibald MacLeish later told Murrow, "You have destroyed the superstition that what is done beyond 3,000 miles of water is not really done at all."[18]

Murrow and his wife were in Washington on Sunday to attend a private dinner with FDR and Eleanor at the White House that evening. After learning of the attack on Pearl Harbor, Murrow assumed that the dinner would be canceled, but Eleanor insisted that they come anyway. The president was busy, so the Murrows dined with Eleanor, who served her standard Sunday dinner of scrambled eggs. When the dinner ended, an aide asked Murrow to wait; the president still wanted to see him. While his wife returned to their hotel room, Murrow sat on a bench in the hallway outside the president's study, chain-smoking, watching top officials scurry in and out of meetings with FDR.

Years later, when charges first surfaced that the president's men had been part of a vast conspiracy to precipitate the attacks, Murrow recalled the expressions on the faces that night as evidence of genuine shock and surprise. If Hull, Stimson, and Knox were not surprised, he said, "then that group of elderly men were putting on a performance which would have excited the admiration of any experienced actor. I cannot believe that their expressions, bearing and conversation were designed merely to impress a correspondent who was sitting outside in the hallway."[19]

At one point, a ghostly looking Harry Hopkins came out and saw Murrow sitting alone on the bench. "What the hell are you doing here?" he asked. Hopkins invited Murrow to join him in his room two doors down. As they talked, Hopkins prepared for bed by putting on a pair of striped pajamas that seemed too big for his thin, gaunt physique. "His body was frail," Murrow recalled, "and he looked like a death's-head." Just before he climbed into bed, Hopkins spoke, in a very low tone: "Oh God

— If I only had the strength."[20]

FDR summoned Murrow to his study shortly after midnight. Over beer and sandwiches, Roosevelt asked him about the morale in England and how they were standing up to the bombing in London. While Murrow talked about the resolve and the sacrifices of the British people, FDR was clearly still privately fuming about the day's events. Without prompting, FDR shared with Murrow the detailed damage reports that he had refrained from giving to members of Congress. According to Murrow, FDR pounded the table with his fist when repeating the figures of planes destroyed on the ground. "On the ground, by God, on the ground!"[21]

According to the White House log, Murrow was never alone with the president. He was joined by Colonel William "Wild Bill" Donovan, soon to be director of the Office of Strategic Services. Murrow, however, recalled that Donovan joined them later in the conversation. When he did, the topic changed to discussing the Philippines. At 12:30, the president cleared everybody out and announced that he was going to bed.[22]

Murrow left his meeting realizing that he had been given the scoop of the century. Roosevelt had not instructed him to keep the information confidential. At no point had he stated that the meeting was off the record. Murrow returned to the CBS offices, where everyone looked at him, wondering what he had learned. Murrow kept silent. All he said was, "It's pretty bad."[23]

Later that night, he returned to his hotel room and paced back and forth for hours. Should he report the information, or should he keep quiet? "The biggest story of my life," he repeated. "I can't make up my mind whether it's my duty to tell it, or to forget it." He concluded that the conversation should be kept confidential. The president was using him as a sounding board, and although he did not specifically say it was off the record, Murrow felt that he was bound to protect the president's confidentiality.[24]

After Murrow and Donovan left, James Roosevelt entered the room and prepared his father for bed. FDR would soon be a wartime president. War was more than an abstraction to him. All four of his sons were in the service. FDR's oldest son, Franklin, served in the naval reserve. John was an ensign in the navy, and Elliott was in the army air force. James, a marine, was stationed in Washington, working as a liaison between the marine headquarters and what would become the Office of War Information. To this day, only one other president, Abraham Lincoln, had a son serving in the military while he was commander in chief during war.[25]

James recalled that as he lifted his father into bed that evening, they "talked of the long, dark tunnel we had entered, one which had no end in sight at that time." James told his father that he wanted to be transferred to combat duty. "Although I did not say it to him, I felt that as the son of the president I had to seek combat." His father worried about his son's health. James had survived major surgery for an ulcer a few years earlier that had removed two-thirds of his stomach. James, however, would soon get his wish. Within a year, he, along with his brothers, would see combat. In the Map Room at the White House, FDR would have a special pin designated for the ship on which Franklin Jr. served. FDR always looked at that pin first when he came into the room.[26]

15

"I HOPE MR. CAPONE DOESN'T MIND"

A White House switchboard operator woke FDR at 7:00 a.m. on Monday morning with an urgent call from Grace Tully. The American ambassador in Britain, Gil Winant, had contacted her to let her know that Churchill was planning to go before Parliament and ask for a declaration of war against Japan. Winant asked "if the President might wish to request a delay in London to allow our own declaration to come first." Realizing the political sensitivity of the issue, Tully called the White House switchboard and told them to wake up the president to give him the message. "In a few minutes he was on the wire to me and dictated a message to Churchill suggesting the British declaration be deferred long enough to permit him to go before the Congress."[1]

Roosevelt understood that in the wake of Pearl Harbor, Americans were likely to be far more enthusiastic about fighting a war in the Pacific than they were about joining forces in the European effort. For now, he wanted to avoid tying the two wars together, hoping that Hitler would solve the problem for him by declaring war on the United States. "I think it best on account of psychology here that Britain's declaration of war be withheld until after my speech at 12:30 Washington Time," he wrote, adding, "Any time after that would be wholly satisfactory."[2]

Unfortunately, Roosevelt's message arrived too late. Early in the afternoon in Britain, Churchill stood before a packed House of Parliament to deliver his speech, announcing Britain's declaration of war against Japan. With typical eloquence, the British leader said that "a state of war" existed between England and Japan. "It only remains now for the two great democracies to face their tasks with whatever strength God may give them." The House erupted with applause.[3]

For the next few hours, Roosevelt scanned the morning newspapers and the latest dispatches from the Pacific. "The news continued very bad," Stimson wrote in his diary. Japanese troops had attacked Hong Kong, Wake Island, and Midway Island. Naval aide Admiral Beardall arrived shortly after 8:00 a.m. to brief the president and to show him the most recent cables. The reports the previous day had contained only fragments of information, some of it false. By Monday morning, military officials had pieced together the snippets of evidence, weeded out some of the misinformation, and presented FDR with a more accurate narrative of what had taken place.

The information was uniformly depressing. The cables from Pearl Harbor pointed out that the raid on American aircraft on the ground was so effective that "practically none" were able to respond except for ten planes that had already been airborne at the time of the attack. "Dive bombing and torpedoing were most effective," stated a cable that Beardall handed to FDR at 8:45, "and in spite of magnificent and courageous work by gun crews, not more than a dozen of the enemy were shot down." The reports described the damage as "great," but the full extent was still unknown. FDR read that the Japanese had sunk three battleships, all the others had suffered some damage, and a large number of planes had been destroyed on ground. The cable estimated 2,800 casualties at Pearl Harbor, about half of those fatalities. The number must have been shocking to Roosevelt, who was learning for the first time about the deadly blast that had destroyed the *Arizona*. "The *Arizona* blew up and most of her officers and men including rear admiral Kidd were lost," the report said. In addition to the Pearl update, FDR was briefed on the other Japanese offensives. "Wake reports heaving damage from bombing by 30 planes. Guam reported air attack."[4]

The reports from Pearl Harbor were shocking, but the news from the Philippines must have been infuriating to Roosevelt. He was getting his full account of the destruction that had taken place during the overnight hours. He likely was shown a report based on a phone call from MacArthur about conditions in the Philippines. "Heavy damage was sustained at Clark Field with 23 dead and 200 wounded," MacArthur stated. "Our air losses here were heavy, while enemy air losses were light or medium."[5]

It was hard enough to understand why the navy and army in Hawaii were caught off guard, but how could MacArthur, who had been informed about Pearl Harbor and warned of an imminent attack, have been so unprepared? For now, Roosevelt kept his anger under control and simply updated his speech, jotting down additions to provide the nation with the most up-to-date information on Japanese movements in the Pacific.

Scanning the papers, Roosevelt likely noticed the mood of the nation had shifted overnight from fear and uncertainty to anger and determination. "What was the silence of shock last night, today was the cold, determined hatred of an outraged people," observed wire service reporter Jerry Greene, describing the mood in Washington on December 8. Arthur Krock, writing in the *New York Times,* said that "national unity was an instant consequence" of the Japanese attack. "You could almost hear it click into place in Washington today," he observed. "The lives, armament and property lost in Hawaii are a heavy price to pay for anything," Krock wrote. "But they were not spent in vain, for national unity — which has been a distant and unattained goal since and before Hitler invaded Poland in 1939 — seemed visibly to arise from the wreckage at Honolulu."[6]

The attack on Pearl Harbor indeed forged unprecedented unity in America. "Probably never in all American history was there provided such a spectacle of unity of purpose as stamped the dramatic sequence of events today," observed the *Pittsburgh Post-*

Gazette. "In the flash of a few bombs dropped without warning on territory under the American flag, isolationism puffed out in thin air. Republicans and Democrats dropped their differences. It was quickly apparent that President Roosevelt would have a vigorously united government behind him in the epochal days ahead."[7]

Overnight the battle cry "Remember Pearl Harbor!" had taken its place alongside other great battle slogans, such as "Remember the *Maine*," which came into existence shortly after the USS *Maine* sank in Havana Harbor in 1898, and "Remember the Alamo," voiced by General Sam Houston before the battle of San Jacinto against Mexico in 1836. Hundreds of telegrams continued pouring into the White House, expressing outrage and demanding retribution against Japan. "Today," announced the head of the Aplington, Iowa, Baptist Church, "we are no longer a divided people, but a united one."[8]

But amid the calls for unity were subtle reminders of the deep divisions that could not be glossed over with patriotic fervor. Capp Jefferson, an African American living in Oklahoma City, wrote the president on December 8 to "pledge the loyalty of every Negro in the United States and its allied possessions to the protection of our flag and the policies of our government." But his pledge of support came with a request. He asked that the president, along with the governors and mayors throughout the United States, proclaim an end to discrimination, poor housing, and poor transportation and "grant us the full rights of any and all American citizens."[9]

For any president giving a speech before a joint session of Congress, knowing that millions of Americans would be huddled next to their radios listening to every word would be stressful enough. Roosevelt had the added physical burden of strapping on his metal braces, traveling to the Capitol, and navigating the path to the rostrum in full glare of the newsreels.

Even a task as simple as getting dressed required enormous effort. At 11:00 a.m., valet Arthur Prettyman entered FDR's bedroom and began the laborious task of dressing the president for his trip to the Capitol. While laying FDR flat in bed, Prettyman would remove the president's pajamas and slip his legs into the heavy metal braces, which weighed roughly five pounds each. The braces had a hinge at the knee that could be locked into place, along with three straps: One went below FDR's knee, another across his thigh, and a third was positioned at the top of the brace just below the hip. When pulled tight, the straps would keep his legs rigid. FDR's black dress shoes were attached to the bottom of the braces through a hole drilled into the heel. The most difficult part of the process for Prettyman was trying to fit the lifeless feet into the shoes.[10] Once the braces were strapped on and the shoes secured, Prettyman proceeded to dress the president. FDR chose formal morning clothes — black cutaway coat, striped trousers, and a gray and white tie. Roosevelt insisted on an added feature: a black armband he wore in memory of his mother. With the president still lying flat on the bed, his assistant would rock FDR to the right and then the left, gradually working his trousers over the shoes and braces and up his legs. Once the pants were on, Prettyman lifted the president to a sitting position on the bed and helped him put on his shirt, tie, and jacket. Once Roosevelt was dressed, Prettyman hoisted him into his wheelchair for the trip to the Capitol. The whole process took about forty-five minutes.[11]

Before leaving the White House, however, FDR made another brief visit to his physician's office. He arrived at 11:55 a.m. and stayed for ten minutes. McIntire probably sprayed FDR's nose to clear up any congestion and probably applied an ointment on his throat and mouth to keep his vocal cords moist.

After his brief stopover with McIntire, Roosevelt was wheeled to the north portico of the White House. As he emerged into the open air, Roosevelt would have seen ten highly polished black limousines bearing the seal of the president. Up ahead, and reaching nearly to the west gate, stood a dozen escorting police on motorcycles. Never before had a president been so well protected. There were more Secret Service agents and police gathered around him than at any other time in his presidency, including his three inaugurals. Many agents carried sawed-off shotguns. Despite the cold weather, they had decided not to wear topcoats because they feared the extra clothing would hamper their ability to draw their .38-caliber service revolvers.[12]

Roosevelt must have been surprised to see a new, shiny limousine waiting to transport him to the Capitol. Since government rules prevented spending more than $750 for a single automobile, the president did not have an armored car. "We could pay a million and a half dollars for a cannon if we thought that would protect the President," Mike Reilly observed, "but the book said $750 for a car, and when the book says anything in the government that's it." Although the car was billed as bulletproof, in reality, only the windows were able to stop bullets.[13]

As Roosevelt approached the car, he said to Reilly, "What's that thing, Mike?"

"Mr. President, I've taken the liberty of getting a new car. It's armored, I'm afraid it's a little uncomfortable, and I know it has a dubious reputation."

"Dubious reputation?" FDR asked inquisitively.

"Yes, sir. It belonged to Al Capone. The Treasury Department had a little trouble with Al, you know, and they got it from him in the subsequent legal complications. I got it from treasury."

Roosevelt seemed amused. "I hope Mr. Capone doesn't mind," he said.[14]

Reilly and Roosevelt's son James, dressed in his Marine Corps officer uniform, then lifted FDR to a standing position and maneuvered him into the car for the short ride. Eleanor, wearing a black hat, black suit, and a silver-fox fur, stood by his side, watching his every step. James jumped in with his father, while Eleanor took a backup car.

Although FDR rode in a closed, bulletproof car, a Secret Service man stood on the running board to shield him from a potential assassin. Both sides of his car were flanked by an open Secret Service car with three men on each of the running boards armed with .38-caliber service revolvers. Four more agents were huddled inside with sawed-off riot guns at the ready. Another Secret Service car followed FDR. In front of the president's auto was a car the Secret Service dubbed "Big Bertha" or "the Queen Mary," because it held a rolling arsenal of firepower. "If ever a President rode in a mechanized division it was Roosevelt today," observed journalist Felix Belair Jr.[15]

The president's route along Pennsylvania Avenue to the Capitol was lined with soldiers and heavily armed policemen. "We turned out every policeman in Washington, and we virtually soaked the halls of Congress with Secret Service operatives summoned from New York, Philadelphia, and other Eastern cities," recalled Reilly. The Secret Service took other unprecedented steps to protect the presidential motorcade: Street intersections were blocked off so that the motorcade could maintain a constant thirty-mile-an-hour speed. According to Wilson, all "manholes on the route were inspected for hidden bombs, and then sealed."[16]

In 1917, President Woodrow Wilson had traveled the same route to deliver his message. Large and enthusiastic crowds, which embraced Wilson's idealistic crusade to make the world safe for democracy, greeted him along the way. On this day, the crowds were small, somber, and silent. Roosevelt occasionally waved and smiled at the crowds, although, as one reporter noted, "the hand waving was a little less vigorous and the smile was not from ear to ear."[17]

Roosevelt arrived at a Capitol swarming with police, Secret Service agents, and soldiers. More than two hundred Secret Service men guarded the Capitol. Another four hundred police officers were stationed in and around the building. Marines with fixed bayonets guarded each entrance. Everyone was on edge. When a reporter absentmindedly walked into the Capitol with a rolled-up newspaper in his hands, police snatched it away. A Secret Service agent forcefully pushed back another journalist who was trying to get into the press gallery without a pass.[18]

Roosevelt's car pulled up to the ground-floor entrance under the south entrance of the Capitol. It was a secure area, away from public view. The Secret Service took his wheelchair from the trunk before helping FDR out of the car. James stood by his side, while Mrs. Roosevelt left her husband and was escorted to the elevator to the Executive Gallery, where she would watch the speech. It was there that she met her invited guest: Mrs. Woodrow Wilson.[19]

Roosevelt entered the building using the same ramp that he originally used for his first inaugural in March 1933. Since FDR became president in 1933, the Secret Service had installed wooden ramps at all the key buildings in Washington that Roosevelt routinely visited. James trailed a few feet behind, carrying his father's speech. The Secret Service pushed him to the Speaker's Room, a chamber just off the House floor. There he waited to give one of the most important speeches ever delivered by an American president.

While FDR waited in the Speaker's Room, members of Congress and the press crowded into the House chamber. With the exception of the first few rows of seats, which were reserved for the Senate, the Supreme Court, members of the cabinet, and the leaders of the armed forces, every inch of the ornate hall was filled to capacity. People were jammed into doorways, standing on chairs, and leaning on the narrow ledge of the panels on the wall. The 86 seats available in the press gallery could not begin to cover the accredited corps of 590 correspondents who had turned out to hear the speech.[20]

At 12:15 Speaker Sam Rayburn gaveled the House to order. Most members of Congress were already in their seats. About a dozen members had brought their children onto the floor with them to witness the historic occasion. Doorkeeper Joe Sinnott announced a message had been received from the Senate. It was passage of House Concurrent Resolution 61, agreeing that a joint session of Congress be convened.

A few minutes later, members of the Senate filed into the House chamber. Vice President Henry Wallace led the delegation, escorting octogenarian Carter Glass of Virginia. He was followed by a delegation of Democratic and Republican leaders. As a demonstration of solidarity, isolationist Republican Hiram Johnson of California linked arms with silver-haired Elmer Thomas, a Democrat from Oklahoma.[21]

The cabinet followed, led by the white-headed Cordell Hull. "He looked almost like a ghost risen for the occasion," observed one reporter. "Tall, slightly stooped, he seemed almost exhausted. His face was deeply lined, sad. His white hair was neatly brushed, set off by his blue suit, black tie and white soft-collar shirt." Admiral Stark and General Marshall followed in full uniform. Next in line were the members of the Supreme Court, in their long black robes. "There was no laughter, and none of the boisterous horseplay which customarily accompanies the preliminary stages of such gatherings," noted a reporter. "There was only a subdued hum of conversation."[22]

At 12:29 a voice cried out, "The President of the United States." There was a moment of silence before FDR appeared in the back of the center aisle. His presence in the hall produced a burst of thunderous applause. For the first time in years, Republicans stood and applauded Franklin Roosevelt. The president stood, propped up on the arm of his son James. A House and Senate delegation of six members surrounded them. Their presence underscored the bipartisan nature of Roosevelt's message, but it also helped to disguise FDR's awkward movement to the podium before the full glare of the world's media.[23]

A reporter noted that FDR appeared oblivious to the ovation that greeted him. The president, he observed, "appeared to be lost in deep thought." He assumed that Roosevelt was "thinking of the gravity of the pronouncement he was about to make, a statement which, however inevitable it was, nevertheless was something to make any man think seriously."[24]

While Roosevelt no doubt appreciated the gravity of the moment, James believed that his father was far more focused on the difficult task of appearing to walk down the aisle and then force his way up the wooden ramp that led to the rostrum. "His uppermost thought," James later wrote, "was that he get one braced foot after the other in the right position; that he hold his balance over his hips and pelvis just so; that he shift his great shoulders forward, left, and right just so; that he not fall down. This concentration caused him to break out into a sweat as, indeed, it always did."[25]

As James helped his father to the rostrum, the outburst of applause grew louder, joined by cheers and rebel yells, until Speaker Rayburn stilled the demonstration and presented the president. Once at the podium, the president grasped the firm sides of the platform. He adjusted his glasses and took a long, steady look at the assembled leaders of government that stood before him. He gazed almost directly into a battery of floodlights that had been set up for photographers.

If he could see past the lights, Roosevelt would have noticed how much Washington had changed since he first stood before Congress in 1933. Seeing the members of the Supreme Court sitting to his left would have reminded him both of the partisan legal wrangling of his presidency and of the remarkable impact he had on the judiciary. The average age of the Court he had inherited in 1933 was seventy-one, and it was then dominated by conservatives who did not share his faith in activist government. After it invalidated key New Deal programs, FDR announced an ill-conceived plan to reform the Supreme Court. The plan went down in defeat, but he still managed to transform the Court over the next few years, as many older, more conservative members resigned. He could take note that he had appointed seven of the nine members sitting before him and that the average age was now in the midforties, making it the youngest Court since the Civil War.[26]

Behind the cabinet sat the senators and

members of the House. There were more Republicans in the seats than earlier, and many of the Democrats were from southern states that were unsympathetic to his liberal agenda. Gone were the massive majorities of 1937, when Democrats commanded margins of 331 to 89 in the House and 76 to 16 in the Senate. The margins on December 8 were 267 to 162 in the House, and 66 to 28 in the Senate.

After scanning the audience, Roosevelt looked down and flipped open his black leather loose-leaf notebook holding his speech, which was typed on special paper that would not rustle as he turned the pages. Reporters noted how a year earlier, while giving his State of the Union address, Roosevelt had seemed tired and worn. His hands had trembled, and he had almost dropped his glasses as he prepared to read his speech. It was a different story today. "Today, that tremor was gone," noted an observer. "His hand was firm, its muscles bulging as he gripped the desk." His voice was "steely, brittle with determination."[27]

As he began to read his speech, the gallery fell silent. "Yesterday," he said in a strong resonant voice, "December 7th, 1941 — a date which will live in infamy — the United States of America was suddenly and deliberately attacked by naval and air forces of the Empire of Japan." His tone became indignant as he outlined the dishonesty of a Japanese government that launched attacks even as it negotiated for peace. "The United States was at peace with that nation and, at the solicitation of Japan, was still in conversation with its government and its emperor looking toward the maintenance of peace in the Pacific." He told the nation how "one hour after Japanese air squadrons had commenced bombing in the American island of Oahu," the Japanese ambassador had given the secretary of state a message that "contained no threat or hint of war or of armed attack." The only conclusion to draw was that "the Japanese government has deliberately sought to deceive the United States by false statements and expressions of hope for continued peace."

Roosevelt made only a brief, vague reference to the damage at Pearl Harbor. The attack, he said, "has caused severe damage to American naval and military forces. I regret to tell you that very many American lives have been lost." Then he moved quickly into cataloging the list of Japanese targets in the past twenty-four hours:

American ships have been reported

torpedoed on the high seas between San Francisco and Honolulu.

Yesterday, the Japanese government also launched an attack against Malaya.

Last night, Japanese forces attacked Hong Kong.

Last night, Japanese forces attacked Guam.

Last night, Japanese forces attacked the Philippine Islands.

Last night, the Japanese attacked Wake Island.

And this morning, the Japanese attacked Midway Island.

There was little applause during this early part of his speech. The first sustained outburst came when he declared that no matter how long it might take, the United States would win through "to absolute victory." As he proceeded, and the applause broke in, he appeared anxious to curtail the demonstrations. This was not a political campaign speech; it was about the grim business of war, although the line that Hopkins added was clearly designed to produce applause. "With confidence in our armed forces — with the unbounding determination of our people — we will gain the inevitable triumph — so help us God." The line brought the chamber to its feet. Even the ordinarily restrained members of the Supreme Court stood to applaud.[28]

As Roosevelt's war message culminated, Congress once again rose and gave him a standing ovation. "I ask that the Congress declare that since the unprovoked and dastardly attack by Japan on Sunday, December 7, a state of war has existed between the United States and the Japanese Empire." Only two members remained sitting: Republicans Jeanette Rankin of Montana and Clare Hoffman from Michigan.

Roosevelt appeared oblivious to the demonstration. He had sat in the same chamber as an assistant secretary of the navy and recalled the wild cheering that had greeted Wilson's declaration of war. He remembered how the harsh reality of war ultimately quieted the cheers and how disillusion with the postwar settlement had endured for a generation. More than anyone in the chamber that day, FDR was in a position to understand the challenges that lay ahead. Unlike the applauding members of Congress, he knew the full extent of the devastation in Hawaii. With a tight-lipped smile, FDR waved his right hand in acknowledgment and turned swiftly to leave the rostrum.[29]

Eleanor Roosevelt, who had been seated behind a construction beam in one of the worst seats of the House, stood applauding with everyone else. But she had mixed feelings that evening. "I was living through it again, it seemed to me, the day that President Wilson addressed Congress to announce our entry into World War I. Now the president of the United States was my husband, and for the second time in my life I heard a president tell the Congress that this nation was engaged in a war. I was deeply unhappy. I remembered my anxieties about my husband and brother when World War I began; now I had four sons of military age."[30]

Roosevelt had spoken for only six minutes and thirty seconds. The speech attracted the largest audience in the history of radio. The response was overwhelmingly positive. The New York Times reported that Roosevelt "spoke concisely, clearly and to the point to an already convinced audience already stirred to belligerency by the wantonness of the Japanese attack." Columnist Ernest Lindley observed that FDR "delivered his address soberly and unfalteringly." The Philadelphia Inquirer described Roosevelt as "serious and tired looking. His face was lined and his eyes were somber. But his voice had all of the resonance and confidence that has thrilled millions of Americans over the last nine years. There was no hint of hesitation in his manner; only cold, grim determination."[31]

In all of the coverage of events that day, not a single journalist made mention of FDR's disability. Even when describing his "walk" down the aisle, reporters noted only that he leaned on the arm of his son. Later they said he "slowly" made his way out of the hall. In its live radio broadcast of the speech, the CBS announcers described the scene as Roosevelt was "walking up to the battery of microphones" on the Speaker's platform. No one mentioned the cane that he gripped with his right hand or the effort that he seemed to expend to make it up and down the aisle.[32]

The speech's reception in London was less enthusiastic. Churchill was hoping that Roosevelt would use his address to declare war on Germany and Italy. Now he worried that Lend-Lease shipments would be curtailed and that the United States would move resources from the war in the Atlantic to the Pacific. "America is fighting for her own life," editorialized the *Daily Express.* "Arms workers of Britain and Russia must be ready to provide from their own factories some of the weapons they had expected from America."[33]

Congress moved with unprecedented speed to pass the war resolution. After Woodrow Wilson delivered his war message, a divided Congress debated the resolution for four days. It passed, but with 56 dissenting votes. The nation, however, had not been attacked in 1917. As soon as Roosevelt left the building, the Senate returned to their chamber to begin debate.

Senator Connally introduced the resolution at 12:51 p.m. He made clear that he wanted no speeches, and he refrained from giving one. However, Senator Arthur Vandenberg, a Republican from Michigan, and leading isolationist, said he desired "to make the record clear." He told the Senate that "when war comes to us," partisan differences disappear and the nation unites behind the commander in chief. If Japan believed that it could exploit America's differences, it was mistaken. "There can be no shadow of a doubt about America's united and indomitable answer to the cruel and ruthless challenge of this tragic hour — the answer not only of the Congress but also of our people at their threatened hearthstones."[34]

Vandenberg's rousing speech signaled the end of the foreign policy debate that had plagued the nation since the end of World War I. For twenty years, isolationists and pacifists had conspired to restrain American power, tying Roosevelt's hands as he struggled to deal with the growing crisis in Europe. While Roosevelt had managed to nudge public opinion toward supporting efforts to aid Britain, the nation remained reluctant to embrace the cause of war. Less than twenty-four hours earlier, FDR's key foreign policy aides were refining their arguments to convince him of the necessity of declaring war if Japan attacked British possessions in the Pacific. In one decisive move, Japan managed to erase those divisions and unite the nation.

As soon as the Michigan senator finished his speech, the Senate began calling the roll. A succession of proud and defiant "ayes" filled the room. By 1:06 the roll had been called. The final tally was 82 to 0. There were 13 senators who missed the vote. A few were ill, but most were unable to make it back to Washington on such short notice. In the chamber were 5 members who had voted on the last war resolution in 1917. One, George Norris, an independent of

Nebraska, voted no then, but supported this resolution.

The process of passing the resolution was slower in the House. Majority Leader John McCormack presented the "unanimous consent" resolution and asked that the rules be suspended so that it could be considered immediately. When he made the request, Jeanette Rankin rose to object. Suffrage was what motivated her, but pacifism would define her career. Rankin had voted against America's entry in the last war and now seemed poised to oppose this one as well. Speaker Rayburn ignored her. "There can be no objection," he declared.

With members shouting from the floor, "Vote, vote, vote," House Republican leader Joseph Martin took the floor. "There can be no peace," Martin declared, "until the enemy is made to pay in a full way for his dastardly deed. Let us show the world that we are a united nation." With restless members shouting for a vote, Rayburn tried calming the crowd. "It won't be long. Let us keep order," he insisted. The cries, which had temporarily died down, picked up again when Martin yielded three minutes to Hamilton Fish (R–NY), who took the floor to renounce his isolationist views and support FDR's call for war. "There is no sacrifice I will not make to annihilate these war-made Japanese devils," he told his colleagues. When Fish concluded, Rankin was standing, seeking recognition from the Speaker. "Sit down, sister," yelled John Dingell of Michigan. Rayburn continued to ignore her and recognized two more speakers.

At 1:04 p.m., Rayburn ordered the roll call. Rankin tried to interrupt, but the Speaker again ignored her. The clerk of the House needed to read each name and register their vote on the resolution. Taking the roll call was often a slow and laborious process, complicated by the chaos on the floor. Irving Swanson, the twenty-nine-year-old clerk taking the roll call, remembered this day as different. "You could hear the drop of a pin," he reflected. "Everybody was quiet. Very serious."[35]

As the roll call proceeded, Representative Everett Dirksen of Illinois sat next to Rankin, pleading with her to vote "present" rather than "no" to allow the vote to be unanimous. He failed. When the clerk called her name, Rankin declared in a firm soprano voice, "Nay." Spectators in the gallery hissed as the clerk recorded her vote, forcing Rayburn to pound the gavel and restore order. Rankin was the only dissenting vote. At 1:26 p.m., the House passed the resolution with a vote of 388 to 1. A cheer followed Rayburn's announcement that the resolution had passed.[36]

Under parliamentary rules, one chamber must approve the resolution adopted by the other. Since the Senate acted first, Rayburn substituted its version, Senate Joint Resolution 116, which was identical to the House resolution. "Without objection, the joint resolution is read a third time and passed," the Speaker announced. At 1:32 p.m., fifty-two minutes after FDR finished his address, Congress had voted for war against Japan.[37]

Speaker Rayburn signed the resolution on behalf of the House at 3:14 p.m. The vice president, representing the Senate, placed his signature on the document at 3:25 p.m. The resolution was carried to the White House, where Roosevelt signed it at 4:10 p.m. — three hours and thirty-seven minutes from the time he started his address.

Roosevelt's finely tuned political instincts had proven correct. His short speech rallied the Congress and inspired the nation. Shortly after the final vote, FDR cabled Churchill in London. "Today all of us are in the same boat with you and the people of the Empire," he wrote, "and it is a ship which will not and cannot be sunk."[38]

EPILOGUE

The Japanese attack on Pearl Harbor represented the single most significant event of the twentieth century. The Japanese mistakenly believed the assault would intimidate the American people, making them less willing to fight. Instead, it aroused the full fury of an angry nation, provided a decisive advantage to the Allies, and prevented Hitler's plan for global domination.

By the end of the day on December 7, it was clear to administration officials that Japan had launched a brilliant surprise attack that dealt a major blow to the American fleet at Pearl Harbor and left behind 3,566 American casualties.

Although tactically brilliant, the attack was a strategic disaster. The United States managed to repair and restore all but two of the hundred ships in port that day. The two lost were both old battleships of limited capability: the *Arizona,* commissioned in 1913, and the *Oklahoma,* commissioned in 1914. The *Utah* was also destroyed, and while it has often been counted among the battleships sunk that day, it had long been considered obsolete and was being used as target practice for American aircraft. Of the 120 damaged planes, 80 percent were salvaged. (Many of the ones that were not were already out of commission at the time of the attacks.) In addition, the army sent 29 new B-17s from the mainland shortly after the attack. Within two weeks, the army had almost as many planes in Hawaii as before December 7. The Japanese failed to hit half of the light cruisers, 86 percent of the destroyers, or any of the heavy cruisers or submarines in the harbor. They failed to inflict any damage on the massive oil tanks. Most important, the three aircraft carriers were out of port that day, and they would prove to be the decisive weapons of the naval war.[1]

Instead of demoralizing Americans, Japan stirred a patriotic fervor that would inspire the nation to fight. Thousands of young men packed recruiting stations across the country following Roosevelt's message. In Chicago, around 2,000 men — more than ten times the normal number — turned up at recruiting stations. There were more than

60 waiting outside the door of the army-recruiting center when the door opened at 8:00 a.m. on December 8. Army-recruitment centers in New York City reported three times as many enlistments following Roosevelt's war address when compared to the response to Woodrow Wilson's address in 1917.[2]

American political divisions dissolved in the wake of the attack. While there had been domestic opposition to the War of 1812, the Mexican War, the Spanish-American War, and World War I, support for America's entry into World War II was nearly unanimous. Never before, and never again, would the nation experience such unity in time of war. Many isolationists either fell silent or publicly endorsed war. Aviator Charles Lindbergh released a statement saying, "Our country has been attacked by force of arms and by force of arms we must retaliate." Herbert Hoover, the man FDR defeated in the 1932 presidential election, announced, "American soil has been treacherously attacked by Japan. Our decision is clear. It is forced upon us. We must fight with everything we have." Hamilton Fish, a leading isolationist who despised Roosevelt, called upon the American people "to present a united front in support of the

President." The Pittsburgh Chapter of the America First Committee dissolved, passing a resolution declaring, "The war into which we have been plunged by Japanese treachery demands unity of effort by all Americans, as well as unity of support for our government in its prosecution of the war."[3]

Organized labor pledged its full support to the war effort. "Labor knows its duty," William Green, president of the American Federation of Labor, announced after the declaration of war. "It will do its duty, and more. No new laws are necessary to prevent strikes. Labor will see to that. American workers will now produce as the workers of no other country have ever produced." In a radio address, Philip Murray, president of the Congress of Industrial Organizations, said his members "were ready and eager to defend our country against the outrageous aggression of Japanese imperialism, and to secure the final defeat of the forces of Hitler."[4]

The press was unanimous in praising FDR for his handling of the crisis. "All who have seen and talked with him during the last week testify that he has been magnificently calm and resolute," observed *Washington Post* columnist Ernest Lindley. "All over Washington — and I suppose all over the country — people have been going around in a daze. . . . The President, all report, has gone about his job with clear-minded efficiency." Lindley was one of the few contemporary journalists to speculate about the connection between Roosevelt's struggle with polio and his response to Pearl Harbor. Although he never used the word "polio," he mentioned that the "personal ordeal" that FDR endured two decades earlier had prepared him to deal with adversity. "From the shadow of death he emerged to be consigned to an invalid's life," he wrote in surprisingly stark language. "He determined to treat the disaster which had overtaken him as if it had never happened." Over the next few years, he proved that there "was iron in him, and the fires of that personal ordeal tempered it into the hardest steel."[5]

Writing in the *New York Times,* Frank Kluckhohn observed a new burst of energy from Roosevelt and a strength that he had not previously displayed. "Before Japan moved, the lines — which years of responsibility had etched on his face — appeared to sag; now those lines have hardened and Mr. Roosevelt's face appears to be carved of granite," he wrote. "Gone is his almost happy-go-lucky air of early New Deal days;

gone is the latter-day fatigue and occasional irritability. He stands more firmly than for some time, his head held higher, his chin thrust out."[6]

Germany followed Japan's strategic blunder by declaring war on the United States four days after Pearl Harbor. In October 1943, FDR told Stalin that had it not been for the German declaration of war, he would not have been able to send vast numbers of American troops across the Atlantic.[7]

Roosevelt's major challenge in the days after December 7, however, was to convince the American people that Germany, with its Nazi ideology, military might, and industrial production, presented a far graver threat to America's interest than tiny Japan.

FDR had expected Hitler to declare war on the United States in response to America's declaration of war against Japan. When Hitler failed to do so, FDR reminded Americans of the connection between the war in the Pacific and the battle for Europe. Unwilling to declare war on Germany first, FDR instead issued a statement a few hours after his address to Congress, laying blame for the Japanese attack on Hitler. "Obviously Germany did all it could to push Japan into war," he said. "It was the German hope that if the United States and Japan could be pushed into war that such a conflict would put an end to the Lend-Lease Program."[8]

The next day, Tuesday, December 9, FDR gave a fireside chat at 10:00 p.m. on the East Coast. A radio audience estimated at 60 million listened to the address. Resisting the State Department's effort to give a long recital of U.S.-Japanese relations, he instead chose to tie the attacks to the war in Europe. The "criminal attacks," he said, represented the culmination of a course Japan had followed "for the past ten years in Asia" and that "paralleled the course of Hitler and Mussolini in Europe. Today it has become more than parallel. It is actual collaboration so well calculated that all continents of the world, and all the oceans, are now considered by the Axis strategists." He wanted America to think globally, recognizing that the war against Japan was part of a larger struggle that was playing out in Europe. "We expect to eliminate the danger from Japan," he concluded, "but it would serve us ill if we accomplished this and found that the rest of the world was dominated by Hitler and Mussolini."[9]

Hitler was not obligated under the terms of the treaty with Japan to go to war with the United States. His foreign minister advised him that the Tripartite Pact obligated Germany only in the event that Japan was attacked. His advisers were aware that Roosevelt would have had a difficult time getting Congress to declare war against Germany and that U.S. military leaders would prefer to avoid a two-front war. Hitler, blinded by his contempt for Roosevelt and his disdain for the United States, ignored the advice and opted for war. "I cannot be insulted by Roosevelt, for I consider him mad, just as Wilson was," he declared. He claimed that Roosevelt wanted war to distract the American people from the failures of his New Deal programs. On December 11, Germany and Italy declared war against the United States.[10]

Roosevelt did not go before Congress to make another war address. Instead, he sent Congress a brief note, asking that it recognize a state of war with the Axis powers. Congress unanimously adopted the resolution, with Jeanette Rankin this time voting "present."

The attack on Pearl Harbor set in motion a series of changes that would transform the postwar world. The nation, mired in depression for the previous decade, experienced an unprecedented economic expansion. Unemployment, which stood at 17 percent when Japanese planes attacked Pearl Harbor, plummeted to nearly immeasurable levels by 1942. National income more than doubled, from $81 billion in 1940 to $181 billion five years later. The war also improved the distribution of income — an accomplishment that had eluded New Deal planners.

The growing centralization of power in Washington, begun during the New Deal, accelerated enormously during World War II. Between 1940 and 1945, the number of civilian employees in government posts rose from 1 million to 3.8 million. Total spending for the war came to more than $251 billion, a sum greater than the total of all government spending in the history of the United States to that point.

Bigger government meant more regulation and a pressing need to raise money to pay for the war effort. Most Americans had never filed an income tax return before World War II because the income tax, on the books since 1913, had been a small tax on upper-income families. Beginning in 1942, anyone earning $600 or more annually had to file a return. Income-tax withholding from paychecks went into effect in 1943.

FDR's response to the Depression and World War II fundamentally changed the institution of the presidency. On issues of both international diplomacy and domestic government, the people and Congress now looked to the president for leadership. The entire twelve years that Roosevelt spent in the White House were a time of crisis. Whether solving the problems of the Depression or rallying the nation to global war, Roosevelt made the presidency the focus of the public's hopes and expectations. Recognizing the growing power of the office, Congress delegated enormous power to the president, who in turn delegated it to the sprawling bureaucracy he controlled.

The struggle forced Americans to rethink their relationship with the rest of the world. The American victory in the fight against Germany and Japan shattered the myth of isolationism that had dominated thinking during the 1930s and introduced a new consensus in favor of internationalism. Many leaders, including former isolationists, came to believe that appeasement had been a tragic mistake that allowed Hitler's war machine to thrive. By the end of World War II, they were arguing that the United States needed to play a more active role in world affairs. "No more Munichs!" declared former isolationist leader Senator Arthur Vandenberg in 1945. "America must behave like the number one world power which she is." The rhetoric of economic as well as military internationalism echoed through the halls of Congress and down Pennsylvania Avenue to the White House.

America emerged from the struggle as the leading economic and military power in the world. Flush from victory, the United States prepared to launch a new crusade against communism, armed with enormous military might and confidence in the universal relevance of American values. The experience of total war against absolute evil, however, did little to prepare Americans for the prospect of limited war or for the moral ambiguity of conflicts in third world countries such as Vietnam.

The memory of Franklin Roosevelt's decisive leadership in the wake of the attacks on Pearl Harbor shadowed George W. Bush in the weeks and months following the terrorist attacks of September 11, 2001. That evening, after returning to the White House, Bush scribbled in his diary, "The Pearl Harbor of the 21st century took place today."

President Bush was not alone in drawing

parallels between the two attacks. "This is the second Pearl Harbor. I don't think that I overstate it," said Nebraska Republican senator Charles Hagel. Newspaper headlines across the country screamed "INFAMY!" recalling FDR's description of Japanese treachery on December 7, 1941. "This is our generation's Pearl Harbor," observed a writer in the *New Republic*.[11]

The United States confronted a very different crisis in 2001, but the Bush administration was eager to draw parallels between past and present. "In the 21st century, freedom is again under attack," he declared on Pearl Harbor Remembrance Day in 2006, "and young Americans have stepped forward to serve in a global war on terror that will secure our liberty and determine the destiny of millions around the world. Like generations before, we will answer history's call with confidence, confront threats to our way of life, and build a more peaceful world for our children and grandchildren."[12]

There can be no doubt that Franklin Roosevelt, and the generation that he inspired, created a more democratic and peaceful world. Whether the generation leading the nation today can achieve the same goals remains to be seen. The effort to link the modern struggle against terrorism with the fight against fascism reveals that both in history and in memory, Pearl Harbor remains a day that will truly live in infamy.

ACKNOWLEDGMENTS

I could not have written this book without the support of the University of Oklahoma and the History Channel, the dedication of skilled archivists, the insights of many colleagues and scholars, and the encouragement of friends.

At the Franklin D. Roosevelt Library, my thanks to chief archivist Robert Clark, who possesses a nearly encyclopedic knowledge of the collection and a seemingly limitless supply of patience in dealing with pesky researchers. David Woolner, senior fellow and resident historian for the Roosevelt Institute, read a draft of the manuscript and provided many constructive comments. Mike Sampson offered valuable resources from the archives of the United States Secret Service.

A number of people read the manuscript at various stages and offered helpful comments. My mentor, James T. Patterson, read the manuscript with extraordinary care, offering his usual blend of gentle encouragement, detailed criticism, and thoughtful commentary. At Basic Books, the talented editor Lara Heimert guided the project from beginning to end. She made this a much better book. My friend Gary Ginsberg volunteered to read the manuscript and, as always, offered encouragement, suggestions, and support.

Dr. Matthew Miller of the Harvard School of Public Health tracked down sources that helped me to understand medical practices for dealing with sinus infections in the 1940s. Dr. Jordan S. Josephson, director of the New York Nasal and Sinus Center, was especially helpful and shared with me his considerable knowledge of sinus infections and how physicians have treated them over the years.

A number of research assistants helped along the way. Anthony Carlson, Eric England, and Doug Miller — all graduate students in history at the University of Oklahoma — copied articles, combed through newspapers, and read early drafts. At the FDR Library, Geraldine Hawkins tracked down a handful of documents.

At the History Channel, Nancy Dubuc and David McKillop commissioned a two-hour special based on the book and placed it in the capable hands of Emmy Award–winning producer Anthony Giacchino.

This book is dedicated to Abbe Raven. Every once in a while, if you are lucky, you meet someone special who manages to change your life. For me, Abbe has been one of those special people. I first met her around eighteen years ago when she was the head of programming for a fledging network called the History Channel and I was an assistant professor of history at Yale University. Although I lacked both experience and talent, she decided to put me on the air, hosting a show, *HistoryCenter,* which ran for the next eight seasons. Since then, she has provided me with a world of new opportunities and experiences that I never could have imagined. Her career has also blossomed. After managing the History Channel, she took over A&E before being named president and CEO of AETN.

While Abbe has many remarkable qualities, what I find most unique has been her ability to climb the corporate ladder while still managing to keep her feet, and her ego, planted firmly on the ground. She skillfully balances the tough decisions of corporate governance with an instinctive compassion and ingrained empathy for her employees.

NOTES

Preface

1. "Nation's Full Might Mustered for All-Out War," *Newsweek,* December 15, 1941, 15.
2. The "back door" theory, like most conspiracy theories, fails the test of logic. It assumes that the President of the United States, along with Secretary of State Cordell Hull, Secretary of War Henry Stimson, Secretary of the Navy Frank Knox, Army Chief of Staff George Marshall, and Chief of Naval Operations Admiral Harold Stark, knowingly risked the lives of thousands of servicemen in pursuit of a policy option that could easily have been achieved by other, less costly, means. Roosevelt did not need to sacrifice his Pacific Fleet to inflame public opinion. The nation would have been aroused to fight had the commanders been fully prepared and the damage less extensive.

Also, it was by no means clear that the Japanese attack on an American military base in Hawaii would have allowed FDR to lead the nation into the European war. Had Hitler not declared war on the United States, FDR would likely have been forced to focus all of America's resources on defeating Japan, leaving Britain to fend for itself against Germany. Although it defies the rules of common sense and lacks evidence, the "back door" theory refuses to go away. For an excellent discussion of the theory and why it persists, see Emily S. Rosenberg, *A Date Which Will Live: Pearl Harbor in American Memory* (Durham, NC: Duke University Press, 2003), 34–52.

3. Harold I. Gullan, "Expectations of Infamy: Roosevelt and Marshall Prepare for War, 1938–41," *Presidential Studies Quarterly* (Summer 1998): 510–522.

4. Max Hastings, *Winston's War: Churchill, 1940–1945* (New York: Alfred A. Knopf, 2010), 165.

5. Ibid.

6. Grace Tully, *FDR: My Boss* (New York: Scribner's, 1949), 257.

7. The "disaster of Pearl Harbor," concluded the Joint Congressional Committee, "was the failure . . . of the Army and the Navy to institute measures designed to detect

an approaching hostile force, to effect a state of readiness commensurate with the realization that war was at hand, and to employ every facility at their command in repelling the Japanese." *Report of the Joint Committee on the Investigation of the Pearl Harbor Attack,* 79th Cong., 2nd sess., document 244, final report, pt. 5, *Conclusions and Recommendations* (Washington, DC: U.S. Government Printing Office, 1946), 251.

Chapter 1

1. Robert Sherwood, *Roosevelt and Hopkins: An Intimate History* (New York: Enigma Books, 2008), 161; "Draft Article on FDR," Box 10, Marguerite A. ("Missy") LeHand Papers, Tully Archive, Franklin D. Roosevelt Library.

2. Doris Kearns Goodwin, *No Ordinary Time* (New York: Simon and Schuster, 1994), 17; William Seale, *The President's House: A History* (Baltimore: Johns Hopkins University Press, 2008), 2:971.

3. "Draft Article on FDR"; Seale, *President's House,* 987.

4. Sherwood, *Roosevelt and Hopkins,* 160; Seale, *President's House,* 984–985; Goodwin, *No Ordinary Time,* 34.

5. Goodwin, *No Ordinary Time,* 34; Seale,

President's House, 986.

6. Hugh Gregory Gallagher, *FDR's Splendid Deception* (Arlington, VA: Vandamere Press, 1994), 91–92.

7. "Roosevelt Appeals Direct to Emperor as Japan Masses More Men, Proclaims Crisis Is at Hand," *Washington Post,* December 7, 1941, 1; "Roosevelt Appeals to Hirohito," *New York Times,* December 7, 1941, 1; "Navy Is Superior to Any, Says Knox," *New York Times,* December 7, 1941, 1.

8. Frank Freidel, "FDR vs. Hitler: American Foreign Policy, 1933–1941," *Proceedings of the Massachusetts Historical Society,* 3rd ser. (1987): 25–43.

9. Ibid., 39.

10. Ibid., 25–43.

11. Jean Edward Smith, *FDR* (New York: Random House, 2008), 434; Freidel, "FDR vs. Hitler," 25–43.

12. Freidel, "FDR vs. Hitler," 25–43.

13. Harold I. Gullan, "Expectations of Infamy: Roosevelt and Marshall Prepare for War, 1938–41," *Presidential Studies Quarterly* (Summer 1998): 510–522.

14. Goodwin, *No Ordinary Time,* 61–62.

15. David F. Schmitz, *Henry L. Stimson: The First Wise Man* (Wilmington, DE: Scholarly Resources, 2001), xiii–xv.

16. Goodwin, *No Ordinary Time,* 380.
17. Ibid., 187.

Chapter 2

1. Jean Edward Smith, *FDR* (New York: Random House, 2008), 291–292.
2. Admiral Harold Stark, *Hearings Before the Joint Committee on the Investigation of the Pearl Harbor Attack,* 79th Cong., 1st sess., pt. 32, Navy Court of Inquiry, August 7, 1944, and August 17, 1944 (Washington, DC: U.S. Government Printing Office, 1946), 28, 283–285.
3. Doris Kearns Goodwin, *No Ordinary Time* (New York: Simon and Schuster, 1994), 265.
4. Ibid., 266.
5. J. E. Smith, *FDR,* 510.
6. Ibid., 511.
7. Ibid., 512–513.
8. Francis Biddle, *In Brief Authority* (New York: Doubleday, 1962), 180; J. E. Smith, *FDR,* 525; Conrad Black, *Franklin Delano Roosevelt: Champion of Freedom* (New York: Public Affairs, 2003), 337; Harold I. Gullan, "Expectations of Infamy: Roosevelt and Marshall Prepare for War, 1938–41," *Presidential Studies Quarterly* (Summer 1998): 510–522; Frank Freidel, *Franklin D. Roosevelt: A Rendezvous with*

Destiny (New York: Little, Brown, 1990), 108.

9. Cordell Hull, *Hearings Before the Joint Committee,* 1st sess., pt. 2, 409, 413.

10. J. E. Smith, *FDR,* 516.

11. Ibid., 518.

12. Robert Dallek, *Franklin D. Roosevelt and American Foreign Policy, 1932–1945* (New York: Oxford University Press, 1995), 302–303.

13. J. E. Smith, *FDR,* 518–523.

14. Goodwin, *No Ordinary Time,* 272.

15. Ibid.

16. *Hearings Before the Joint Committee,* pt. 19, exhibit 160, "Remarks of the President," December 7, 1941, 3503.

17. J. E. Smith, *FDR,* 525; "Day of Infamy," *Time,* December 2, 1991, 30.

18. Testimony of Cordell Hull, *Hearings Before the Joint Committee,* 1st sess., pt. 2, 432.

19. Ibid., 433.

20. J. E. Smith, *FDR,* 526–527.

21. Testimony of Honorable Henry L. Stimson, *Hearings Before the Joint Committee,* Army Pearl Harbor Board, 1st sess., pt. 29, September 26, 1944, 2070; J. E. Smith, *FDR,* 526–530.

22. http://www.arlingtoncemetery.net/hrstark.htm.

23. Dallek, *Franklin D. Roosevelt and American Foreign Policy,* 309; Testimony of Admiral Harold R. Stark, *Hearings Before the Joint Committee,* 1st and 2nd sess., pt. 5, 2122–2124, 2316–2321.

24. Ibid., 2124–2125.

25. Rufus Bratton, *Hearings Before the Joint Committee,* 1st sess., pt. 29, Army Pearl Harbor Board, September 30, 1944, 2442, 45; Hull, *Hearings Before the Joint Committee,* 441.

26. *Report of the Joint Committee on the Investigation of the Pearl Harbor Attack,* 79th Cong., 2nd sess., document 244, appendix D, "The Last Hours" (Washington, DC: U.S. Government Printing Office, 1946), 427.

27. Gordon W. Prange, *December 7, 1941: The Day the Japanese Attacked Pearl Harbor* (New York: Wings Books, 1991), 12–13.

28. Ibid., 28.

Chapter 3

1. Robert Sherwood, *Roosevelt and Hopkins: An Intimate History* (New York: Enigma Books, 2008), 4–5.

2. Ibid., 5.

3. Robert E. Sherwood, "Harry Hopkins,"

New Republic, February 11, 1946, 180; Sherwood, *Roosevelt and Hopkins,* 4.

4. William Seale, *The President's House: A History* (Baltimore: Johns Hopkins University Press, 2008), 2:991.

5. Sherwood, *Roosevelt and Hopkins,* 95–96.

6. Ibid., 136; Doris Kearns Goodwin, *No Ordinary Time* (New York: Simon and Schuster, 1994), 88.

7. Geoffrey C. Ward, "A (White) House Divided," *American Heritage* (October 1994); Sherwood, *Roosevelt and Hopkins,* 6.

8. *Report of the Joint Committee on the Investigation of the Pearl Harbor Attack,* 79th Cong., 2nd sess., document 244, appendix D, "The Last Hours" (Washington, DC: U.S. Government Printing Office, 1946), 434–435; Robert Dallek, *Franklin D. Roosevelt and American Foreign Policy, 1932–1945* (New York: Oxford University Press, 1995), 309–310; Stanley Weintraub, *Long Day's Journey into War: December 7, 1941* (New York: Dutton, 1991), 108–109.

9. Admiral Harold Stark, *Hearings Before the Joint Committee on the Investigation of the Pearl Harbor Attack,* 79th Cong., 1st

sess., pt. 32, Navy Court of Inquiry, August 7, 1944 (Washington, DC: U.S. Government Printing Office, 1946), 28.

10. Gordon W. Prange, *December 7, 1941: The Day the Japanese Attacked Pearl Harbor* (New York: Wings Books, 1991), 31.

11. Ibid., 33.

12. Testimony of Rear Admiral John R. Beardall, United States Navy, *Hearings Before the Joint Committee,* 2nd sess., pt. 11, 5283–5284; *Report of the Joint Committee on the Investigation of the Pearl Harbor Attack,* 79th Cong., 2nd sess., document 244, appendix D, "The Last Hours," 436; Weintraub, *Long Day's Journey into War,* 183; Bratton, *Hearings Before the Joint Committee,* Army Pearl Harbor Board, September 30, 1944, 1st sess., pt. 29, 2344–2345.

13. Sherwood, *Roosevelt and Hopkins,* 429.

14. Ibid., 337.

15. Weintraub, *Long Day's Journey into War,* 34–35; Frank E. Beatty, "The Background of the Secret Report," *National Review,* December 13, 1966, 1261.

16. Statement by Henry L. Stimson, Former Secretary of War, *Hearings Before the Joint Committee,* 79th Cong., 2nd sess., pt. 11, March 1946, 5440–5441.

17. Bratton, *Hearings Before the Joint Committee*, Army Pearl Harbor Board, September 30, 1944, 1st sess., pt. 29, 2346–2347; Bratton, *Hearings Before the Joint Committee*, 2nd sess., pt. 9, 4517.

18. Prange, *December 7, 1941*, 60–61; Weintraub, *Long Day's Journey into War*, 185–186.

19. In his testimony before the Joint Congressional Committee, Bratton said, "General Miles and I both said that we were convinced it meant Japanese hostile action against some American installation in the Pacific at or shortly after 1 o'clock that afternoon." Bratton, *Hearings Before the Joint Congressional Committee*, 2nd sess., pt. 9, 4518.

20. Weintraub, *Long Day's Journey into War*, 212; Stark, Roberts Commission, http://www.ibiblio.org/pha/pha/roberts/roberts.html, 1082; Stark, *Hearings Before the Joint Committee on the Investigation of the Pearl Harbor Attack*, Navy Court of Inquiry, 136; Bratton, *Hearings Before the Joint Committee*, Army Pearl Harbor Board, 2346–2347.

21. Prange, *December 7, 1941*, 247–248; Weintraub, *Long Day's Journey into War*, 220–221.

22. David Brinkley, *Washington Goes to War* (New York: Random House, 1999), 86.

23. Earl Rickard, "Henry L. Stimson: The Ever-Present Presence," *World War II* (July–August 2004): 22–24.

Chapter 4

1. Dan Van der Vat, *Pearl Harbor: The Day of Infamy — an Illustrated History* (New York: Basic Books, 2001), 22–25.

2. Jean Edward Smith, *FDR* (New York: Random House, 2008), 531.

3. Ibid., 531–532.

4. Van der Vat, *Pearl Harbor,* 20; "The Attack on Pearl Harbor," USS *Arizona* Preservation Project, 2004, http://www.pastfoundation.org/Arizona/PearlHarbor Attack.html.

5. Van der Vat, *Pearl Harbor,* 21–22.

6. Ibid., 23.

7. J. E. Smith, *FDR,* 533–534.

8. Gordon W. Prange, *December 7, 1941: The Day the Japanese Attacked Pearl Harbor* (New York: Wings Books, 1991), 84.

9. Van der Vat, *Pearl Harbor,* 60; Prange, *December 7, 1941,* 88–90.

10. Prange, *December 7, 1941,* 108.

11. Ibid., 108–109.

12. Van der Vat, *Pearl Harbor,* 80; Prange, *December 7, 1941,* 109–110.

13. Prange, *December 7, 1941,* 120; "Day of Infamy," *Time,* December 2, 1991, 30.

14. http://www.military.com/Resources/pearlharbor.htm.

15. Robert S. LaForte and Ronald E. Marcello, eds., *Remembering Pearl Harbor: Eyewitness Accounts by U.S. Military Men and Women* (Wilmington, DE: Scholarly Resources, 1991), 19.

16. Prange, *December 7, 1941,* 118–119.

17. "The Attack on Pearl Harbor," USS *Arizona* Preservation Project.

18. Ibid.

19. David Reynolds, *From Munich to Pearl Harbor: Roosevelt's America and the Origins of the Second World War* (Chicago: Ivan R. Dee, 2001), 166. The figures on American casualties are supplied by the National Park Service: http://www.nps.gov/nr/twhp/wwwlps/lessons/18arizona/18arizona.html.

Chapter 5

1. Stanley Weintraub, *Long Day's Journey into War: December 7, 1941* (New York: Dutton, 1991), 238; *Report of the Joint Committee on the Investigation of the Pearl Harbor Attack,* 79th Cong., 2nd sess., document 244, appendix D, "The Last Hours" (Washington, DC: U.S. Government Printing Office, 1946), 439; Gor-

don W. Prange, *December 7, 1941: The Day the Japanese Attacked Pearl Harbor* (New York: Wings Books, 1991), 248.

2. "Memorandum: December 7, 1941," Harry Hopkins Papers, Box 6, Folder 19, Georgetown University Library, Special Collections Research Center.

3. Fred Blumenthal, "The White House Is Calling," *Washington Post,* July 7, 1957; "December 7 in DC Chapter," Gordon Prange Papers, Box 12, Special Collections, University of Maryland Library (UML).

4. Prange, *December 7, 1941,* 252–253; "Conference with Grace Tully," December 15, 1970, Prange Papers, Box 20, UML.

5. "Monday, December 8, 1941," Henry Lewis Stimson Diaries (microfilm edition, reel 7), Manuscripts and Archives, Yale University Library.

6. Ibid.

7. Weintraub, *Long Day's Journey into War,* 180.

8. Ragsdale to David Hulburd, *War Comes to the U.S. — Dec. 7, 1941: The First 30 Hours as Reported to the Time-Life-Fortune News Bureau from the U.S. and Abroad* (New York, 1942); *Report of the Joint Committee on the Investigation of the Pearl Harbor Attack,* 79th Cong., 2nd sess.,

document 244, appendix D, "The Last Hours," 439–440; "Memorandum: December 7, 1941."

9. *Report of the Joint Committee on the Investigation of the Pearl Harbor Attack*, 79th Cong., 2nd sess., document 244, appendix D, "The Last Hours," 441.

10. Prange, *December 7, 1941*, 250; Archie Satterfield, *The Day the War Began* (Westport, CT: Praeger, 1992), 121.

11. "Mr. Early's Press Conference," December 6, 1941, Stephen Early Papers, Box 71, Franklin D. Roosevelt Library (FDRL).

12. Prange, *December 7, 1941*, 251.

13. Linda Lotridge Levin, *The Making of FDR: The Story of Stephen T. Early, America's First Modern Press Secretary* (New York: Prometheus Books, 2008), 251–252.

14. "Press release, December 7, 1941, 2:25 pm," Early Papers, Box 71, FDRL.

15. Prange, *December 7, 1941*, 250–251; "December 7 in DC Chapter."

Chapter 6

1. Gordon W. Prange, *December 7, 1941: The Day the Japanese Attacked Pearl Harbor* (New York: Wings Books, 1991), 253; James Roosevelt, *My Parents: A Differing*

View (New York: Playboy Press, 1976), 266.

2. Testimony of Rear Admiral John R. Beardall, United States Navy, *Hearings Before the Joint Committee on the Investigation of the Pearl Harbor Attack,* 79th Cong., 2nd sess., pt. 2 (Washington, DC: U.S. Government Printing Office, 1946), 5275–5276.

3. Stanley Weintraub, *Long Day's Journey into War: December 7, 1941* (New York: Dutton, 1991), 300–301.

4. "Memorandum: December 7, 1941," Harry Hopkins Papers, Box 6, Folder 19, Georgetown University Library, Special Collections Research Center.

5. "Call to President, December 7, 1941," microfilm copy of U.S. Adjutant General's Office, Far Eastern Situation, November 27, 1941–January 1, 1942," John Toland Papers, Series V, Infamy, "December 7, 1941," Box 126, Franklin D. Roosevelt Library; Larry I. Bland, ed., *The Papers of George Catlett Marshall* (Baltimore: Johns Hopkins University Press, 1991), 3:7.

6. "Memorandum: December 7, 1941."

7. Grace Tully, *FDR: My Boss* (New York: Scribner's, 1949), 255.

8. "Memorandum: December 7, 1941"; Tully, *FDR: My Boss,* 255.

9. Eric Larrabee, *Commander in Chief: Franklin Delano Roosevelt, His Lieutenants & Their War* (New York: Harper and Row, 1987), 316–317.

10. Bland, *Papers of George Catlett Marshall,* 3:8.

11. "Memorandum: December 7, 1941."

12. George Herring, *From Colony to Superpower: U.S. Foreign Relations Since 1776* (New York: Oxford University Press, 2008), 500–501.

13. Ibid., 528–529.

14. John F. Bratzel and Leslie B. Rout Jr., "FDR and the 'Secret Map,' " *Wilson Quarterly* (New Year's 1985): 167–173.

15. "Memorandum: December 7, 1941."

16. Alice Goldfarb Marquis, "Written on the Wind: The Impact of Radio During the 1930s," *Journal of Contemporary History* (July 1984): 385–415.

17. Betty Houchlin Winfield, *FDR and the News Media* (Urbana: University of Illinois Press, 1990), 104–105.

18. Ibid., 105–106.

19. Tully, *FDR: My Boss,* 254.

20. *Report of the Joint Committee on the Investigation of the Pearl Harbor Attack,* 79th Cong., 2nd sess., document 244, appendix D, "The Last Hours" (Washington,

DC: U.S. Government Printing Office, 1946), 441; Tully, *FDR: My Boss,* 254.

21. Ed Lockett to David Hulburd, *War Comes to the U.S. — Dec. 7, 1941: The First 30 Hours as Reported to the Time-Life-Fortune News Bureau from the U.S. and Abroad* (New York, 1942).

22. Winfield, *FDR and the News Media,* 172; Richard W. Steele, "The Great Debate: Roosevelt, the Media, and the Coming of the War, 1940–1941," *Journal of American History* (June 1984): 69–92.

23. Lockett to Hulburd, *War Comes to the U.S.*

Chapter 7

1. Jonathan Alter, *The Defining Moment: FDR's Hundred Days and the Triumph of Hope* (New York: Simon and Schuster, 2007), 209–211.

2. Grace Tully, *FDR: My Boss* (New York: Scribner's, 1949), 256.

3. "FDR's 'Day of Infamy' Speech: Crafting a Call to Arms," *Prologue* (Winter 2001); Tully, *FDR: My Boss,* 256.

4. "FDR's 'Day of Infamy' Speech."

5. There are conflicting reports of when this conversation took place. Tully said they made the connection in the afternoon, shortly after they received word of the at-

tack. Another official with the governor in Hawaii said the call went through at 12:40 Pacific time, which would be after 6:00 p.m. in Washington. See "Diary of Charles M. Hite, the Secretary of Hawaii, December 7, 1941," John Toland Papers, Series V, December 7, 1941, Box 126, Franklin D. Roosevelt Library (FDRL).

6. Stanley Weintraub, *Long Day's Journey into War: December 7, 1941* (New York: Dutton, 1991), 395.

7. "5:55 Press Briefing," Stephen Early Papers, Box 71, FDRL.

8. Steven Lomazow and Eric Fettmann, *FDR's Deadly Secret* (New York: Public Affairs, 2010), 52.

9. Ross T. McIntire, *White House Physician* (New York: G. P. Putnam, 1946), 57; Lomazow and Fettmann, *FDR's Deadly Secret,* 53; Kenneth R. Crispell and Carlos Gomez, *Hidden Illness in the White House* (Durham: Duke University Press, 1989), 96.

10. Leon Pearson, "Washington, April 1941," Dr. Ross McIntire Papers, Box 2, FDRL.

11. George Creel, "The President's Health," *Colliers,* March 3, 1945, 15.

12. McIntire, *White House Physician,* 64.

13. Leon Pearson, "Washington, D.C., April

1941," McIntire Papers, Box 2, FDRL.

14. Francis Biddle, *In Brief Authority* (New York: Doubleday, 1962), 207.

15. Dr. Murray Grossan, interview by the author, December 13, 2010.

16. Lester Grinspoon and James B. Bakalar, "Coca and Cocaine as Medicines: An Historical Review," *Journal of Ethnopharmacology* 3 (1981): 149–159; Robert D. Priest, M.D., "Nasal Allergy," in *Fundamentals of Otolaryngology: A Textbook of Ear, Nose, and Throat Diseases,* ed. Lawrence R. Boies, M.D., 3rd ed. (Philadelphia: W. B. Saunders, 1959), 208; Nicholas L. Schenck, M.D., "Cocaine: Its Use in Otolaryngology," *Western Journal of Medicine* (September 1975): 187.

17. Grinspoon and Bakalar, "Coca and Cocaine as Medicines," 149–159.

18. Dr. Jordon S. Josephson, interview by the author, December 16, 2010; Grossan interview; Dr. Robert Lofgren, interview by the author, March 27, 2010.

19. Josephson interview; Grossan interview; Lofgren interview.

20. Francis Lederer, *Diseases of the Ear, Nose, and Throat: Principles and Practice of Otorhinolaryngology* (Philadelphia: F. A. Davis, 1939), 741; Eleanor Roosevelt, *This*

I Remember (Santa Barbara: Greenwood Press Reprints, 1975), 232–233. Some medical historians have speculated that Dr. McIntire destroyed FDR's medical records in 1945 to hide his possible misdiagnosis of the president's deteriorating heart condition. This information suggests another possible motive: McIntire did not want the public to learn that he had been treating the President of the United States on a regular basis with cocaine — a treatment that was both legal and medically sound at the time — but would also have been politically controversial.

Chapter 8

1. Edward Bliss Jr., *Now the News: The Story of Broadcast Journalism* (New York: Columbia University Press, 1991), 135–136.
2. Ibid., 136.
3. Betty Houchin Winfield, *FDR and the News Media* (Urbana: University of Illinois Press, 1990), 55–57.
4. Merriman Smith, *Thank You, Mr. President: A White House Notebook* (New York: Harpers, 1946), 118.
5. Wm. C. Murphy Jr., "Roosevelt to Give Message on War to Congress Today," *Philadelphia Inquirer,* December 8, 1941, 1.

6. M. Smith, *Thank You, Mr. President,* 118–119.

7. "Press Conference — 4:30 pm," Stephen Early Papers, Box 71, Franklin D. Roosevelt Library (FDRL).

8. M. Smith, *Thank You, Mr. President,* 118–119.

9. Steven M. Gillon, *The Kennedy Assassination — 24 Hours After: Lyndon B. Johnson's Pivotal First Day as President* (New York: Basic Books, 2009), 98–99.

10. "December 7 in DC Chapter," Gordon Prange Papers, Box 12, Special Collections, University of Maryland Library.

11. Shirley Povich, "War's Outbreak Is Deep Secret to 27,102 Redskin Game Fans," *Washington Post,* December 8, 1941, 24.

12. Calhoun to Hulburd, *War Comes to the U.S. — Dec. 7, 1941: The First 30 Hours as Reported to the Time-Life-Fortune News Bureau from the U.S. and Abroad* (New York, 1942).

13. James to Hulburd, ibid.

14. Howland to Hulburd, ibid.

15. James to Hulburd, ibid.

16. Archie Satterfield, *The Day the War Began* (New York: Praeger, 1992), 133.

17. James to Hulburd, *War Comes to the U.S.*
18. "Calm About News," *Kansas City Times,* December 8, 1941, 4.
19. "Memorandum for General Watson," 12-11-41, Official File, OF4661–OF4674, "World War II — 1941," Box 1, FDRL.
20. Calhoun to Hulburd, *War Comes to the U.S.;* "What Do Angelenos Think of War?" *Los Angeles Times,* December 8, 1941, E1.
21. "What Do Angelenos Think of War?"
22. Satterfield, *Day the War Began,* 129; "Public Believed First War Reports Only Gag," *Los Angeles Times,* December 8, 1941, 2.
23. Stanley Weintraub, *Long Day's Journey into War: December 7, 1941* (New York: Dutton, 1991), 462.
24. "J-Day in Hawaii," John Toland Papers, Series V, December 7, 1941, Box 126, FDRL; "Journal, 001 7 December to 2400 7 December, 1941," Toland Papers, Series V, December 7, 1941, Box 126, FDRL.
25. "Rumors and Facts as Jotted Down by Mrs. Robert Thompson," Toland Papers, Series V, December 7, 1941, Box 126, FDRL.
26. "Journal, 001 7 December to 2400 7 December, 1941," Toland Papers, Series

V, December 7, 1941, Box 126, FDRL.

27. Ibid.

28. T. H. Davies, "Intelligence Summary #1," December 7, 1941, 2100, Toland Papers, Series V, December 7, 1941, Box 126, FDRL.

29. Weintraub, *Long Day's Journey into War,* 534.

30. Ibid., 318–319, 542.

31. "La Guardia Acts to Guard Cities," *New York Times,* December 8, 1941, 3.

32. "War Brings White House a Tense Day," *Washington Post,* December 8, 1941, 2; "Memorandum: December 7, 1941," Harry Hopkins Papers, Box 6, Folder 19, Georgetown University Library, Special Collections Research Center; Murphy, "Roosevelt to Give Message on War to Congress Today."

33. "Memorandum for General Miles: 'Chronology,' Sunday — December 7, 1941," Toland Papers, Series V, Box 125, FDRL.

34. Satterfield, *The Day the War Began,* 166–167.

35. Robert Sherwood, *The White House Papers of Harry L. Hopkins* (London: Eyre and Spottiswoode), 1:440.

36. Ragsdale to Hulburd, *War Comes to the U.S.;* Edmund W. Starling, Duty Log,

December 7–8, 1941, United States Secret Service Archive.

37. "Dingell Urges Court-Martial for Officers He Says Were 'Napping at Pearl Harbor,' " *New York Times,* December 9, 1941, 7.

Chapter 9

1. Frank Wilson and Beth Day, *Special Agent* (New York: Holt, Rinehart, and Winston, 1965), 144.

2. Morgenthau Diaries, December 3, 1941, Box 515, Franklin D. Roosevelt Library (FDRL); Michael F. Reilly, *Reilly of the White House* (New York: Simon and Schuster, 1947), 4.

3. Wilson and Day, *Special Agent,* 141.

4. Ibid., 142.

5. Merriman Smith, *Thank You, Mr. President: A White House Notebook* (New York: Harpers, 1946), 117.

6. Frank Wilson, "Survey Regarding the Protection of the President," September 6, 1940, Secret Service Records, Box 25, File 71, 7–10, FDRL.

7. Ibid.

8. Wilson and Day, *Special Agent,* 142.

9. M. F. Reilly to Frank J. Wilson, December 11, 1941, United States Secret Service Archive (USSSA), in author's possession;

Wilson and Day, *Special Agent,* 143.

10. Reilly, *Reilly of the White House,* 44; Wilson and Day, *Special Agent,* 143; Reilly to Wilson, December 11, 1941, USSSA.

11. Grace Tully, *FDR: My Boss* (New York: Scribner's, 1949), 259; Jean Edward Smith, *FDR* (New York: Random House, 2008), 118; William Seale, *The President's House: A History* (Baltimore: Johns Hopkins University Press, 2008), 2:975–977; Ed Lockett to David Hulburd, *War Comes to the U.S. — Dec. 7, 1941: The First 30 Hours as Reported to the Time-Life-Fortune News Bureau from the U.S. and Abroad* (New York, 1942); "Blackout Ordered for Capitol Dome," *New York Times,* December 10, 1941, 18; Wilson and Day, *Special Agent,* 145.

12. Wilson and Day, *Special Agent,* 150.

13. Wilson, "Survey Regarding the Protection of the President," 7–10.

14. Reilly, *Reilly of the White House,* 18, 26–27, 54–55.

15. Seale, *President's House,* 2:976.

16. Reilly to Wilson, December 11, 1941, USSSA.

17. "Heavy Guard Thrown Around Capital's Most Vital Spots," *Washington Post,* December 8, 1941, 3.

18. Morgenthau Diaries, December 7,

1941, 6:35 p.m., Box 515, FDRL.

19. Reilly, *Reilly of the White House,* 6; M. Smith, *Thank You, Mr. President,* 118.

20. Morgenthau Diaries, December 7, 1941.

21. Ibid.

22. Wilson and Day, *Special Agent,* 146.

23. Reilly to Wilson, December 11, 1941, USSSA.

24. Reilly, *Reilly of the White House,* 37.

25. Gaston to Morgenthau, December 15, 1941, Morgenthau Diaries, Box 515, FDRL; Seale, *President's House,* 975–976.

26. Tully, *FDR: My Boss,* 259.

27. Wilson and Day, *Special Agent,* 147–148.

28. Reilly, *Reilly of the White House,* 39; Eleanor Roosevelt, *This I Remember* (Santa Barbara: Greenwood Press Reprints, 1975), 237.

29. Frank Wilson, "Protective Rostrum," October 31, 1943, Secret Service Records, Box 13, File 103-A-1-5, FDRL.

30. Michael F. Reilly, "Movements of the President," September 25, 1943, Secret Service Records, Box 25, File 7-1–File 7-10, FDRL.

31. Robert J. Lewis, "White House Architect Winslow to Visit Daughter Here," *Haiti Sun,* February 5, 1961. For security reasons, the Winslow memoirs are now clas-

sified and housed with the office of the White House curator. William Seale had access to the memoirs before they became classified and quoted from them extensively for his book *The President's House.*

32. Lockett to Hulburd, *War Comes to the U.S.*

33. Greg Robinson, *By Order of the President: FDR and the Internment of Japanese Americans* (Cambridge: Harvard University Press, 2001), 11–37.

34. Roger Daniels, "Incarceration of the Japanese Americans: A Sixty-Year Perspective," *History Teacher* (May 2002): 299–300.

35. http://www.digitalhistory.uh.edu/learning_history/japanese_internment/munson_report.cfm.

36. Robinson, *By Order of the President,* 75.

37. James to Hulburd, *War Comes to the U.S.;* "Japanese Aliens' Roundup Starts," *Los Angeles Times,* December 8, 1941, 1.

38. "Entire City Put on War Footing," *New York Times,* December 8, 1941, 1.

39. Robinson, *By Order of the President,* 75; "Begin Arresting Japs Classified as 'Dangerous,' " *Chicago Daily Tribune,* December 8, 1941, 4; John Crider to Hulburd, *War Comes to the U.S.*

40. Eugene V. Rostow, "The Japanese American Cases: A Disaster," *Yale Law Journal* (June 1945): 489–533; Doris Kearns Goodwin, *No Ordinary Time* (New York: Simon and Schuster, 1994), 321.

41. J. E. Smith, *FDR,* 551–553.

42. Roosevelt later regretted "the burdens of evacuation and detention which military necessity imposed on these people." Quoted in Goodwin, *No Ordinary Time,* 322; Francis Biddle, *In Brief Authority* (New York: Doubleday, 1962), 219.

Chapter 10

1. Pamela Harriman, "When Churchill Heard the News," *Washington Post,* December 7, 1991; Max Hastings, *Winston's War: Churchill, 1940–1945* (New York: Alfred A. Knopf, 2010), 180.

2. Frank Freidel, *Franklin D. Roosevelt: A Rendezvous with Destiny* (New York: Little, Brown, 1990), 333.

3. Jean Edward Smith, *FDR* (New York: Random House, 2008), 445.

4. Hastings, *Winston's War,* 155–157.

5. Ibid., 153.

6. J. E. Smith, *FDR,* 498–501; Kenneth Davis, *FDR: The War President* (New York: Random House, 2000), 259.

7. Robert Dallek, *Franklin D. Roosevelt and*

American Foreign Policy (New York: Oxford University Press, 1995), 281–285.

8. Hastings, *Winston's War,* 169.

9. Ibid., 170–171.

10. Ibid., 176–181.

11. Welsh to Hulburd, *War Comes to the U.S. — Dec. 7, 1941: The First 30 Hours as Reported to the Time-Life-Fortune News Bureau from the U.S. and Abroad* (New York, 1942).

12. Harriman, "When Churchill Heard the News."

13. Stanley Weintraub, *Long Day's Journey into War: December 7, 1941* (New York: Dutton, 1991), 339; Richard Snow, *A Measureless Peril: America in the Fight for the Atlantic, the Longest Battle of World War II* (New York: Scribner's, 2010), 146.

14. Weintraub, *Long Day's Journey into War,* 340.

15. Freidel, *Franklin D. Roosevelt,* 410.

16. Jeffrey Mark to Hulburd, *War Comes to the U.S.*

17. Ibid.

18. H. L. Trefousse, "Germany and Pearl Harbor," *Far Eastern Quarterly* (November 1951): 35–50.

19. Weintraub, *Long Day's Journey into War,* 297–298; Snow, *Measureless Peril,* 148.

20. Weintraub, *Long Day's Journey into War*, 298–299.

21. Snow, *Measureless Peril*, 148.

22. Denis Mack Smith, *Mussolini* (New York: Alfred A. Knopf, 1982), 273; R. J. B. Bosworth, *Mussolini* (New York: Oxford University Press, 2002), 281; Weintraub, *Long Day's Journey into War*, 596.

23. Wayne S. Cole, "The America First Committee," *Journal of the Illinois State Historical Society* (Winter 1951): 305–322.

24. "Press Release," America First Committee, Pittsburgh Chapter, America First Committee Papers (AFCP), Box 233, Hoover Institution on War, Revolution, and Peace (HIWR); Hagy to Hulburd, "Pittsburgh and the War," in *War Comes to the U.S.*

25. Hagy to Hulburd, "Pittsburgh and the War," in *War Comes to the U.S.*

26. Executive Vice Chairman to William S. Foulis, December 9, 1941, Box 230, AFCP-HIWR; Hagy to Hulburd, "Pittsburgh and the War," in *War Comes to the U.S.*

27. Hagy to Hulburd, "Pittsburgh and the War," in *War Comes to the U.S.;* Weintraub, *Long Day's Journey into War*, 310–312.

28. Hagy to Hulburd, "Pittsburgh and the War," in *War Comes to the U.S.*

Chapter 11

1. Grace Tully, *FDR: My Boss* (New York: Scribner's, 1949), 257; Gordon W. Prange, *December 7, 1941: The Day the Japanese Attacked Pearl Harbor* (New York: Wings Books, 1991), 386.
2. *Report of the Joint Committee on the Investigation of the Pearl Harbor Attack,* 79th Cong., 2nd sess., document 244, appendix D, "The Last Hours" (Washington, DC: U.S. Government Printing Office, 1946), 441.
3. "Naval Message," December 7, 1941, 5:28 p.m., Map Room Papers, Box 36, Franklin D. Roosevelt Library (FDRL).
4. "December 7 in DC Chapter," Gordon Prange Papers, Box 12, University of Maryland Library; Alonzo Fields, *My 21 Years in the White House* (New York: Coward-McCann, 1961), 80.
5. "Memorandum: December 7, 1941," Harry Hopkins Papers, Box 6, Folder 19, Georgetown University Library, Special Collections Research Center.
6. "Notes taken of conversation between Admiral Stark and Admiral Bloch," John Toland Papers, Box 126, FDRL.

7. Ibid.

8. Ibid.

9. "Record of Telephone Conversation Between Gen. Gerow, WPD, and Gen. MacArthur in Manila, P.I., About 7:00 p.m.," Toland Papers, Series V, December 7, 1941, Box 126, FDRL.

10. Michael Schaller, *Douglas MacArthur: The Far Eastern General* (New York: Oxford University Press, 1989), 55–57.

11. Eric Larrabee, *Commander in Chief: Franklin Delano Roosevelt, His Lieutenants & Their War* (New York: Harper and Row, 1987), 316–317; Archie Satterfield, *The Day the War Began* (Westport, CT: Praeger, 1992), 94–95.

12. "Memorandum for General Miles: Chronology of December 7," Toland Papers, Series V, "Chronology," Box 125, FDRL.

13. William Seale, *The President's House: A History* (Baltimore: Johns Hopkins University Press, 2008), 2:984.

14. Landon to the President, December 7, 1941; Keen to the President, December 7, 1941; Dixon to the President, December 7, 1941, Official File, OF4675, World War II, Support: Governors, Mayors, Box 5, FDRL. These letters are a small sample

of the wires and letters of support that fill more than a dozen boxes at the Roosevelt Library.

15. Mrs. Peace Tungruito to the President, n.d., Official File, OF4675, World War II, Support: "P," Box 5, FDRL.
16. Merriman Smith, *Thank You, Mr. President: A White House Notebook* (New York: Harpers, 1946), 115–116.

Chapter 12

1. "Memoir, Mrs. Charles Hamlin," December 7, 1941, John Toland Papers, Series V, December 7, 1941, Box 126, Franklin D. Roosevelt Library (FDRL); Gordon W. Prange, *December 7, 1941: The Day the Japanese Attacked Pearl Harbor* (New York: Wings Books, 1991), 248.
2. Eleanor Roosevelt, "My Day," December 7, 1941; Eleanor Roosevelt, *This I Remember* (Santa Barbara: Greenwood Press Reprints, 1975), 232–233; Prange, *December 7, 1941,* 248.
3. Carl Anthony Sferrazza, "The First Ladies: They've Come a Long Way, Martha," *Smithsonian,* October 1992, 135.
4. James Roosevelt, *My Parents: A Differing View* (New York: Playboy Press, 1976), 10–11.
5. Ibid., 12.

6. Jean Edward Smith, *FDR* (New York: Random House, 2008), 44; J. Roosevelt, *My Parents,* 17.

7. J. E. Smith, *FDR,* 46–47; Frank Freidel, *Franklin D. Roosevelt: A Rendezvous with Destiny* (New York: Little, Brown, 1990), 12–13.

8. J. Roosevelt, *My Parents,* 33.

9. Jonathan Alter, *The Defining Moment: FDR's Hundred Days and the Triumph of Hope* (New York: Simon and Schuster, 2007), 43–44; J. E. Smith, *FDR,* 160.

10. J. E. Smith, *FDR,* 161; J. Roosevelt, *My Parents,* 101.

11. J. Roosevelt, *My Parents,* 102; J. E. Smith, *FDR,* 161.

12. Eleanor Roosevelt Oral History, "The Roosevelt Years," Robert Graft Papers, Box 4, p. 5, reel 1, FDRL.

13. E. Roosevelt, *This I Remember,* 232–233.

14. Alter, *Defining Moment,* 25; J. Roosevelt, *My Parents,* 7.

15. J. E. Smith, *FDR,* 23.

16. Doris Kearns Goodwin, *No Ordinary Time* (New York: Simon and Schuster, 1994), 80.

17. J. E. Smith, *FDR,* 6, 25.

18. Freidel, *Franklin D. Roosevelt,* 6.

19. Geoffrey C. Ward, *A First-Class Tempera-*

ment: *The Emergence of Franklin Roosevelt* (New York: Harper and Row, 1989), 607–608.

20. Freidel, *Franklin D. Roosevelt*, 7.

21. Ibid., 41.

22. J. E. Smith, *FDR*, 191.

23. J. Roosevelt, *My Parents*, 72–73.

24. Ward, *First-Class Temperament*, 600.

25. E. Roosevelt Oral History, "The Roosevelt Years," Graft Papers, Box 4, p. 5, reel 1, FDRL; J. Roosevelt, *My Parents*, 73–74.

26. J. Roosevelt, *My Parents*, 73–74.

27. Hugh Gregory Gallagher, *FDR's Splendid Deception* (Arlington, VA: Vandamere Press, 1994), 63.

28. Ibid., 65.

29. J. Roosevelt, *My Parents*, 92–93; Ward, *First-Class Temperament*, 694–695.

30. Ward, *First-Class Temperament*, 696–697.

31. J. E. Smith, *FDR*, 197–198.

32. Ibid., 204; Freidel, *Franklin D. Roosevelt*, 45–56.

33. Ward, *First-Class Temperament*, 715, 728; Alan Brinkley, *Franklin Delano Roosevelt* (New York: Oxford University Press, 2009), 16–17.

34. Ward, *First-Class Temperament*, 750.

35. Alter, *Defining Moment*, 64–65, 327.

36. Ibid., 51–52.
37. A. Brinkley, *Franklin Delano Roosevelt,* 18–19.
38. Ward, *First-Class Temperament,* 782–783.
39. J. B. West, *Upstairs at the White House* (New York: Warner Books, 1974), 17; A. Brinkley, *Franklin Delano Roosevelt,* 20.
40. E. Roosevelt, *This I Remember,* 165–166.
41. The full text of her remarks can be found online at: http://www.gwu.edu/~erpapers/teachinger/q-and-a/q21-pearl-harbor-address.cfm.

Chapter 13

1. Frances Perkins, *The Roosevelt I Knew* (New York: Viking, 1946), 378.
2. Ibid.
3. Ibid., 379; Francis Biddle, *In Brief Authority* (New York: Doubleday, 1962), 206.
4. "Memorandum: December 7, 1941," Harry Hopkins Papers, Box 6, Folder 19, Georgetown University Library, Special Collections Research Center; Perkins, *The Roosevelt I Knew,* 379.
5. Perkins, *The Roosevelt I Knew,* 379.
6. "December 7, 1941," Claude Wickard Papers, Box 13, Cabinet Meetings, 1941–1942, Franklin D. Roosevelt Library

(FDRL). Attorney General Francis Biddle noted in his diary that FDR "expected the possibility of war with Germany and Italy." "December 7, 1941," Francis Biddle Papers, Box 1, Cabinet Meetings, 1941, FDRL.

7. "December 7, 1941," Biddle Papers, Box 1, Cabinet Meetings, 1941, FDRL; "December 7, 1941," Wickard Papers, Box 13, Cabinet Meetings, 1941–1942, FDRL; Perkins, *The Roosevelt I Knew,* 379.

8. "December 7, 1941," Wickard Papers, Box 13, Cabinet Meetings, 1941–1942, FDRL; Donald J. Young, *First 24 Hours of War in the Pacific* (Shippensburg, PA: Burd Street Press, 1998), 157.

9. "December 7, 1941," Biddle Papers, Box 1, Cabinet Meetings, 1941, FDRL; "December 7, 1941," Wickard Papers, Box 13, Cabinet Meetings, 1941–1942, FDRL.

10. Perkins, *The Roosevelt I Knew,* 379–380.

11. "December 7, 1941," Wickard Papers, Box 13, Cabinet Meetings, 1941–1942, FDRL.

12. Ibid.

13. Monday, December 8, 1941, Henry Lewis Stimson Diaries (microfilm edition, reel 7), Manuscripts and Archives, Yale University Library (MA-YUL).

14. "December 7, 1941," Biddle Papers,

Box 1, Cabinet Meetings, 1941, FDRL; Robert Dallek, *Franklin D. Roosevelt and American Foreign Policy, 1932–1945* (New York: Oxford University Press, 1995), 312.

15. Dallek, *Franklin D. Roosevelt and American Foreign Policy,* 312; "Monday, December 8, 1941," Stimson Diaries, MA-YUL.

16. "December 7, 1941," Wickard Papers, Box 13, Cabinet Meetings, 1941–1942, FDRL; "December 7, 1941," Biddle Papers, Box 1, Cabinet Meetings, 1941, FDRL.

17. Bernard Asbell, *The FDR Memoirs* (Garden City, NY: Doubleday, 1973), 249.

18. Jean Edward Smith, *FDR* (New York: Random House, 2008), 207, 248.

19. Ibid., 494.

20. J. E. Smith, *FDR,* 495; Doris Kearns Goodwin, *No Ordinary Time* (New York: Simon and Schuster, 1994), 246.

21. McIntire to Johnson, November 25, 1941; Johnson to McIntire, November 14, 1941, McIntire Papers, Box 9, FDRL.

22. Goodwin, *No Ordinary Time,* 294.

Chapter 14

1. George N. Green, "Connally, Thomas Terry," *Handbook of Texas Online,* http://www.tshaonline.org/handbook/online/

articles/fco36.

2. Tom Connally, *My Name Is Tom Connally* (New York: Thomas Y. Crowell, 1954), 248.

3. "Memorandum: December 7, 1941," Harry Hopkins Papers, Box 6, Folder 19, Georgetown University Library, Special Collections Research Center; C. P. Trussell, "Congress Decided," *New York Times,* December 8, 1941, 1.

4. Connally, *My Name Is Tom Connally,* 248.

5. Frank McNaughton to Hulburd, December 8, 1941, *War Comes to the U.S. — Dec. 7, 1941: The First 30 Hours as Reported to the Time-Life-Fortune News Bureau from the U.S. and Abroad* (New York, 1942); *Hearings Before the Joint Committee on the Investigation of the Pearl Harbor Attack,* 79th Cong., pt. 19, exhibit 160, "Remarks of the President," December 7, 1941 (Washington, DC: U.S. Government Printing Office, 1946), 3503.

6. *Hearings Before the Joint Committee on the Investigation of the Pearl Harbor Attack,* 79th Cong., pt. 19, exhibit 160, "Remarks of the President," December 7, 1941, 3504.

7. Ibid.

8. "Monday, December 8, 1941," Henry Lewis Stimson Diaries (microfilm edition,

reel 7), Manuscripts and Archives, Yale University Library.

9. Connally, *My Name Is Tom Connally,* 249.

10. *Hearings Before the Joint Committee on the Investigation of the Pearl Harbor Attack,* 79th Cong., pt. 19, exhibit 160, "Remarks of the President," December 7, 1941, 3504.

11. Connally offered an embellished account of this confrontation in his memoir. He claimed to have followed up with a series of pointed questions directed at Knox. "Didn't you say last month that we could lick the Japs in two weeks? Didn't you say that our navy was so well prepared and located that the Japanese couldn't hope to hurt us at all? When you made those public statements, weren't you just trying to tell the country what an efficient secretary of the navy you were?" While Knox "fumbled around" searching for words, Roosevelt said nothing. "President Roosevelt sat perfectly quiet with a blank expression on his face." Connally, *My Name Is Tom Connally,* 249. This exchange cannot, however, be found in the transcript of the meeting. See *Hearings Before the Joint Committee on the Investigation of the Pearl Harbor Attack,* 79th Cong., pt. 19, exhibit 160, "Remarks of the Presi-

dent," December 7, 1941, 3505.

12. "Memorandum: December 7, 1941."

13. *Hearings Before the Joint Committee on the Investigation of the Pearl Harbor Attack,* 79th Cong., pt. 19, exhibit 160, "Remarks of the President," December 7, 1941, 3504; "December 7, 1941," Wickard Papers, Box 13, Cabinet Meetings, 1941–1942, FDRL.

14. "Memorandum: December 7, 1941."

15. C. P. Trussell, "Congress Decided," *New York Times,* December 8, 1941, 1; Raymond Z. Henle, "Roosevelt May Ask War on Axis," *Pittsburgh Post Gazette,* December 8, 1941, 1.

16. "Nearly All Congressional Opposition to Roosevelt's Foreign Policy Fades," *Wall Street Journal,* December 8, 1941, 3; Trussell, "Congress Decided"; Wm. C. Murphy Jr., "Roosevelt to Give Message on War to Congress Today," *Philadelphia Inquirer,* December 8, 1941, 1.

17. Henle, "Roosevelt May Ask War on Axis," 1.

18. "From Brick Dust to Bouquets," *Time,* December 15, 1941, 50.

19. Alexander Kendrick, *Prime Time: Life of Edward R. Murrow* (New York: Littlehampton, 1970), 240.

20. Frank Costigliola, "Broken Circle: The Isolation of Franklin D. Roosevelt in World War II," *Diplomatic History* 32 (November 2008): 693.

21. Kendrick, *Prime Time,* 240.

22. A. M. Sperber, *Murrow: His Life and Times* (New York: Fordham University Press, 1999), 207; "Memorandum: December 7, 1941."

23. Ibid., 207.

24. Kendrick, *Prime Time,* 240–241.

25. James Roosevelt, *My Parents: A Differing View* (New York: Playboy Press, 1976), 266.

26. William Seale, *The President's House: A History* (Baltimore: Johns Hopkins University Press, 2008), 2:989–990.

Chapter 15

1. Grace Tully, *FDR: My Boss* (New York: Scribner's, 1949), 258.

2. Stanley Weintraub, *Long Day's Journey into War: December 7, 1941* (New York: Dutton, 1991), 625.

3. "British Declare War on Japan Without Waiting for America," *Los Angeles Times,* December 9, 1941, 1.

4. CINCPAC Cable, "Shown to President by Naval Aide, 8:30 am, December 8," Map Room Papers, Military Files, Series

I, Box 36, Franklin D. Roosevelt Library (FDRL); CINCPAC Cable, "Shown to President by Naval Aide, 8:45 am, December 8," Map Room Papers, Military Files, Series I, Box 36, FDRL.

5. "Phoned from Operations Duty Officer," December 8, 1941, Map Room Papers, "Warfare: Philippines, 1941–1943," Box 99, FDRL.

6. Greene to Hulburd, *War Comes to the U.S. — Dec. 7, 1941: The First 30 Hours as Reported to the Time-Life-Fortune News Bureau from the U.S. and Abroad* (New York, 1942); Arthur Krock, "Unity Clicks into Place," *New York Times,* December 8, 1941, 6.

7. Raymond Z. Henle, "Nation Set to Avenge Jap Blows," *Pittsburgh Post-Gazette,* December 9, 1941, 1.

8. C. Fred Lehr to President, December 8, 1941, Official File, OF4675, World War II, Support: "M-L," Box 5, FDRL.

9. Jefferson to President, December 8, 1941, Official File, OF4675, World War II, Support: "J," Box 5, FDRL.

10. The FDR Library also has in its possession aluminum braces that belonged to Roosevelt. It is unclear, however, when Roosevelt wore these braces. The aluminum design is similar to that of the steel

braces, but they weigh only three and a half pounds each.

11. William C. Murphy Jr., "U.S. Declares War on Japs," *Philadelphia Inquirer,* December 9, 1941, 1; Hugh Gregory Gallagher, *FDR's Splendid Deception* (Arlington, VA: Vandamere Press, 1994), 163.

12. Felix Belair Jr. to Hulburd, *War Comes to the U.S.*

13. Michael F. Reilly, *Reilly of the White House* (New York: Simon and Schuster, 1947), 27.

14. Ibid., 27–28. Reilly says the conversation took place on December 9, the day after FDR's address to Congress. In fact, it was December 8.

15. James Reston, "Capital Swings into War Stride," *New York Times,* December 9, 1941, 1; Belair to Hulburd, *War Comes to the US.*

16. Frank Wilson and Beth Day, *Special Agent* (New York: Holt, Rinehart, and Winston, 1965), 147.

17. "Memoir, Mrs. Charles Hamlin," December 7, 1941, John Toland Papers, Series V, Infamy, "December 7, 1941," Box 126, FDRL; Gordon W. Prange, *December 7, 1941: The Day the Japanese At-*

tacked *Pearl Harbor* (New York: Wings Books, 1991), 248; Gallagher, *FDR's Splendid Deception,* 164–165; Frank L. Kluckhohn, "Unity in Congress," *New York Times,* December 9, 1941, 1; Belair to Hulburd, *War Comes to the U.S.*

18. Belair to Hulburd, *War Comes to the U.S.*

19. Gallagher, *FDR's Splendid Deception,* 97, 165.

20. Louis M. Lyons, "Again a U.S. President Asks for Declaration of War," *Boston Daily Globe,* December 8, 1941, 1.

21. McNaughton to Hulburd, *War Comes to the U.S.*

22. Ibid.

23. Ibid.

24. Murphy, "U.S. Declares War on Japs," 1.

25. James Roosevelt, *My Parents: A Differing View* (New York: Playboy Press, 1976), 92–93.

26. Kenneth Davis, *FDR: The War President* (New York: Random House, 2000), 206–208.

27. McNaughton to Hulburd, *War Comes to the U.S.*

28. Murphy, "U.S. Declares War on Japs," 1.

29. Ibid.

30. Eleanor Roosevelt, *This I Remember* (Santa Barbara: Greenwood Press Reprints, 1975), 234.

31. Kluckhohn, "Unity in Congress," 1; Ernest Lindley, "The President in Crisis," *Washington Post,* December 14, 1941, 7; Murphy, "U.S. Declares War on Japs," 1.

32. Audio Recording, "FDR's Address to Congress," December 8, 1941, FDRL.

33. Laird to Hulburd, *War Comes to the U.S.*

34. C. P. Trussell, "Unanimous Senate Acts in 15 Minutes," *New York Times,* December 9, 1941, 1.

35. http://clerk.house.govhighlights.html.

36. Hulburd to McNaughton, *War Comes to the U.S.*

37. Ibid.

38. FDR to "For the Former Naval Person," December 8, 1941, Map Room Papers, Warfare, Box 99, FDRL.

Epilogue

1. John Mueller, "Pearl Harbor: Military Inconvenience, Political Disaster," *International Security* (Winter 1991–1992): 172–203.

2. "Chicagoans Rush to Join Forces Fighting Japan," *Chicago Daily Tribune,* December 9, 1941, 7.

3. "Minutes of the Special Meeting of the Advisory Board," December 8, 1941, America First Committee Papers, Box 162, Hoover Institution on War, Revolution, and Peace; "Isolation Groups Back Roosevelt," *New York Times,* December 9, 1941, 44; Kenneth Davis, *FDR: The War President* (New York: Random House, 2000), 348–349.

4. "Labor for Ending Defense Strikes," *New York Times,* December 9, 1941, 37.

5. Ernest Lindley, "The President in the Crisis," *Washington Post,* December 14, 1941, 7.

6. Frank L. Kluckhohn, "The Commander-in-Chief," *New York Times Magazine,* December 14, 1941, 10.

7. Frank Freidel, "FDR vs. Hitler: American Foreign Policy, 1933–1941," *Proceedings of the Massachusetts Historical Society* (1987): 25–43.

8. Press Release, December 8, 1941, Official File, World War II, OF4675, Box 1, Franklin D. Roosevelt Library.

9. Davis, *FDR: The War President,* 349–350.

10. Frank Freidel, *Franklin D. Roosevelt: A Rendezvous with Destiny* (New York: Little, Brown, 1990), 408.

11. Emily S. Rosenberg, *A Date Which Will*

ABOUT THE AUTHOR

Steven M. Gillon earned his Ph.D. at Brown, taught for several years at Yale and Oxford, and is now a Professor of History at the University of Oklahoma, as well as Resident Historian for The History Channel. He is the author of numerous books and articles on modern American history and politics, including, *The Kennedy Assassination — 24 Hours After* and *Ten Days That Unexpectedly Changed America.* He lives in New York and Oklahoma.

The employees of Thorndike Press hope you have enjoyed this Large Print book. All our Thorndike, Wheeler, and Kennebec Large Print titles are designed for easy reading, and all our books are made to last. Other Thorndike Press Large Print books are available at your library, through selected bookstores, or directly from us.

For information about titles, please call:
  (800) 223-1244

or visit our Web site at:
  http://gale.cengage.com/thorndike

To share your comments, please write:
  Publisher
  Thorndike Press
  10 Water St., Suite 310
  Waterville, ME 04901